Lecture Notes
in Business Information Processing 482

LNBIP reports state-of-the-art results in areas related to business information systems and industrial application software development – timely, at a high level, and in both printed and electronic form.

The type of material published includes

- Proceedings (published in time for the respective event)
- Postproceedings (consisting of thoroughly revised and/or extended final papers)
- Other edited monographs (such as, for example, project reports or invited volumes)
- Tutorials (coherently integrated collections of lectures given at advanced courses, seminars, schools, etc.)
- Award-winning or exceptional theses

LNBIP is abstracted/indexed in DBLP, EI and Scopus. LNBIP volumes are also submitted for the inclusion in ISI Proceedings.

Marcela Ruiz · Pnina Soffer

Editors

Advanced Information Systems Engineering Workshops

CAiSE 2023 International Workshops
Zaragoza, Spain, June 12–16, 2023
Proceedings

Springer

Editors
Marcela Ruiz 🆔
Zurich University of Applied Sciences
Winterthur, Switzerland

Pnina Soffer 🆔
University of Haifa
Haifa, Israel

ISSN 1865-1348   ISSN 1865-1356 (electronic)
Lecture Notes in Business Information Processing
ISBN 978-3-031-34984-3   ISBN 978-3-031-34985-0 (eBook)
https://doi.org/10.1007/978-3-031-34985-0

This Springer imprint is published by the registered company Springer Nature Switzerland AG
The registered company address is: Gewerbestrasse 11, 6330 Cham, Switzerland

Preface

Over the last two decades, the Conference on Advanced Information Systems Engineering (CAiSE) has been established as a leading venue for information systems engineering research on innovative topics with rigorous scientific theories. The theme of this year's CAiSE, "Cyber-Human Systems", reflects the interdisciplinary and diverse nature of information systems engineering. CAiSE 2023 was held in Zaragoza, Spain on 12–16 June 2023. Each year CAiSE is accompanied by a significant number of high-quality workshops. Their aim is to address specific emerging challenges in the field, to facilitate interaction between stakeholders and researchers, to discuss innovative ideas, and to present new approaches and tools. Six workshops were held at the conference this year:

- 3rd International Workshop on Information Systems Engineering for Smarter Life (ISESL)
- 1st International Workshop on Hybrid Artificial Intelligence and Enterprise Modelling for Intelligent Information Systems (HybridAIMS)
- 1st Workshop on Knowledge Graphs for Semantics-Driven Systems Engineering (KG4SDSE)
- International Workshop on Blockchain and Decentralized Governance Design for Information Systems (BC4IS and DGD)
- 2nd International Workshop on Agile Methods for Information Systems Engineering (Agil-ISE)
- 3rd International Workshop on Model-driven Organizational and Business Agility (MOBA)

These workshops received a total of 32 submissions, of which 10 are included in the proceedings as full papers and 9 as short ones. While some of the workshops opted to be discussion-oriented without a formal publication, the papers in the proceedings are related to three workshops:

- 1st International Workshop on Hybrid Artificial Intelligence and Enterprise Modelling for Intelligent Information Systems (HybridAIMS)
- 1st Workshop on Knowledge Graphs for Semantics-Driven Systems Engineering (KG4SDSE)
- International Workshop on Blockchain and Decentralized Governance Design for Information Systems (BC4IS and DGD)

We would like to thank the chairs of the workshops for their excellent job. Also, we thank the reviewers for their timely and constructive work, as well as the publicity chairs for their activities that helped attract submissions. We thank the proceedings chair, Pierluigi Plebani, and Springer for the swift communication and support of the proceedings production process. Finally, we warmly thank Carlos Cetina and Oscar

Pastor—the General Co-chairs of CAiSE 2023—and Iris Reinhartz-Berger and Marta Indulska—the PC Co-chairs of CAiSE 2023—for continuously helping us in the process.

June 2023   Pnina Soffer
                                                                         Marcela Ruiz

Organization

CAiSE Workshops Chairs

Pnina Soffer   University of Haifa, Israel
Marcela Ruiz   Zürich University of Applied Sciences,
                                      Switzerland

Contents

BC4IS and DGD

HybridAIMS

1st International Workshop on Hybrid Artificial Intelligence and Enterprise Modelling for Intelligent Information Systems (HybridAIMS'23)

Hybrid Artificial Intelligence is the research direction that focuses on the combination of two prominent fields: sub-symbolic AI (e.g., machine learning, deep learning, neural networks) and symbolic AI (e.g., knowledge graphs, knowledge representation and reasoning, knowledge engineering, knowledge-based systems). Approaches from the two fields have complementary strengths and enable the creation of Intelligent Information Systems (IIS). For example, whilst neural networks can recognize patterns in large amounts of data, knowledge-based systems contain domain knowledge and enable logical reasoning and explainability of conclusions. AI approaches are typically integrated with application systems, which provide data for the AI approaches and use the results of these approaches for further processing. Thus, the creation of IIS requires high expertise in both AI approaches, knowledge about the application domain and IT knowledge. An early inclusion of domain experts in the engineering process is beneficial as it promotes the high quality of an IIS and reduces its building time. Such an early inclusion is, however, challenging because stakeholders from business and IT have complementary skills and speak different languages: one more technical and one more business oriented. Enterprise Modelling (EM) can tackle this challenge as it supports business and IT alignment. It is an established approach for the conceptual representation, design, implementation, and analysis of information systems. This is of relevance for AI approaches. Graphical notation of enterprise models fosters human interpretability, hence supporting communication and decision-making, involving stakeholders from the application domain, IT and AI. The convergence of Hybrid Artificial Intelligence and Enterprise Modelling promises to deliver high value in the creation of Intelligent Information Systems. The workshop featured 2 keynote speakers from industry and academia, and hosted a World Café to discuss and delineate the next challenges in the field.

June 2023

Emanuele Laurenzi
Hans-Friedrich Witschel
Peter Haase

Organization

HybridAIMS23 Workshop Co-chairs

Emanuele Laurenzi   FHNW University of Applied Sciences and
                                 Arts Northwestern Switzerland,
                                 Switzerland
Hans-Friedrich Witschel   FHNW University of Applied Sciences and
                                 Arts Northwestern Switzerland,
                                 Switzerland
Peter Haase   Metaphacts, Germany

HybridAIMS23 Workshop Program Committee

Karsten Böhm   University of Applied Sciences Kufstein
                                 Tirol, Austria
Dominik Bork   Vienna University of Technology, Austria
Simone Braun   University of Applied Sciences Offenburg,
                                 Germany
Robert Andrei Buchmann   University Babeş-Bolyai din Cluj-Napoca,
                                 Romania
Fabrizio Fornari   University of Camerino, Italy
Giancarlo Guizzardi   University of Twente, The Netherlands
Gregor Heinrich   Creditshelf Solutions GmbH, Germany
Knut Hinkelmann   FHNW University of Applied Sciences and
                                 Arts Northwestern Switzerland,
                                 Switzerland
Bo Hu   Barclays Bank, UK
Lutz Maicher   HTWK Leipzig University of Applied
                                 Sciences, Germany
Andreas Martin   FHNW University of Applied Sciences and
                                 Arts Northwestern Switzerland,
                                 Switzerland
Heiko Maus   DFKI Deutsche Forschungszentrum für
                                 Künstliche Intelligenz GmbH, Germany
Raghava Mutharaju   IIIT-Delhi, India
Andrea Polini   University of Camerino, Italy
Uwe Riss   OST University of Applied Sciences of
                                 Eastern Switzerland, Switzerland
Ben Roelens   Open Universiteit, The Netherlands
Kurt Sandkuhl   University of Rostock, Germany

Md Kamruzzaman Sarker	University of Hartford, USA
Hanlie Smuts	University of Pretoria, South Africa
Alta van der Merwe	University of Pretoria, South Africa
Frank van Harmelen	Vrije Universiteit Amsterdam, The Netherlands

A Morphological Box for AI Solutions: Evaluation, Refinement and Application Potentials

Jack Daniel Rittelmeyer[1]([✉]) [iD] and Kurt Sandkuhl[1,2] [iD]

[1] Institute of Computer Science, University of Rostock, Albert-Einstein-Str. 22, 18059 Rostock, Germany
{jack.rittelmeyer,kurt.sandkuhl}@uni-rostock.de
[2] School of Engineering, Jönköping University, Jönköping, Sweden
kurt.sandkuhl@ju.se

Abstract. The understanding of the concepts of AI is still one of the major problems for companies that want to implement AI solutions, from our own experience. Because of that, we presented an initial version of a morphological box that supports the understanding of AI solutions in previous work [1]. We now evaluated the morphological box with expert interviews from different domains and a short literature search. We present the planning, conduction and analysis of the interviews as well as a refined version of the morphological box for AI solutions. For the analysis we used the approach of qualitative content analysis by Mayring & Fenzl [2]. The interviews helped to identify several new features and values and they offered interesting insights into important aspects for AI introduction and into the introduction process itself from practitioners' perspectives. Furthermore, we illustrate some of the boxes application potential along the information system development process and future improvement and application potentials.

Keywords: Morphological box · organizational AI solutions · artificial intelligence · AI context

1 Introduction

Technological advances in the last years have made artificial intelligence (AI) solutions very attractive for enterprises in various industry domains. The advantages commonly attributed to AI solutions include that they open for automation potential, support process innovation or lead to new kinds of products. Many researchers consider AI as one of the cornerstones of digital transformation (e.g., [3] and [4]). Recent studies claim that more than 75% of all large enterprises and 50% of enterprises with less than 1.000 employees work on AI solutions [5]; in the sector of small and medium-sized enterprises, more than 45% are interested in AI solutions and 21% consider AI as an essential topic for the future and started to investigate the use of AI in the own business [6].

However, what also has been observed during the introduction of AI solutions into organizations is that development processes of AI solutions create different challenges

M. Ruiz and P. Soffer (Eds.): CAiSE 2023 Workshops, LNBIP 482, pp. 5–16, 2023.
https://doi.org/10.1007/978-3-031-34985-0_1

than development of other, more established kinds of IT or information systems (IS). Some of the challenges are related to the current technology-hype concerning AI technologies and solutions [7], which can "blur the distinction between what the technology can actually do and what potential users imagine" [8]. Other challenges relate to the specific needs of AI solutions when it comes to the availability and quality of large datasets or domain knowledge, and workflows to be supported.

We argue that methodical support for the organizational introduction of AI solutions is needed that not only addresses the IT-related aspects but also supports decision making, scoping and requirements definition for AI solutions, i.e., coordination and alignment of business and IT-related aspects. Our approach is to support understanding and managing complexity of organizational AI solution by decomposing this complexity into aspects that represent the features of AI solutions. More concretely, we propose a morphological box for the use in organizational AI solution development. In previous work, we developed an initial version of this morphological box [1]. This paper focuses on improving the box by using results from expert interviews and illustrating its application potential.

The main contributions of our work are (a) results from expert interviews on utility and applicability of a morphological box in AI solution development, (b) an improved version of the morphological box, and (c) a discussion of application potential along the information system development processes.

The paper is structured as follows: Sect. 2 summarizes previous work and related research. Section 3 introduces the research method used in our work. Section 4 addresses the planning of expert interviews for evaluating the first version of the morphological box. Section 5 presents the findings from the interviews. In Sect. 6, the refined version of the box is presented. Section 7 discusses application potential, limitations and future work.

2   Theoretical Background and Related Work

In this chapter, we will summarize the most relevant background and related work for the morphological box (Sect. 2.1) and AI solution development (Sect. 2.2).

2.1   Morphological Box for AI Solutions

According to Zwicky [9], a morphological box is a tool from product development that can help to solve problems by dividing them into several smaller problems for which solutions can be found easier. These smaller problems can then be seen as features for which solutions should be provided as values for the features. A morphological box is often represented as a table with features in the first row and then the values for each feature in the following rows. The development starts with a problem statement, followed by gathering an initial set of features and values.

In previous work [1], we presented a morphological box that supports the development and integration of AI solutions in companies (see Fig. 1). The box was developed on four own industrial use cases for AI solutions from different application domains. We further applied the box to the AI context model presented in [10] and showed that it can help with the introduction of AI by improving different steps of the context model.

This showed that the application led to more complete requirements for AI solutions. Nevertheless, the development of the box was only based on four use cases and its application showed some room for improvement. Because of that, we decided to enhance the empirical basis of the box with expert interviews as a qualitative approach next. The primary purpose was to analyze the box for completeness and potential overlaps.

Feature	Values			
Computing source	cloud	local	device	hybrid
Maturity	COTS	Commercial components	Open source components	Individual
Special hardware required	Computing	Data capture	Data visualization	Data output
Data source	Own data	Open data	Commercial collection	Synthetic data
Data and model update frequency	Continuously	None	In case of changes in regulation	In case of quality problems
Time to decision	Real-time	Near real-time	Several hours	Not time critical
Primary data type	Audio / Video	Raster image / Vector image	Transaction records	Time series data
Primary purpose	assistance / decision making	forecasting	classification	anomaly detection
AI use in solution development	Design time	Runtime	Accompanying runtime	Hybrid
AI focus	Processing input	Generating output		Computing task
Extent of effect on enterprise	Isolated solution	Effect on single process / Complete process	Work system	Business model
Reliability and precision of results	100% required	Defined by enterprise		Defined by domain

Fig. 1. Morphological box for AI solutions from [1]

2.2 AI Solution Development

In previous work, we conducted a literature analysis to identify procedural approaches for the introduction of AI solutions into organizations [11]. The main finding of this work was that the general phases to be taken are basically identical to the introduction of information systems or software systems, and differences are visible within these general phases. Thus, for the general process of introducing AI solutions, the following phases typically are recommended by IS development methods [12]. For the realization phase, refinements from software development methods were included [13]:

The first phase is used for decision-making and can include different tasks depending on the starting point. An analysis of the AI potential should take place if no specific AI application has yet been defined, but the possibilities are to be considered in general. Here, examples of AI applications of other companies from the own industry or the analysis of the business model can be relevant. A feasibility analysis is the right step if the purpose of the AI use is already clear, but there are technical uncertainties regarding sufficient data quality or accuracy of the AI. A context analysis is important when the analysis of potential has identified promising AI applications, but it is not clear which departments, processes or data would be affected and what all would need to be changed. This is basically where the company's readiness for AI implementation is examined. Budget estimation and potential suppliers or development partners should also be explored in the process. The result of the first phase is the decision for which purpose and where in the company AI should be introduced.

The second phase is the specification of the operational integration and technical features of the AI solution. This also includes how these will be checked (evaluation). Operational integration is sometimes very simple (e.g., installing an AI component in a machine with no impact on processes), but often it changes processes and places new demands on employees and the entire organization. This must be recognized early on and specified accordingly. The technical specifications for the development (functionality of the AI, specifications for accuracy and speed) should also be defined, especially if the solution is developed or delivered and installed by external parties.

The third phase is then usually the contracting and realization. Few companies will be able to develop the planned AI in-house, so contracting out is necessary. During realization, there is usually involvement of the company in the project when it comes to concretizing processes or providing data.

The final phase is acceptance and introduction. The defined properties from the specification phase can then be used for acceptance of the AI solution. Likewise, the operational changes defined there help with their implementation.

3   Research Approach

From our own experience and projects, we discovered a need for an artifact that can support companies with the introduction of AI. Using the Design Science Research (DSR) approach by Hevner et al. [14] as a guideline, we started to identify and motivate the problem on hand with a structured literature review [11]. In the next step, we developed our artifact, a morphological box to assist in the design and evaluation of AI solutions (see Sect. 2.2) [1]. For a first evaluation of our artifact, we decided to conduct a qualitative evaluation, which is presented in this paper. Additionally, we wanted to demonstrate some first application potentials for the box.

To ensure that our artifact included all relevant features and values and that the existing features and values were truly relevant, we chose guideline-based interviews as a qualitative method. Participants for the interviews were selected based on their experience in developing and/or introducing AI applications. By targeting this audience, we were able to gain insights from experts who had real-world experience with the challenges and opportunities of AI applications.

To analyze the results of the interviews, we used qualitative content analysis according to Mayring & Fenzl [2]. This approach allowed us to use our existing features and values as a starting set for the categories used to label the data. The advantage of this approach was that it allowed us to leverage our existing knowledge and understanding of the field, while also gaining insights from the experiences and perspectives of the interview participants. By combining our current knowledge with the insights gained from the interviews, we were able to refine and improve the morphological box as a tool for designing and evaluating AI solutions.

4 Interview Planning and Conduction

The purpose of the interviews was to evaluate the morphological box and its individual parts. To achieve this, we employed a mixed-method approach by combining two standard interviewing techniques: narrative and focused interviews. While focused interviews are guideline-based and concentrate on a specific object of research, narrative interviews allow interviewees to talk openly about a topic without the influence of already existing theories or leading questions. As our goal was to identify new features and values, we chose to incorporate the four phases of the narrative interview into a guideline to combine both approaches.

The interview guideline comprised seven parts: the greeting, entry questions, a narrative phase, a question phase, the evaluation of the morphological box itself, a summary and finally the ending. Before conducting the interviews, we assigned two researchers for each interview. One researcher conducted the interview by asking questions and the other researcher directly wrote down important statements about the morphological box and any potential features and values. We recorded all interviews using Zoom to transcribe and analyze them thoroughly later.

The greeting served as an icebreaker to help the interviewee feel comfortable and familiar with the interview topic. This was followed by entry questions such as age, gender, and work experience to ease the interviewee into the interview. These two phases served as our opening phase.

Next, we proceeded to the narrative phase, where we asked the interviewee to describe one of their past AI projects and guide us through its development and introduction process. This approach helped us gain an unaffected view of an AI project and all its potentially relevant aspects. During this phase, the interviewee mostly spoke, and the interviewers observed and listened.

Following the narrative phase, we proceeded to the question phase, where the interviewee was asked to clarify any unclear points and elaborate on features or values. The interviewee was also asked to reflect on lessons learned, what worked well or not, and the most critical aspects for a successful AI development and introduction. The questions were formulated openly to elicit unaltered responses.

After the narrative part of the interview, we introduced the morphological box to the interviewee. Since the box had six features with up to six values each, we showed and explained only two features with their respective values at a time so that the interviewee could comprehend the information. After every two features and values were explained, the interviewee was given time to think about them and was asked to agree or disagree with all values for the corresponding feature. Finally, the interviewee was asked whether the values were sufficient to describe all possible characteristics of the feature, or if additional values were necessary.

At the end of this phase, the interviewee was asked again to reflect on what aspects are relevant for successful AI development and integration, and whether the features of the box represent all of them or if further features are necessary. The interviewee was also asked to identify which aspects are fundamental and which are less critical for successful AI development and integration.

Finally, the recording interviewer summarized the most important points of the interview and asked the interviewee if everything was understood correctly and whether they wished to add anything. For the closing, the interviewee was asked to provide feedback about the interview, whether they enjoyed it, what they liked/did not like, if any answers were too complex, and if they wished to add anything we may have missed. The interviewee was thanked for their time and effort.

5 Interview Findings

We conducted three interviews between June and August 2022 with male participants aged between 20 and 40. Each interview lasted 45–60 min. In this chapter, we will summarize the findings from each interview, including the interviewees' AI projects and their thoughts on the various features and values of the morphological box.

Interviewee A was the head of sales for a company that develops AI solutions for other companies. His AI example was a photo/picture analysis software that extracts information from photos of insurance policy documents, adds the data to a customer relationship management system, and then makes a counteroffer. The solution replaced a process that generally took around 15–20 min for an employee, but the AI-based solution only needed about two seconds. The recognition rate is approximately 97%, which was only possible due to close cooperation between the developers and the relevant department of the customer. The project took them twelve instead of six months because they had insufficient suitable data. In this case, the AI must be trained continuously to hold the 97% precision rate, especially when new documents occur. The interviewee also mentioned that data security was important for the customer because the AI would work with very personal and confidential data.

Regarding the morphological box, Interviewee A thought that the cloud option was the most important computing source, and the term "device" was unclear to him. In an ideal case, only own data would be used, and open data would be difficult to use. Continuous updating of the AI is crucial to maintain precision, and any failure to update the model or data could be dangerous. In his opinion, an AI's decision is always time-critical, so the value "not time-critical" would be unrealistic. It would be best to use the AI in all steps of solution development, with the AI focus combining input and output. After explaining the difference between "effects on a single process" and "complete process," he suggested "workflow" as a suitable term. A precision of 100% is not realistic, and the goal should instead be 99.9%. Another relevant aspect for him is how well his market competitors are performing. According to him, the most essential features for a successful AI implementation are the data and computing source, update frequency, time to decision, data type, the primary purpose, and reliability/decision.

Interviewee B was a developer for a financial company with eight months of experience in this role. He worked on a project where an AI for fraud detection in the financial sector was developed. During the narrative part, he quickly emphasized that close cooperation with the relevant departments was important. On one side, the end-users wanted to understand the AI. On the other side, the developers needed to understand the data. They were able to reach an error detection rate on the same level a human could achieve. But to hold this level, the application has to be updated continuously, mainly to prevent mistakes when customer behaviour changes, which happens occasionally in the financial industry according to him. They also had to acquire new servers and virtual machines for their application. He also states that a new application needs to provide additional value to a company to be accepted by the employees.

Interviewee B did not provide as much feedback as Interviewee A regarding the morphological box. However, he noted the importance of continuous updating to prevent mistakes and maintain a high error detection rate.

Interviewee C was a director for a company that develops AI applications for their customers, with eight years of experience in this role. He chose a project where they developed an AI for document processing. He mentioned the importance of data quality and quantity for AI applications and he emphasized the importance of knowing what level of knowledge the employees in the companies have and if the AI has to be trained continuously after implementation by themselves. For example, if they are not IT-savvy, the user interface and experience must be as simple as possible. Also, the question arises if the employees may need some training before they can update the AI continuously. He also highlighted the importance of data security, which can be a concern when handling sensitive data that cannot be stored on a cloud-based solution.

Considering the morphological box, the interviewee suggested adding "augmented data" as a new value for data sources and emphasized the importance of context and content understanding for the primary purpose feature. He doubted that 100% reliability could ever be achieved and suggested that pursuing such a goal could hinder development. In terms of computing source, he considered cloud computing to be the most crucial factor, although it would need to be supported by appropriate hardware. He identified the most critical features as data source, required hardware, and time to decision. The interviewee stressed the importance of careful consideration and planning when developing and implementing AI applications. Factors such as data quality and security, user interface and experience, and ongoing employee training and support are all crucial elements that must be addressed to ensure the successful implementation and adoption of AI technologies.

The three interviews highlighted the importance of close cooperation between the developers and the relevant departments of the customer to develop successful AI solutions. All three interviewees emphasized the importance of data quality and quantity for AI applications and the need for continuous updating of the AI to hold a high precision rate. The interviewees also discussed the importance of data security, particularly when handling personal and confidential data. Regarding the morphological box, the computing source and data source were identified as the most important features, while 100% reliability was deemed unrealistic. The primary purpose of the AI solution and the time to decision were also highlighted as essential features. Overall, the interviews provided insights into the challenges and key factors involved in developing and implementing successful AI solutions.

6 Analysis and Discussion

The interviews with three AI experts revealed new features and values. Additionally, they revealed room for improvement regarding some values and confirmed the current features and values as relevant according to their opinion.

The following new features emerged from the interviews with the interviewees that mentioned them in parenthesis: Data quantity (A, C), data quality (A, C), data security

(A, B, C), communication/coordination with end-user departments (A, B), added value for the Company (B) and ease of use/usability (C).

The interviews showed quite clearly that a number of features were missing so far, especially regarding the data aspect. This is a fascinating observation because the vast amount of data required for practical AI applications is one of the main aspects that differentiates them from "classical" software. In the course of this, two interviewees mentioned "Data Quantity" and "Data Quality" as essential aspects because a considerable amount of high-quality data is usually required to train e.g., neural networks. How much data is actually needed depends on the specific use case. The quality of data could be measured with different data quality metrics like consistency, completeness, noisiness or duplicate records. The third data-related feature is "Data Security" which should also include legal requirements and, therefore could be measured by aspects like compliance, data encryption, access control or data integrity. This feature contains dependencies to the features computing source and data source because it can be relevant for data security where the data is processed (e.g., in a cloud on a server somewhere in the USA or on a device in ones company) and which data is processed (e.g. personal or user data compared to open data).

The next feature "Communication" with the end-user (department), is especially relevant if the AI development will be outsourced to another company and the interviewees emphasized that this aspect highly influences the success of an AI project because the end-users have to use the application later and are often the ones who deliver the training data. This leads to the fact that most of the time a frequent, detailed and active communication is required, but depending on the size and impact of the application, less communication or communication only at specific points during the development process could be enough.

This also leads to the last possible new features "Added Value" for the company and "Ease of Use". As mentioned, the end-users are often other people than the developers of an application, making it important first to know who the end-user will be (IT-expert, IT-savvy or no IT knowledge at all) and then to design the user interface and experience as easy as possible for the user group. This also connects to the data and model update frequency because if they have to be updated continuously, e.g., trained further with new data to stay up-to-date, the end-user could also be responsible for this. And if this is the case, it must also be as easy as possible for him to update the model. It could also be the case that the end-user needs to be trained first to be able to update the model continuously. Because the level of accessibility of the application as well as other aspects depend on the end-user, we decided to add a feature "End-User" instead of "Ease of Use". The values can then be determined as "IT-Expert", "IT-Savvy", and "No IT Knowledge".

To know the added value of an AI application is highly important to calculate if the investments in developing and integrating it (time, money, personnel, etc.) are worth the effort in the long term. The added value can also be an important aspect for accepting a new application, especially because often employees are sceptical regarding AI applications because they cannot completely understand how they function or are afraid to lose their jobs because of them. To be able to show them how they can also benefit from a new application could potentially help with the acceptance and boost the integration as well. Besides that, the main problem with this possible feature is how can you determine the value? This is highly individual and depends on many different aspects of a company. Because of that, we chose not to include added value as a feature, but we still want to emphasize its importance of it at this point.

Similarly to the features, the following new values were revealed: One interviewee suggested "prototype" as a new step between open-source components and individual for maturity (A) as well as "Augmented Data" as another data source (C).

Regarding the update frequency of the data and the model, two new cases were revealed. According to the experience of the interviewees, the AI should be trained with new data, especially when new additional documents need to be recognized (in the case of document recognition applications and similar cases) (A, B) and when customer behaviour changes (B). It could be argued that both values are rather specific and could be covered by the "in the case of quality problems" value. In our opinion, both cases are two events that could be relevant for many AI applications similar to the "changes in regulation" value. Furthermore, as the box itself should also help companies that have no knowledge about AI, it would be helpful for them to provide them with as many different scenarios as possible so that they can decide if those events could occur for them in the future.

A new primary purpose could be the context and content understanding (C). According to the interviewee, this understanding of the relevant content from images, documents, etc., builds the basis for other values like decision-making, classification or anomaly detection. The question that arises now is, is context and content understanding a value of its own? Are there AI applications that only understand the context and content and then do nothing else based on that? In our opinion, there will always be another action after the understanding. Because all existing values indirectly already include the context and content understanding as a necessary part of their purpose, we decided not to add this as a new value.

Regarding reliability and precision, all interviewees agreed that an absolute precision rate of 100% is impossible and not practical (A, B, C). They suggested lowering it to approximately 99,9%. Additionally, two interviewees made it clear that the necessary reliability and precision are often determined by their competitors and how well their solutions perform (A, B).

Finally, two values were marked as not possible or correct. First, no data or model updates at all would be unrealistic because there would always be change and if the AI were not updated, it would be guaranteed to be outdated at one point and then produce wrong results (B). Similarly, it would never be the case that the time to decision would entirely not be time critical (A). Even if the results are not needed directly or in a few hours at some point, they will be required (even after days, months, etc.) because otherwise, the application itself would be unnecessary. A suggestion was to use days or just at a "later" time as a value instead.

Also, some values were not clear and precise enough for the interviewees: For the computing source, "device" was unclear (A), and for the extent of the effect the difference between "single" and "complete process" was unclear. To make the wording of our values more precise, we changed the values "device" to "end-device" and "complete process" to "workflow". The difference here is that a single process consists of only one process, and a workflow can consist of several processes.

Feature	Values				
Computing Source	Cloud	Local computing center		End-Device	Hybrid
Maturity	COTS	Commercial Components	Open Source Components	Prototype	Individual
Special Hardware Required	Computing	Data Capture		Data Visualization	Data Output
Data Source	Own Data	Augmented Data	Open Data	Commercial Collection	Synthetic Data
Data Quantity	Very High	High	Moderate	Low	Very Low
Data Quality	Inconsistent	Duplicate	Incomplete	Outdated	Biased	Noisy	Corrupted
Data Security	Compliance	Data Encryption	Access Control	Data Integrity	Data Privacy	Incident Management	Audit & Monitoring
Data and Model Update Frequency	Continuously	In Case of Changes in Regulation	In Case of New Documents/Data	In case of Changes in Customer Behavior	In Case of Quality Problems
End-User	IT-Expert	IT-Savvy		No IT-Knowledge	
Time to Decision	Real-time	Near Real-Time	Several Hours	Later	
Primary Data Type	Audio	Video	Raster Image	Vector Image	Transaction Records	Time Series Data
Primary Purpose	Assistance	Decision Making	Forecasting	Classification	Anomaly Detection
Point in Time of AI Use in Solution Development	Design-Time	Runtime		Accompanying Runtime	Hybrid
AI Focus	Processing Input	Generating Output		Computing Task	
Extent of Effect on Enterprise	Isolated Solution	Single Process	Workflow	Work System	Business Model
Reliability and Precision of Results	~ 99,9 % Required	Defined by Enterprise	Defined by Domain	Defined by Competitors	
Communication	Frequent & Detailed, Active Collaboration	Regular, Some Collaboration	Minimal, Minimum Collaboration	Specific Moments	None

Fig. 2. Revised version of the morphological box for AI solutions (Color figure online)

All of the discussed new and updated features and values (in green) led to a revised version of the morphological box (see Fig. 2). As we could not extract values for all new features, we conducted a literature search for suitable values. Especially for the features data quantity, quality and security it was difficult to define precise values. As we try to help to implement AI solutions with the morphological box, one could naturally argue for values in a range from very high to very low in regard of what the requirements for the solutions are. But we want to achieve more tangible values that can be measured. For data quality and security, we found suitable values that can be analyzed. However, those values are still on another level of abstraction than the remaining values. Because of that, further research is required regarding the values of the new features to refine them. One possibility could be to create different views for the morphological box depending on the user (e.g., AI expert or no AI knowledge). Because of the increased number of features, grouping the features into categories like technical features (e.g., computing source, data source) and business features (e.g., extent of effect on enterprise, communication, end-user) could also be useful.

7   Application Potentials and Future Work

One of the core contributions of this paper is a new version of the morphological box supporting the organizational introduction of AI solutions. In this context, the applicability of the box during the different phases is an important topic. In an initial step, we evaluate the applicability by using the different phases and steps discussed in Sect. 2.2. Table 1 shows the phases and steps and how the box could be used.

Table 1. Application potential of the morphological box along the IS development process

Phase	Step	Use of the morphological box
Decision Making	Analysis of AI potential	Features support the understanding of the variety of possible AI applications
	Feasibility analysis	Features support the understanding of the general preconditions for AI
	Readiness check	Features support the understanding of the general preconditions for AI
Specification	Specify operational integration	Features and values contribute to an analysis of the AI solution context in an organization, as demonstrated in [1]
	Technical specification	No significant application potential
Contracting & realization	Make or buy decision	Features and values contribute to outlining the desired AI solution from which the company's experts can use to decide if they have the knowledge to develop it themselves
	Development of AI solution	Features and values contribute to requirements engineering as demonstrated in [1]
	Integration of AI solution	Values help to know the end-user if training will be necessary, the extent of impact the solution will have on the company and how much communication will be required
Acceptance and introduction	Acceptance test	No significant application potential
	Implementation of operational integration	No significant application potential
	Training	"End-user" helps to determine the end-user and necessary training early

As shown in Table 1, the box could potentially be helpful in several stages of the AI solution development process. Future work will be a further validation of the new version of the box. An established taxonomy development process should be consolidated and followed for additional orientation. Following such an approach, quality metrics should be used to evaluate the maturity of the box. After the theoretical evaluation is completed, the box also needs to be used and evaluated in practical use cases.

References

1. Rittelmeyer, J.D., Sandkuhl, K.: Features of AI Solutions and their Use in AI Context Modeling. Gesellschaft für Informatik e.V (2022)

2. Mayring, P., Fenzl, T.: Qualitative Inhaltsanalyse Handbuch Methoden der empirischen Sozialforschung, pp. 633–648. Springer, Wiesbaden (2019). https://doi.org/10.1007/978-3-658-21308-4_42

3. Bordeleau, F.-È., Felden, C.: Digitally transforming organisations: a review of change models of industry 4.0. In: Proceedings of the 27th European Conference on Information Systems (ECIS) (2019)

4. Hirsch-Kreinsen, H., Hompel, M.T.: Digitalization of industrial work. Development perspectives and design approaches. Manual Industry, vol. 4 (2017)

5. IDG: Studie Machine Learning 2021 (2023). https://www.lufthansa-industry-solutions.com/de-de/studien/idg-studie-machine-learning-2021

6. Vitera, J., et al.: On the Importance of Digital Transformation for SME-Results from a Survey among German SME (2020)

7. Panetta, K.: 5 Trends Emerge in the Gartner Hype Cycle for Emerging Technologies (2018). https://www.gartner.com/smarterwithgartner/5-trends-emerge-in-gartner-hype-cycle-for-emerging-technologies-2018/

8. Hedman, J., Gimpel, G.: The adoption of hyped technologies: a qualitative study. Inf. Technol. Manage. **11**, 161–175 (2010)

9. Zwicky, F.: Discovery, invention, research through the morphological approach (1969)

10. Sandkuhl, K., Rittelmeyer, J.D.: Use of EA Models in Organizational AI Solution Development, pp. 149–166. Springer, Cham (2022). https://doi.org/10.1007/978-3-031-11520-2_10

11. Rittelmeyer, J.D., Sandkuhl, K.: Effects of artificial intelligence on enterprise architectures - a structured literature review. In: 2021 IEEE 25th International Enterprise Distributed Object Computing Workshop (EDOCW). IEEE (2021). https://doi.org/10.1109/edocw52865.2021.00042

12. Avison, D., Fitzgerald, G.: Information Systems Development: Methodologies, Techniques and Tools. McGraw-Hill, New York (2003)

13. Sommerville, I.: Software Engineering. Pearson, New York (2011)

14. Hevner, M., Park, R.: Design science in information systems research. MIS Q. **28**, 75 (2004). https://doi.org/10.2307/25148625

Enriching Enterprise Architecture Models with Healthcare Domain Knowledge

Valeriia Afonina[1]([⊠]) (iD), Knut Hinkelmann[1,3]([⊠]) (iD),
and Devid Montecchiari[1,2]([⊠]) (iD)

[1] FHNW University of Applied Sciences and Arts Northwestern Switzerland,
Windisch, Switzerland
valeriia.afonina@alumni.fhnw.ch,
{knut.hinkelmann,devid.montecchiari}@fhnw.ch
[2] School of Science and Technology, UNICAM University of Camerino,
Camerino, Italy
[3] Department of Informatics, University of Pretoria, Pretoria, South Africa

Abstract. Enterprise architecture (EA) modeling gives an opportunity to have an overview of the enterprise architecture supporting business-IT alignment within the rapidly changing environment. Visual representation of enterprise architecture models is appropriate for interpretation by humans. Machines, however, cannot interpret labels associated with the model element, as well as its domain-specific concepts. To make EA models machine-interpretable, a graphical representation of models shall be connected to domain knowledge. This research demonstrates an approach to enriching the EA model of a medical institution with healthcare domain knowledge. Evaluation of the developed solution proves that a human and a machine could equally understand the ontology-based EA model.

Keywords: Domain Knowledge · Conceptual Modeling ·
Ontology-based Modeling · Enterprise Architecture Modeling ·
Ontology Engineering · Medical Domain Knowledge · Semantic Lifting

1 Introduction

Enterprise architecture modeling is the process of creating models of an organization's business elements and information technology. It involves capturing the interrelationships and dependencies between the different architecture components in order to understand how they interact, identify areas of conflict, and adapt to change by creating strategies and making decisions for improving the organization's efficiency and effectiveness. It makes organizations more flexible and adaptive in the rapidly changing environment and enables a better alignment of business and IT in the Digital Age [17,21,31].

Graphical models are appropriate for use by humans. Interpretation of models requires knowledge about the modeling elements and the domain. Knowledge about the modeling elements is captured in the metamodel and can be interpreted by a machine. For example, it is possible to retrieve all elements of a

M. Ruiz and P. Soffer (Eds.): CAiSE 2023 Workshops, LNBIP 482, pp. 17–28, 2023.
https://doi.org/10.1007/978-3-031-34985-0_2

specific type (e.g. all business processes and business services) that are connected with a specific relation (e.g. realize). For a complete interpretation of a model, it is required that one can also interpret the labels of elements. For example, if a business process is labeled as "send invoice", we as humans can interpret the meaning. For a machine, however, the label is just a string without specific meaning. Enriching EA models with explicit representation of domain knowledge - as it is known from symbolic Artificial Intelligence - can increase the level of machine-interpretability.

An ontology is an explicit specification of a conceptualization of domain knowledge [16] and introduces terminology [8]. It thus can be a basis for a shared understanding of EA models. While a visual representation of EA models can be understood by a human, an ontology-based representation of the models can be interpreted also by a machine. In [20] it is shown how an ontology about APQC process framework can be used to represent the functionality of a business process - enabling the selection of appropriate cloud services.

This research explores how a medical ontology can be connected to an enterprise architecture model, making this model understandable by both humana and machines. We chose the medical domain because there already exist several medical ontologies which can be reused. They provide a good basis for a shared understanding of the knowledge represented in the EA model in healthcare. This work takes a pragmatic standpoint. We examine the combination of enterprise architecture models and medical ontologies in the scenario of ophthalmological appointments.

In Sect. 2 we describe the state of the art in ontology-based EA modeling in healthcare. Section 3 described the research method. The suggested solution is presented in Sect. 4. The process of implementation of the solution is presented in Sect. 5 using an example of one of the EA model elements. Finally, an evaluation of the developed solution is conducted using the SPARQL [39] query of the constructed enterprise ontology and is presented in Sect. 6.

2 Literature Review

This section introduces Enterprise Modeling and Ontology-based Modeling with a focus on the medical domain. Then the current state of using EA models and medical ontologies is discussed. In conclusion, the identified knowledge gap and the research problem are described.

2.1 Enterprise Modeling

Enterprise Modeling is about representing knowledge about an enterprise. It can be applied in many different domains for different purposes, for instance, strategic planning, and information support, but it has to be supported by specific domain knowledge and controlled by people with a high level of expertise in this domain in order to "produce results of satisfactory completeness and quality" [4].

An Enterprise Model (EM) represents elements of an enterprise, including structure, processes, information resources, actors, products, etc. [11]. Management of the EA has become increasingly recognized as a crucial part of both business and IT management [40]. Enterprise Architecture Modeling can be used to provide a description of how an enterprise operates at the current time; a "blueprint" of how it should operate in the future, and a roadmap for getting to the target state" [34]. To perform effective EA management, a model - a visual representation of an EA should be created following the special methodologies, frameworks, and modeling languages. One of the widely used EA modeling languages is ArchiMate [43].

2.2 Enterprise Modeling in Healthcare

The increasing effectiveness and efficiency of a hospital using the EA modeling approach were proven by various researchers [14,22]. Ahsan et al. [1], after developing and analyzing an enterprise architecture model of a hospital in the UK, concluded that enterprise architecture could help hospital management analyze a hospital's current performance and develop a set of recommendations for improvements. Enterprise architecture supports decision-making and can be used as a planning tool by enabling a conceptual view of the enterprise [1].

In a case study conducted in Dharmais Cancer Hospital, Girsang and Abimanyu [14] identified four main performance issues: lack of ownership from business users, lack of alignment between business strategy and IT strategy, lack of awareness to use IT as a tool for competitive advantage, and low quality of IT operation performances. After modeling the hospital architecture, Girsang and Abimanyu [14] identified some issues in the primary activities of the hospital that lack guidance and governance, such as education and training activities, research activities, etc. Further, they provided a set of recommendations to the hospital, that could help them to improve the quality of the performance.

2.3 Semantic Lifting of Enterprise Models

Ontologies provide a vocabulary of domain-specific concepts with defined machine-interpretable semantics. Enhancing the human-interpretable graphical model with a machine-interpretable ontology is called semantic lifting [19]. There have been several approaches for semantic lifting, which provide semantic annotations of conceptual models [9], create knowledge graphs for Enterprise Architecture [15] or process models [2], link diagrammatic models with ontologies [5] or create ontology-based metamodels [25].

Semantic lifting of enterprise models can be achieved by enhancing models with enterprise ontologies [7]. Many enterprise and business ontologies and frameworks have been proposed [26]. There are generic enterprise ontologies (EO) such as TOVE [10,11], EO [44], EKD [27], REA [12], CEO [3], BMO [38]. Some more specific like the North American Industry Classification System (NAICS) that contains definitions of 1800 categories for classifying business establishments [41] and the OntoWeb ontology for e-commerce [24]. ArchiMEO [21] is a recent enterprise ontology that is based on the metamodel of the standardized Archimate modeling language for EA [43]. It can be extended for various application domains.

2.4   Medical Ontologies and Their Usage in Information Systems

One of the most widely used medical ontologies is the International Classification of Diseases [23], a collection of descriptions of diseases, their symptoms, signs, and abnormal findings, known by medicine to date, which healthcare specialists use for different clinical purposes. There are many ontologies in the healthcare domain, that could be used for a specific purpose, for instance, the DRON ontology contains data about medicaments [42], Traditional Indian Medicine (TIM) Ontology [45], the gene ontology GO [13]. Ontology of Medically Related Social Entities OMRSE [37] covers the domain of healthcare-related social entities, medical subject headings ontology MESH [33] hierarchically organized biomedical and health-related information. Medical Dictionary for Regulatory Activities MedDRA is an ontology of international medical terminology designed for the registration, documentation, and safety monitoring of medicinal products through all phases of the drug-development cycle [32].

There are applications of medical ontologies and medical domain knowledge in information systems, like Automating Medical Text Report Classification [46], process mining in healthcare [30,35], in machine learning for disease prediction [47], the effective handling of IT-based healthcare system problems [48], and knowledge management and cooperative work in a healthcare network [6].

2.5   Research Problem: Semantic Lifting of Enterprise Architecture Models in Healthcare

While there are several approaches for the semantic lifting of enterprise model with enterprise ontologies (see Sect. 2.3) and several approaches for integrating medical ontologies with information systems applications (see Sect. 2.4), there is no semantic lifting of EA model with medical ontologies. This is the focus of the research.

3   Research Method

The research objective is to prove that a medical ontology can be connected to a visual representation of an EA model to make it understandable by a machine. To achieve the goal of this research, we applied the Design Science Research (DSR) methodology described by [18] because of its constructive approach. The fundamental principle of design science research is that knowledge and understanding of a design problem and its solution are acquired by building and applying an artifact. The artifact developed during this study is an ontology-based enterprise architecture model of patient admission and ophthalmological appointment represented in a single modeling environment. According to the DSR methodology, the five phases of the research were performed: problem awareness, suggestion, development, evaluation, and conclusion. The problem awareness phase starts with a literature review of the three main topics: Enterprise Modeling, Ontology-based Modeling, and Medical Enterprise Ontologies (see Sect. 2).

The findings from the literature showed that the ontology-based EA modeling approach is actively discussed among researchers, but has not found a broad application in practice when medical ontologies have already found a broader application for different cases.

In addition to the literature review, to collect the qualitative data during the problem awareness phase, we conducted two interviews with experts from a medical institution called "The Eye Clinic" - a manager of the clinic and an ophthalmologist. Based on the collected data, we modeled the enterprise architecture for ophthalmological appointments in the clinic. The information gathered during these interviews and the modeling experience was used to define the requirements for the developed solution.

In the suggestion phase, we describe a "step-by-step approach" to how to collect, represent and apply medical knowledge to extend the existing enterprise ontology ArchiMEO to the healthcare domain in accordance with the requirements determined in the use case.

The development phase demonstrates how the enriched medical knowledge enterprise architecture model can be represented in one single modeling environment, using as an example the enterprise architecture model of "The Eye Clinic".

Evaluation of the developed solution by querying the developed ontology proves that the artifact correctly displays the medical concepts and that both a human and a machine could understand the ontology-based enterprise architecture model. The conclusion summarizes the results of the research.

4   Ontology-Based Enterprise Architecture Model Development

This section describes how medical knowledge was collected, represented, and applied to support the development of an ontology-based enterprise architecture model.

4.1   Domain Knowledge in Enterprise Architecture Model

"The Eye Clinic" is a private eye clinic located in Switzerland, and it was chosen as a reference medical enterprise for this research. After two interviews with the clinic manager and an ophthalmologist, an EA model of patient admission and an ophthalmological appointment were created. The data gathered during the interviews was further used to identify what medical knowledge is captured in the EA model and should be included in the developed ontology-based EA model. According to the ontology engineering guide of Noy and McGuinness [36], we formulated competency questions to define the scope of an ontology more precisely. These competency questions were used later to evaluate if the solution contains the required knowledge.

- Competency question 1: Does an ophthalmological appointment require an insurance policy?
- Competency question 2: What ophthalmological examinations are included in the ophthalmological appointment?
- Competency question 3: What ophthalmological devices does an ophthalmologist uses to conduct those examinations?
- Competency question 4: What abnormalities could be detected with ophthalmological examinations?
- Competency question 5: Does healthcare insurance cover a medical bill?

Judging from this list of questions and following the further steps suggested by Noy and McGuinness [36], important healthcare-related terms were defined, such as "Patient", "Medical record", "Optic nerve", etc. The terms were derived by analyzing the competency questions and determining the terms that either occur in the questions or that are expected in answer to these questions.

4.2   Representation of Domain Knowledge as an Ontology

Once the EA model was completed and the important terms were enumerated, we started the development of a medical ontology that was later connected to "The Eye Clinic" EA model. The class hierarchy for the enumerated terms was defined as a first step of ontology development [36]. The next step recommended by Noy and McGuinness [36] is considering how the existing ontologies can be reused to cover the defined scope. Since this research deals with EA and healthcare knowledge, we considered reusing medical ontologies and enterprise ontology. We chose the ArchiMEO enterprise ontology because it contains the conceptual model of the ArchiMate modeling language [43], a quasi-standard for EA modeling.

To extend the ArchiMEO ontology to the medical domain, we defined which medical terms refer to which elements of the ArchiMate ontology and visually reflected this correlation using a Fact Model Diagram.

For the constructed ontology, we focused on that part of ArchiMEO that represents the concepts of ArchiMate ("archi:"). This ArchiMate ontology was extended to the scope determined from the competency question using healthcare-related terms. Some terms from ICD-10 ontology [23] were used for a definition of eye diseases, and some terms from OMRSE ontology [37] were used for the definition of insurance-related terms. The medical-related terms are represented as independent classes or sub-classes of ArchiMate concepts, relationships between terms as object properties, and the slot values of those terms as data properties. The developed ontology was named a "hospital ontology" with the prefix "ho:". Overall, the Hospital Ontology includes 96 new owl:Class and 68 owl:NamedIndividual, 36 new owl:ObjectProperty, and 25 new owl:DatatypeProperty, focusing on the presented case. We also referenced these additions to existing concepts, attributes, and relationships from the ArchiMEO, OMRSE, and ICD-10 ontologies.

5 Ontology-Based Enterprise Architecture Model Implementation

This section uses an example to describe how the ontology-based enterprise architecture model was developed and represented the Agile and Ontology-Aided Modeling Environment (AOAME). AOAME is a web application, that allows for semantic lifting by creating an ontology-based EA model and the domain ontology in a single modeling environment [25]. In the enterprise architecture of "The Eye Clinic", the "eye pressure measurement" business process includes an "ophthalmological examination". The ophthalmologic examination is conducted with an "opthalmological device" called "applanation tonometry", and it can determine "abnormalities" such as "increased eye pressure". The following fact model presents the example visually (Fig. 1).

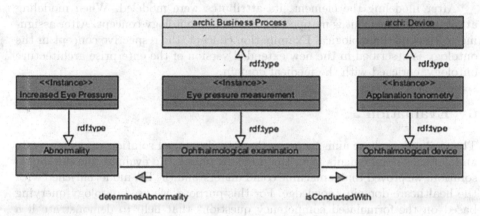

Fig. 1. Resulting fact model regarding the eye pressure measurement example.

The medical-related term "Eye Pressure Measurement" is declared a named individual in the Hospital Ontology (ho) and an instance of the "Ophthalmological examination" class. Its instantiation is representable in ArchiMate as Business process and ArchiMEO as "archi:BusinessProcess"

```
ho:EyePressureMeasurement
    rdf:type          owl:NamedIndividual ,
                      ho:OphthalmologicalExamination,
                      archi:BusinessProcess ;
    ho:examines               ho:EyePressure ;
    ho:isConductedWith    ho:ApplanationTonometry ;
    ho:isIncludedInExamination    ho:OphthalmologicalExamination .
```

Listing 1.1. Declaration of the EPM element in Hospital Ontology

With AOAME, we can use the ontology that describes the modeling language ontology (from ArchiMEO) and the medical domain ontology (our hospital ontology), which will be interpretable by a machine, and the "shape" of the element - the visual representation of instantiation of the ArchiMate business process, that will be understandable by a human.

The shape in AOAME represents the conceptual element declared in the language ontology (e.g. "archi:BusinessProcess"). Modeling of the PRM element in AOAME creates the following declaration of the element:

```
mod:Model_e8198a47-92b0-4a96-91a3-80f4dda6e2e2
    a                  mod:Model ;
    rdfs:label         "EPM" ;
    mod:modelHasShape  mod:BusinessProcess_Shape_f4622de1 .
```

Listing 1.2. Declaration of the EPM element in AOAME

After modeling the element, its attributes were modeled. When modeling attributes, the element is mapped to the domain ontology concept. After assigning to the Ophthalmological Examination concept, the respective concept in the ontology is described in the new extended version of the enterprise architecture ontology, enriched with the medical domain.

6 Evaluation

The evaluation phase aims to prove that the developed solution works correctly and satisfies requirements from the previous phases. To evaluate the developed solution, we proved that a machine could understand the EA model enriched with the healthcare domain knowledge. For this purpose, we used ontology querying based on the formulated competency questions that help to demonstrate if a machine can "understand" the medical knowledge captured in the EA model. In the scope of this research paper, we combined competency questions 4 and 5: "What abnormalities could be detected in a business process doing ophthalmological examinations, and which devices are used?".

Abnormalities are part of the healthcare knowledge, that are not graphically represented in the enterprise architecture model. A human could assume that after conducting examinations, the abnormalities will be detected and used for making a primary diagnosis. In the ontology, abnormalities were defined as the "Abnormality" class with several instantiations. For example, the "ho:EyeRedness" is an instance of the type "ho:Abnormality".

This abnormality can be detected ("ho:isDetectedWith") during the examination "ho:SlitLampExamiation" by the ("ho:isDetectedBy") "ho:SlitLamp". This abnormality was defined as a sign of diseases H10 and H20.0 - instances of the class of diseases "H00-H59" of the imported ontology ICD-10. To answer competency question 4 the following query can be executed:

```
SELECT   ?examination ?device ?abnormality
  WHERE {
  ?examination rdf:type ho:OphthalmologicalExamination.
  ?examination rdf:type archi:BusinessProcess ;
  ?examination ho:isConductedWith ?device .
  ?abnormality ho:isDetectedWith ?examination .
  ?abnormality ho:isSignOfDisease ?disease .
}
```

Listing 1.3. SPARQL query that allows to answer CQ4

The result of the SPARQL query (shown in Fig. 2) displays the relationships between abnormality and disease and what examination and what device should be used to detect these abnormalities.

examination	device	abnormality
EyePressureMeasurement	ApplanationTonometry	IncreasedEyePressure
SlitLampExamination	SlitLamp	CellsInAnteriorChamber
SlitLampExamination	MagnifyingLens	CellsInAnteriorChamber
SlitLampExamination	SlitLamp	MacularEdema

Fig. 2. Results of the query in Protegé (shortened).

The application of ontology querying for evaluating the developed solution allows us to prove that a machine can understand the required scope of medical-domain knowledge. Combined with the visual representation of the ontology-based EA model implemented in AOAME, the developed solution satisfies the defined requirements: The graphical representation is adequate for human interpretation. At the same time, a machine can interpret its representation as ontology.

7   Conclusion and Future Work

The main contribution of this research is the suggested approach to developing ontology-based enterprise architecture models that other researchers can apply and test for different domains.

While reviewing existing ontologies and analyzing the possibility of reusing some, we compiled a fact model with terms taken from different ontologies. We named these terms by adding a prefix of the related ontology. This research validates that the ArchiMEO enterprise ontology, which includes the enterprise architecture concepts from ArchiMate, can be extended to different domains and used to represent an ontology-based enterprise architecture model in the modeling environment AOAME.

Further research directions might be to study possibilities of extending the ArchiMeo ontology with domain knowledge on different levels of specificity, but also with ontologies of different domains and in relation to not only an enterprise architecture but also other enterprise models. It is also possible to recommend more in-depth research on applying ontology-based enterprise models in practice in different domains to assess the potential benefits for enterprises of using such an approach.

References

1. Ahsan, K., Shah, H., Kingston, P.: Healthcare modeling through enterprise architecture: a hospital case. In: 2010 Seventh International Conference on Information Technology: New Generations. pp. 460–465. IEEE (2010)
2. Bachhofner, S., Kiesling, E., Revoredo, K., Waibel, P., Polleres, A.: Automated Process Knowledge Graph Construction from BPMN Models. In: Strauss, C., Cuzzocrea, A., Kotsis, G., Tjoa, A.M., Khalil, I. (eds) Database and Expert Systems Applications. DEXA 2022. Lecture Notes in Computer Science, vol 13426. Springer, Cham. (2022). https://doi.org/10.1007/978-3-031-12423-5_3
3. Bertolazzi, P., Krusich, C., Missikoff, M., Manzoni, V.: An approach to the definition of a core enterprise ontology: CEO. International Workshop on Open Enterprise Solutions: Systems, Experiences, and Organizations. pp. 14–15 (2001)
4. Bubenko, J.A., Kirikova, M.: Improving the Quality of Requirements Specifications by Enterprise Modelling. In: Nilsson, A.G., Tolis, C., Nellborn, C. (eds) Perspectives on Business Modelling. Springer, Berlin, Heidelberg. (1999). https://doi.org/10.1007/978-3-642-58458-9_13
5. Buchmann, R.A., Karagiannis, D.: Enriching linked data with semantics from domain-specific diagrammatic models. Bus. Inf. Syst. Eng. **58**, 341–353 (2016)
6. Dieng-Kuntz, R., et al.: Building and using a medical ontology for knowledge management and cooperative work in a health care network. Comput. Biol. Med. **36**(7–8), 871–892 (2006)
7. Dietz, J.L.: ENTERPRISE ONTOLOGY - UNDERSTANDING THE ESSENCE OF ORGANIZATIONAL OPERATION. In: Chen, CS., Filipe, J., Seruca, I., Cordeiro, J. (eds) Enterprise Information Systems VII. Springer, Dordrecht. (2007). https://doi.org/10.1007/978-1-4020-5347-4_3
8. Enderton, H.B.: Degrees of computational complexity. J. Comput. Syst. Sci. **6**(5), 389–396 (1972)
9. Fill, H.G.: SeMFIS: a flexible engineering platform for semantic annotations of conceptual models. Semant. Web **8**(5), 747–763 (2017)
10. Fox, M.S.: The TOVE project towards a common-sense model of the enterprise. In: Belli, F., Radermacher, F.J. (eds.) IEA/AIE 1992. LNCS, vol. 604, pp. 25–34. Springer, Heidelberg (1992). https://doi.org/10.1007/BFb0024952
11. Fox, M.S., Gruninger, M.: Enterprise modeling. AI magazine **19**(3), 109–109 (1998)
12. Geerts, G. L., McCarthy, W. E.: The ontological foundation of REA enterprise information systems. In: Annual Meeting of the American Accounting Association, Philadelphia, PA. Vol. 362, pp. 127–150 (2000)
13. The Gene Ontology GO, http://geneontology.org, (2023)
14. Girsang, A.S., Abimanyu, A.: Development of an enterprise architecture for healthcare using TOGAF ADM. Emerg. Sci. J. **5**(3), 305–321 (2021)

15. Glaser, PL., Ali, S.J., Sallinger, E., Bork, D.: Model-Based Construction of Enterprise Architecture Knowledge Graphs. In: Almeida, J.P.A., Karastoyanova, D., Guizzardi, G., Montali, M., Maggi, F.M., Fonseca, C.M. (eds) Enterprise Design, Operations, and Computing. EDOC 2022. Lecture Notes in Computer Science, vol 13585. Springer, Cham. (2022). https://doi.org/10.1007/978-3-031-17604-3_4
16. Staab, S., Studer, R. (eds.): Handbook on Ontologies. IHIS, Springer, Heidelberg (2009). https://doi.org/10.1007/978-3-540-92673-3
17. Gustas, R., Gustiené, P.: A Semantically Integrated Conceptual Modelling Method for Business Process Reengineering. In: Zimmermann, A., Schmidt, R., Jain, L.C. (eds.) Architecting the Digital Transformation. ISRL, vol. 188, pp. 163–177. Springer, Cham (2021). https://doi.org/10.1007/978-3-030-49640-1_9
18. Hevner, A., Chatterjee, S.: Design Science Research in Information Systems. In: Design Research in Information Systems. Integrated Series in Information Systems, vol 22. Springer, Boston, MA. (2010). https://doi.org/10.1007/978-1-4419-5653-8_2
19. Hinkelmann, K., Gerber, A., Karagiannis, D., Thöenssen, B., Van der Merwe, A., Woitsch, R.: A new paradigm for the continuous alignment of business and IT: Combining enterprise architecture modeling and enterprise ontology. Comput. Ind. **79**, 77–86 (2016)
20. Hinkelmann, K., Laurenzi, E., Lammel, B., Kurjakovic, S., Woitsch, R.: A semantically-enhanced modelling environment for business process as a service. In: 4th International Conference on Enterprise Systems (ES). pp. 143–152. IEEE (2016)
21. Hinkelmann, K., Laurenzi, E., Martin, A., Montecchiari, D., Spahic, M., Thönssen, B.: ArchiMEO: A Standardized Enterprise Ontology based on the ArchiMate Conceptual Model. In: MODELSWARD. pp. 417–424 (2020)
22. Ilie, L., Moisescu, M. A., Caramihai, S. I., Culita, J.: Enterprise architecture role in hospital management systems development. In: 23rd International Conference on Control Systems and Computer Science (CSCS). pp. 274–279. IEEE (2021)
23. International Classification of Diseases, https://www.who.int/standards/classifications/classification-of-diseases, ICD 10th Revision (2019)
24. Jiajia, L., Wen, S.: OntoWeb: Ontology-based information exchange for knowledge management and electronic commerce. Data Anal. Knowl. Discov. **1**(2), 26–29 (2006)
25. Laurenzi, E., Hinkelmann, K., van der Merwe, A.: An Agile and Ontology-Aided Modeling Environment. In: Buchmann, R.A., Karagiannis, D., Kirikova, M. (eds.) PoEM 2018. LNBIP, vol. 335, pp. 221–237. Springer, Cham (2018). https://doi.org/10.1007/978-3-030-02302-7_14
26. Laurenzi, E., Hinkelmann, K., van der Merwe, A.: An Agile and Ontology-Aided Modeling Environment. In: Buchmann, R.A., Karagiannis, D., Kirikova, M. (eds.) PoEM 2018. LNBIP, vol. 335, pp. 221–237. Springer, Cham (2018). https://doi.org/10.1007/978-3-030-02302-7_14
27. Loucopoulos, P., Kavakli, V., Prekas, N., Rolland, C., Grosz, G., Nurcan, S.: Using the EKD approach: the modeling component. ELEKTRA-Project No. 22927. ESPRIT Programme, 7 (1998)
28. Maedche A., Ontology Learning for the Semantic Web. Kluwer Academic Publishers (2002)
29. Malhotra, A., Younesi, E., Gündel, M., Müller, B., Heneka, M.T., Hofmann-Apitius, M.: ADO: A disease ontology representing the domain knowledge specific to Alzheimer's disease. Alzheimer's Dement. **10**(2), 238–246 (2014)

30. Mans, R. S., Schonenberg, M. H., Song, M., Van der Aalst, W. M. P., Bakker, P. J. M.: Process mining in healthcare. In: International Conference on Health Informatics (HEALTHINF'08). pp. 118–125 (2015)
31. Mayer, N., Aubert, J., Grandry, E., Feltus, C., Goettelmann, E., Wieringa, R.: An integrated conceptual model for information system security risk management supported by enterprise architecture management. Softw. Syst. Model. **18**(3), 2285–2312 (2019)
32. Medical Dictionary for Regulatory Activities, MedRa, https://www.meddra.org/about-meddra/organisation/msso, version 25.0 (2022)
33. Medical subject headings ontology, (MESH), https://www.nlm.nih.gov/mesh/meshhome.html. (2022)
34. Minoli, D.: Enterprise architecture A to Z: frameworks, business process modeling, SOA, and infrastructure technology. Auerbach Publications (2008)
35. Montani, S., Leonardi, G., Quaglini, S., Cavallini, A., Micieli, G.: Improving structural medical process comparison by exploiting domain knowledge and mined information. Artif. Intell. Med. **62**(1), 33–45 (2014)
36. Noy, N. F., McGuinness, D. L.: Ontology development 101: a guide to creating your first ontology (2001)
37. Ontology of Medically Related Social Entities (MRSE), https://github.com/ufbmi/omrse, (2022)
38. Osterwalder, A.: The business model ontology a proposition in a design science approach. Doctoral dissertation, Université de Lausanne, Faculté des hautes études commerciales (2004)
39. Pérez, J., Arenas, M., Gutierrez, C.: Semantics and Complexity of SPARQL. In: Cruz, I., et al. (eds.) ISWC 2006. LNCS, vol. 4273, pp. 30–43. Springer, Heidelberg (2006). https://doi.org/10.1007/11926078_3
40. Simon, D., Fischbach, K., Schoder, D.: An exploration of enterprise architecture research. Commun. Assoc. Inf. Syst. **32**(1), 1 (2013)
41. Sirin, E., Parsia, B., Hendler, J.A.: Template-based Composition of Semantic Web Services. Agents and the Semantic Web, In AAAI Fall Symposium (2005)
42. The Drug Ontology DRON, http://purl.obolibrary.org/obo/dron.owl (2022)
43. The Open Group. ArchiMate® 3.2 Specification https://pubs.opengroup.org/architecture/archimate32-doc/ (2022)
44. Uschold, M., King, M., Moralee, S., Zorgios, Y.: The enterprise ontology. Knowl. Eng. Rev. **13**(1), 31–89 (1998)
45. Vadivu, G., Hopper, S.W.: Ontology mapping of Indian medicinal plants with standardized medical terms. J. Comput. Sci. **8**, 1576–1584 (2012). https://doi.org/10.3844/jcssp.2012.1576.1584
46. Wilcox, A.B., Hripcsak, G.: The role of domain knowledge in automating medical text report classification. J. Am. Med. Inform. Assoc. **10**(4), 330–338 (2003)
47. Yin, C., Zhao, R., Qian, B., Lv, X., Zhang, P.: Domain knowledge guided deep learning with electronic health records. In: 2019 IEEE International Conference on Data Mining (ICDM). pp. 738–747. IEEE (2019)
48. Zeshan, F., Mohamad, R.: Medical ontology in the dynamic healthcare environment. Procedia Comput. Sci. **10**, 340–348 (2012)

Supporting Reuse of Business Process Models by Semantic Annotation

Fabian Baumann[1] , Knut Hinkelmann[1,3](✉) , and Devid Montecchiari[1,2](✉)

[1] FHNW University of Applied Sciences and Arts Northwestern Switzerland, Windisch, Switzerland
fabian.baumann@alumni.fhnw.ch, {knut.hinkelmann, devid.montecchiari}@fhnw.ch
[2] School of Science and Technology, UNICAM University of Camerino, Camerino, Italy
[3] Department of Informatics, University of Pretoria, Pretoria, South Africa

Abstract. Business Process Management (BPM) is a widely applied discipline in many organizations. Creating and maintaining business process models is a task that still requires much human work and is costly and cumbersome. The reuse of business process models is a solution to minimize human effort and increase quality. For reuse, appropriate process models must be discovered in a repository. Enrichment of the models with semantic annotations from domain ontologies can leverage better results for of discovering reusable process models. Although using semantically annotated business process models for the case of reuse has been mentioned and proposed in the literature, the exact requirements and implementation have yet to be analyzed in detail. This paper closes this research gap with an artifact in the form of a methodology to discover business process models. This includes a list of relevant criteria, a base ontology, possible automated annotation techniques, and a query form.

Keywords: Business Process Management · Ontology · Semantic Annotation · BPMN

1 Introduction

Business Process Management (BPM) is the discipline of supporting, managing, and improving business processes and is used by many organizations. BPM has been further developed over the last years due to the ever-increasing automation of processes through systems and technologies such as standard software, workflow systems, or cloud computing [1]. In addition, BPM is now established as a management approach at the management levels of companies.

The development of business process management is divided into different phases. The phases together comprise the entire life cycle of a business process [2]. In the BPM lifecycle in Dumas et al. [3], after a process identification, the process is discovered, and the as-is method is modeled before the process can be analyzed. The identified weaknesses and their impact lead to redesigning the process into the to-be process

M. Ruiz and P. Soffer (Eds.): CAiSE 2023 Workshops, LNBIP 482, pp. 29–35, 2023.
https://doi.org/10.1007/978-3-031-34985-0_3

model. The new process is then implemented and monitored before the cycle starts again. The Process Management Life Cycle (PMLC) by Bayer and Kühn [1] includes more management disciplines, such as quality and risk management. In most lifecycle models [2], a crucial step is modeling the processes, which is the basis for analysis, improvement, implementation, and execution.

Various notations exist for process modeling. BPMN 2.0 by Object Management Group (OMG) has become the de-facto standard for technical and business-process modeling [4, 5].

2 Literature Review

Business Process Management Systems (BPMS) increased the efficiency of creating and maintaining BP management, but many manual activities are still necessary and costly. Reusing existing models may reduce this effort and be more efficient [8, 9]. Most BPMS do not support the reuse of models, and significant improvement have yet to be made [10]. In Semantic Business Process Management (SBPM), the process designer can specify attributes and functionalities of a process using ontology entities [2]. For reuse, the fragments and models are stored in the process repository and are discovered using semantic-based discovery.

Semantic annotation of the business processes for process discovery and reuse is usually done manually without explicit reuse criteria determined from business needs [11, 12]. Annotation approaches can be classified into the categories [13] "extension for BPMN approach," "full semantic approach," "external annotation approach," and "hybrid approach" [13]. In ontology-based modeling, the ontology contains the meta-modeling language and a mapping to the graphical representation with the respective structure and semantics [14]. Since manually creating the semantic annotations for many processes would be time-consuming, Leopold et al. [15] combine semantic similarity with probabilistic optimization.

Automated semantic annotation has been developed for different applications, such as full-text documents [16] or data resources in the Internet of Things [17]. Automating semantic annotation of business process models is challenging because the content of the descriptions is limited, often only keywords [18]. On the other hand, the structured representation of BP models can help to create the annotation.

3 Research Method and Objective

This work aims to semantically annotate existing BPMN models with ontologies to discover business process models for reuse. It combines two approaches: (1) The semantic annotation allows the use of knowledge to discover and identify reusable processes or process fragments. (2) The automated annotation reduces the effort of manually providing semantic context to process models.

This research follows the Design Science Research (DSR) [20], in which an artifact is developed to answer the research question. In the problem awareness phase, we classified business process models according to different criteria to allow the discovery and reuse of BP models. The criteria were derived from literature research, the BPMN specification, analysis of existing modeling tools and query forms, and from expert interviews. In the suggestion phase, these criteria were represented in an ontology, reviewing possible automatic semantic annotation techniques and existing ontologies. The result of the development phase is a methodology - divided into four steps - to support the reusability of BPM models using the developed ontology. The evaluation verified that reusable process models can be discovered from an existing repository.

4 Ontology Development for Model Reuse

Our approach to annotating the process models distinguishes between the base ontology, which represents a business process diagram, and the domain ontologies, which define the semantics. The procedure by Noy and McGuinness [21] was followed to create the ontology. As BPMN ontologies like [22–25] consider only the BPMN elements from the specification but not the tool-specific extensions, which are an essential source of additional information, we partially reused and extended them. Existing domain ontologies were also identified and reused [27]. The developed BPMN ontology included a list of criteria for annotating the BP models, derived from literature research, analysis of existing query forms, and interviews with BP managers, BPM experts, and consultants. The list is clustered into three aspects: (a) Process model procedure and result-in aspect, (b) Organizational aspects (organizational structure, industry), and (c) Model aspect (level of detail, used modeling elements, language). The ontology developed can be found as a.ttl file together with the list of criteria on github[1].

5 Semantic Annotation Approach

The semantic annotation approach (see Fig. 1) prescribes creating an ontology of the process, including all concepts and elements of the BPMN standard and extensions. Compared to other approaches, the full semantic approach does not require performing changes in the model, allowing the usage existing model repository without adaptations.

In step 1, the model shall be retrieved from the BP repository and converted into a "model ontology". Model ontology creation can be supported using a ontology-based modelling tools like AOAME [29].

---

[1] https://github.com/svarcinbah/bpm.

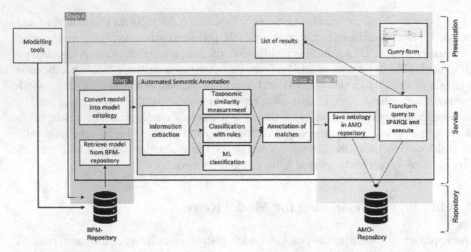

Fig. 1. Reusing business process models by automated semantic annotation

The second step enriches the model ontology by annotating additional information (semantics) from domain ontologies. Based on the literature, different automated annotation techniques, such as taxonomic similarity, rule-based, machine learning (ML) and hybrid approaches, are possible.

Step 3 stores the Annotated Model Ontology (AMO) in a new repository with a link to the original model using a unique identifier.

In step 4, a query form is designed and proposed to discover reusable BP models. The form shall allow using the identified criteria and automatically generate SPARQL queries to search for matching models in the Repository. An exemplary query form is provided in Fig. 2.

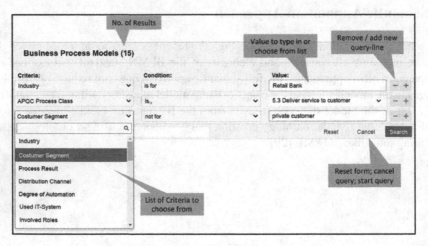

Fig. 2. Query form to discover process models

6 Evaluation

The evaluation proves if the proposed methodology applies to existing process models and if it is possible to find processes for reuse. The review is done by testing the individual steps of this methodology for two publicly available business process models. Both models have been transformed into a model ontology by converting each element of the business process models into instances of the base ontology and linked to the related domain ontologies.

Both annotated model ontologies were stored in an in GraphDB repository. In the last step of the evaluation, several questions defined by business experts were formulated as SPARQL queries and run in GraphDB. As a result, the reusable models could be discovered with the queries.

7 Conclusion and Future Work

The main research contribution is an ontology-based methodology on implementing a service to discover business process models for reuse from an existing process repository. Business process models can automatically be transformed into an ontology and anno-tated with knowledge from domain ontologies. The annotated model ontology (AMO) represents machine-readable and structured data for each criterion to find reusable busi-ness process models. The evaluation of the methodology has confirmed that semantic annotation can be applied to existing process models in BPMN2.0 to discover process models for reuse.

The problem and requirements are now apparent. The proposed methodology presents a basis for how such a system can be implemented and which techniques should be used. In a next research step, the approach shall be applied for a process repository of an actual enterprise. This must include a repository-specific domain ontology. The three proposed techniques for automated annotation need to be elaborated for imple-mentation. A large-scale test should be conducted to validate the service. Furthermore, it can be explored if those annotated model ontologies can be used for purposes other than process reuse.

References

1. Bayer, F., Kühn, H., (eds.): Prozessmanagement für Experten. Springer Berlin Heidelberg (2013). https://doi.org/10.1007/978-3-642-36995-7
2. Wetzstein, B., et al.: Semantic business process management: a lifecycle-based requirements analysis. CEUR Workshop Proc. **251**, 1–11 (2007)
3. Dumas, M., La Rosa, M., Mendling, J., Reijers, H.A.: Fundamentals of business process management. Springer Berlin Heidelberg (2018). https://doi.org/10.1007/978-3-662-56509-4
4. Object Management Group: Business Process Model and Notation (BPMN) (2010)
5. ISO: ISO/IEC 19510:2013. https://www.iso.org/standard/62652.html
6. van der Aalst, W.M.P., van Dongen, B.F., Herbst, J., Maruster, L., Schimm, G., Weijters, A.J.M.M.: Workflow mining: a survey of issues and approaches. Data Knowl. Eng. **47**, 237–267 (2003). https://doi.org/10.1016/S0169-023X(03)00066-1

7. Smeets, M., Erhard, R., Kaußler, T.: Looking to the future—the further development of RPA technology. In: Robotic Process Automation (RPA) in the Financial Sector, pp. 137–141. Springer, Wiesbaden (2021). https://doi.org/10.1007/978-3-658-32974-7_9
8. Markovic, I., Pereira, A.C.: Towards a formal framework for reuse in business process modeling. In: ter Hofstede, A., Benatallah, B., Paik, H.-Y. (eds.) Business Process Management Workshops. Lecture Notes in Computer Science, vol. 4928, pp. 484–495. Springer, Heidelberg (2008). https://doi.org/10.1007/978-3-540-78238-4_49
9. Eid-Sabbagh, R.-H., Kunze, M., Weske, M.: An open process model library. In: Daniel, F., Barkaoui, K., Dustdar, S. (eds.) Business Process Management Workshops. Lecture Notes in Business Information Processing, vol. 100, pp. 26–38. Springer, Heidelberg (2012). https://doi.org/10.1007/978-3-642-28115-0_4
10. Koschmider, A., Fellmann, M., Schoknecht, A., Oberweis, A.: Analysis of process model reuse : where are we now, where should we go from here ? Decision Support Syst. **66**, 9–19 (2014). https://doi.org/10.1016/j.dss.2014.05.012
11. Lin, Y., Strasunskas, D.: Ontology-based semantic annotation of process templates for reuse. CEUR Workshop Proc. **363**, 207–218 (2005)
12. Aldin, L., de Cesare, S., Lycett, M.: A Semantic-based framework for discovering business process patterns, pp. 1–14 (2010)
13. Di Martino, B., Esposito, A., Nacchia, S., Maisto, S.A.: Semantic annotation of BPMN: current approaches and new methodologies. In: 17th International Conference on Information Integration and Web-based Applications & Services (iiWAS) 2015 - Proceedings (2015). https://doi.org/10.1145/2837185.2837257
14. Hinkelmann, K., Gerber, A., Karagiannis, D., Thönssen, B., Van der Merwe, A., Woitsch, R.: A new paradigm for the continuous alignment of business and IT: combining enterprise architecture modelling and enterprise ontology. Comput. Ind. **79**, 77–86 (2016)
15. Leopold, H., Meilicke, C., Fellmann, M., Pittke, F., Stuckenschmidt, H., Mendling, J.: Towards the automated annotation of process models. In: Zdravkovic, J., Kirikova, M., Johannesson, P. (eds.) Advanced Information Systems Engineering. Lecture Notes in Computer Science, vol. 9097, pp. 401–416. Springer, Cham (2015). https://doi.org/10.1007/978-3-319-19069-3_25
16. Erdmann, M., Maedche, A., Schnurr, H., Staab, S.: From manual to semi-automatic semantic annotation: about ontology-based text annotation tools. Group **6**, 79–91 (2000)
17. Zhang, M., Han, L., Yuan, L., Chen, N.: Ontology-based automatic semantic annotation method for IoT data resources. International Conferences on Internet Things (iThings) and IEEE Green Computing and Communications and IEEE Cyber, Physical and Social Computing and IEEE Smart Data and IEEE Congress on Cybermatics, pp. 661–667 (2020)
18. Fengel, J.: Semantic model alignment for business process integration semantic model alignment for business process integration (2014). https://doi.org/10.21427/D72P5M
19. Saunders, M., Lewis, P., Thornhill, A.: Research methods for business students. Pearson Education, Essex (2015)
20. Hevner, A., Chatterjee, S.: Design Research in Information Systems. Springer, US, Boston, MA (2010). https://doi.org/10.1007/978-1-4419-5653-8
21. Noy, N.F., McGuinness, D.L.: Ontology Development 101: A Guide to Creating Your First Ontology. Stanford (2001)
22. Natschläger, C.: Towards a BPMN 2.0 ontology. In: Dijkman, R., Hofstetter, J., Koehler, J. (eds.) Business Process Model and Notation. Lecture Notes in Business Information Processing, vol. 95, pp. 1–15. Springer, Heidelberg (2011). https://doi.org/10.1007/978-3-642-251 60-3_1
23. Kossak, F., et al.: A rigorous semantics for BPMN 2.0 process diagrams. In: A Rigorous Semantics for BPMN 2.0 Process Diagrams, pp. 29–152. Springer International Publishing, Cham (2014). https://doi.org/10.1007/978-3-319-09931-6_4

24. Annane, A., Aussenac-Gilles, N., Kamel, M.: BPMN Based Ontology (BBO). https://www.irit.fr/recherches/MELODI/ontologies/BBO
25. Hinkelmann, K., Laurenzi, E., Martin, A., Montecchiari, D., Spahic, M., Thönssen, B.: ArchiMEO: a standardized enterprise ontology based on the archimate conceptual model. International Conference Model-Driven Engineering and Software Development (MODEL-SWARD 2020), SCITEPRESS, (2020). https://doi.org/10.5220/0009000204170424
26. Woitsch, R., Utz, W.: Business process as a service: model based business and it cloud alignment as a cloud offering. In: Proceedings 3rd International Conference Enterprise Systems ES 2015, pp. 121–130 (2015). https://doi.org/10.1109/ES.2015.19
27. APQC: Process Framework. https://www.apqc.org/process-performance-management/process-frameworks
28. W3C: RDF Repository. https://www.w3.org/egov/wiki/RDF_Repository
29. Laurenzi, E., Hinkelmann, K., van der Merwe, A.: An agile and ontology-aided modeling environment. In: Buchmann, R.A., Karagiannis, D., Kirikova, M. (eds.) The Practice of Enterprise Modeling. Lecture Notes in Business Information Processing, vol. 335, pp. 221–237. Springer, Cham (2018). https://doi.org/10.1007/978-3-030-02302-7_14

Position Paper - Hybrid Artificial Intelligence for Realizing a Leadership Assistant for Platform-Based Leadership Consulting

Stella Gatziu Grivas[✉], Denis Imhof, and Phillip Gachnang

University of Applied Sciences and Arts Northwestern Switzerland FHNW, Olten, Switzerland
{stella.gatziugrivas,denis.imhof,phillip.gachnang}@fhnw.ch

Abstract. Digital technologies enable new forms of value creation, value proposition, and value capturing for all kinds of organizations in all kinds of industries. Often, companies strive to digital transform and obtain consultancy services due to missing expert knowledge on how to approach the transformation. Interestingly, research shows that the consulting industry itself shows a high potential for a digital transformation, but platform-based consulting models and self-service consulting models are still underdeveloped. With this position paper, the authors propose an own approach on how to integrate human expert knowledge and machine learning in a novel hybrid artificial intelligence and platform-based consulting model, which not only offers the potential to transform the consultancy industry but also supports organizations in their transformation efforts. The authors take the area of digital leadership consulting to illustrate this.

Keywords: Digital Leadership · Consulting 4.0 · Hybrid Artificial Intelligence · Enterprise Modelling · Intelligent Information Systems

1 Introduction

Today managers are often left alone to close their gaps towards higher leadership abilities. According to Sahoo (2011), for an organization to work efficiently the so-called "strategic fit", which is a continuous effort from a strategic point of view of aligning business and IT, is essential. Employees are a prominent key success factor in the achievement of such alignment and organizational goals. Empowerment initiatives and empowering leadership practices need to be adopted by organizations to inspire change, increases the degree of individual employee commitment, and to help achieve superior performance and organizational goals (Sahoo 2011; Meyerson 2012). A focus of research today in terms of this empowerment, and achievement of organizational goals, is to combine collective intelligence with leadership approaches, and to learn from mistakes and support a positive mistakes-making culture (Heimann et al. 2023). Collective intelligence in a company can be defined as the shared or group intelligence that emerges from collaboration or collective efforts of many employees and appears in consensus decision-making (Bonabeau 2009). There is a common agreement in the literature that

---

The original version of this chapter was revised: The author Phillip Gachnang and his affiliation has been added. The correction to this chapter is available at
https://doi.org/10.1007/978-3-031-34985-0_20

© The Author(s), under exclusive license to Springer Nature Switzerland AG 2023, corrected publication 2023
M. Ruiz and P. Soffer (Eds.): CAiSE 2023 Workshops, LNBIP 482, pp. 36–42, 2023.
https://doi.org/10.1007/978-3-031-34985-0_4

using collective intelligence can support empowerment, the identification of customer needs, and improve the creation of innovative solutions and business models (Petry 2019).

However, many organizations today, especially small, and medium-sized enterprises, lack the required knowledge related to leadership management qualities needed to make use of the available potential, and to address their challenges. This is problematic in a society that is increasingly oriented towards more inclusive approaches, and fast changing customer needs. Thus, many companies turn to leadership consultancies to obtain support in addressing their challenges and get access to specialized knowledge and expertise, and to get an objective perspective. This is helpful for identifying and addressing issues that a company may not have noticed or may have been too close to see. However, digital leadership consulting today is still a traditional consulting business and lacks the of use of intelligent digital technologies to transform the consulting industry itself. As a result, consulting is cost- and time-intensive, and cannot harvest the potential of digital technologies. Also, the involvement of the employees of an organization is a challenge.

The aim of the paper is to answer the following research questions and identify avenues for future research: (1) What are developments in the consultancy industry related to digital technology enabled consulting models, to support client companies addressing their challenges, described by the literature? (2) What is the current state of digital technology enabled consulting model adoption in the consultancy industry in the DACH region for digital leadership? (3) How could digital technology enabled consulting models to be put into practice, which integrate human knowledge in a hybrid solution?

2   The Use Case – Development of a Platform-Based Digital Leadership Consulting

2.1   State-of-the-Art in Consulting 4.0

Already in 2013 Christensen et al. (2013) prophesied that the digitalization would bring massive changes in the consulting business. In the following years several publications (like Werth and Greff 2017; Nissen and Seifert 2018, Löwer and Gärtner 2019) have discussed areas where a digital transformation of consulting companies takes place. A clear trend of going digital, which also consultancies cannot avoid, to remain relevant and achieve growth and added value is visible in the literature (Alt et al. 2019; Augenstein 2018; Emrich et al. 2018; Greff et al. 2018; Johann et al. 2016; Nissen et al. 2018; Nissen et al. 2018; Werth and Greff 2017). Such new forms of consulting, enabled through digital technologies which have the potential to affect and transform the consulting business model's value proposition, value creation, and value capturing, are in the literature as well referred to as "Consulting 4.0" (Löwer and Gärtner 2019; Crisan and Marincean 2023). In consulting 4.0, examples of a digital transformation are the automation of processes like back-office activities and knowledge management or new services like remote consulting or new business models like crowd consulting. According to Löwer and Gärtner (2019) a promising area for the automation of consulting processes is the usage of online tools to allow customers to answer questions and to collect data autonomously without the intervention of a consultant. The tools can analyze the collected data also using machine learning approaches, and the consultants can bring their value proposition by interpreting the data and by bringing in recommendations for actions. The authors mention that the usage of digital tools plays a role in the acquisition and in up- and cross-selling activities to retain customers and stabilize revenue streams. The new value proposition of the interpretations and recommendations acts as a unique selling.

2.2 Usage of Digital Platforms in Consulting

Digital platforms can have a disruptive impact on businesses models and enable businesses to transform their business models. Even though consultancies support their clients with their transformation, consulting models which exploit the benefits of digital platforms themselves have room for growth, as a study conducted by Nissen et al. (2019) has investigated. Apparently, traditional core only consulting models (IT only to increase efficiency and provision of services) are the most prominent ones. Platform-based consulting models, self-service (clients are empowered to perform consulting related tasks), and algorithmic (computations improve or substitute human consulting) consulting models are less often applied, and show room for development, as compared to core only consulting models. Digital platforms in that sense offer not only the possibility for new platform-based consulting models (Nissen 2022), but also of a combination of the different above presented consulting models is possible, as for example shown by Gatziu Grivas et al. (2022) and their introduction of a platform-based tool for strategic transformation consulting which combines human knowledge (i.e., core only consulting) with machine learning (i.e., algorithmic consulting) and offers self-service properties for clients (i.e., self-service consulting). According to an own analysis of the leadership consulting market in Germany, Austria, and Switzerland (DACH region), conducted in 2023, the authors found that only 18% of the identified leadership consultancies offer some form of an online assessment, resp. online questionnaire. An online questionnaire is the prerequisite to collect and analyze large amounts of data from multiple client companies, and to establish meaningful platform-based consulting services, self-service consulting, and algorithmic consulting models. This shows that also four years after the study by Nissen et al. (2019), the traditional core only consulting models are still prevailing, and the potential for innovative and digital technologies enabled consulting business model lies at hand.

2.3 Challenges for Consultancies to Digitalize the Consulting Industry

On the one hand, consultancies provide support and expertise for client companies to digitally transform and retain competitive advantage. On the other hand, consultancies themselves fall behind and show a high potential for an own digital transformation, and new consulting business models. Several reasons from which two are highlighted in the following lead to this issue. The consulting business is characterized by the provision of highly specific and people-intensive services to individual client companies, which are not easy to automate in the first place (Deelmann 2018). Consulting services are furthermore highly dependent on the consultant's dynamic "human" expert knowledge, which needs to be made available and constantly updated somehow in a machine interpretable format to be of use for digital technology enabled and transformative new consulting business models. It follows that among others, especially the key characteristics of the consulting business, the customer-centricity and the human expert knowledge, pose major challenges for the industry to transform itself.

2.4   Our Vision for Digital Leadership Consulting: The Leadership Assistant

Considering the discussed challenges for client organizations, and consultancies today, and following the trend of consulting 4.0, we propose an own approach to address the digital transformation challenges of client companies and to drive forward the digital transformation of the consulting industry. Our vision is to go beyond offering a tool for collecting and analysing data but also to give recommendations, suggest measures for improvement, and accompany the implementation. The tool called Digital Leadership Guide supports and guides in an effective and efficient way managers and employees to establish digital leadership and to obtain a sustainably successful strategic position. The tool must offer interfaces for the users to conduct maturity assessments and to identify their need for improvement but also for consultants to enter expert knowledge, e.g., best practices, leadership-driven scenarios, or benchmarks, etc. This data will be used for the creation of recommendations for actions which then will be suggested to the users depending on the outcome of the maturity assessment. To do this we consider a knowledge base as the core of the tool. The knowledge base will manage all collected data and suggests based on suitable reasoning appropriate actions to improve the client organization's leadership situation. During the implementation of the actions, a collective intelligence approach will allow to establish empowerment among employees for superior individual, and in turn collective performances (Bonabeau 2009). Thus, our approach is to offer tool-based consulting services based on artificial intelligence-supported domain knowledge acquisition, refinement, and application. This implies the need for an agile and ontology-aided enterprise modelling approach to enable artificial intelligence application in consulting. So, we can support decision-makers with action plans, which will be derived by position assessments and extracted from best practices.

3   The Need for Hybrid Artificial Intelligence

To implement the knowledge base in the backend we consider a knowledge graph, semantic rules and queries and an inference engine. The knowledge graph will represent graphically the enterprise knowledge that is relevant for leadership and could be built using offerings of global players such as Ontotext or Oxford Semantic Technologies.

A knowledge graph will add a semantic layer to the data, which makes human knowledge machine interpretable, thus adding intelligence to the tool. That is, coupling the assessment, recommendations, and the virtual assistant components to a knowledge graph, semantic technology services can be enacted to retrieve information in a contextualized manner accurately, and reasoning via rules can be used to infer new knowledge. Considering recommendations as cases we can also use approaches from case-based reasoning (graph-based and ontology-based). The use of ontologies assists in specifying and clarifying the concepts employed in specific domains and helps formalizing them within the framework of a formal theory with a well-understood logical structure (Guiz-zardi 2012). We will express ontologies with a Resource Description Framework Schema (RDFS) to make use of powerful query and deductive reasoning services. Namely, exploit this ontology language to (1) create automatic recommendation and (2) retrieve relevant and contextual information to intelligent assistant for collective intelligence and interface to input and output domain knowledge.

We can use an ontology-aided modelling approach like AOAME (Laurenzi et al. 2018) and extend it for the modelling of leadership and retrieving the most suitable best practices to be suggested to the users. AOAME implements mechanisms that allow the automatic transformation of domain-specific models into a knowledge graph and vice-versa. The bi-directional consistency between the graphical models and the reflecting machine-interpretable knowledge is then ensured. Therefore, the best practices can be entered directly in the graph database via user-friendly web interfaces.

Our position is that the tool must combine approaches of machine learning (e.g., NLP in the virtual assistant) and knowledge engineering (i.e., semantic technologies), with the human at the core, who interacts with and is supported by the AI. The human-centricity is also a fundamental pillar of the new concept of society 5.0, which builds on industry 4.0. Such combination is aligned with the new trend of hybrid intelligence, which is a new field of research in AI that investigates how humans collaborate with digital actors.

Our idea is to implement a machine learning downstream to the knowledge graph for inductive reasoning. This has the advantage of having well-structured data upon which insights can be identified. From data observation, new knowledge can be inferred in the form of patterns (Hogan et al. 2021). The pattern discovery will be applied in the collective intelligence approach, to identify how employees interact with the virtual assistant and how the data that they input contribute to leadership aspects. This results in applying graph analytics on knowledge graphs or in a combined result of knowledge graphs and machine learning (Hodler and Needam 2019). Such combination reverts to the state of the art in artificial intelligence, where strengths from knowledge engineering and machine learning approaches are combined to create intelligent information systems (Van Harmelen and Ten Teije 2019; Lochbrunner and Witschel 2022).

4   Conclusion and Outlook

There is a broad consensus from both academia and industry that knowledge graphs are becoming essential for realizing AI applications. With our position paper we dis-cuss a concrete use case for the implementation of a platform-based tool, the so-called Leadership Assistant, supporting companies in the definition and implementation of digital leadership transformation. The tool is a contribution in the field of consulting 4.0 which focuses on the digital transformation of the consulting business. The position paper discusses first ideas on an application area how to combine machine learning with knowledge graphs, knowledge representation and reasoning. We show how both fields have complementary strengths and enable the creation of intelligent tools. The presented research also offers some first avenues for future research: Firstly, using AI in a way which has an impact on the people involved, which is clearly the case in the discussed advancements of the consulting industry, always raises ethical questions. Future research might investigate the advancements from an ethical point-of-view, and in terms of potential unintended consequences on the people involved. Secondly, future research could investigate on how client companies make use of the self-service components, how they affect the consulting process, and how they need to be designed for the users to be able to benefit from their full information value.

References

Alt, R., Auth, G., Kögler, C.: Transformation of consulting for software-defined businesses: lessons from a DevOps case study in a German IT company. In: Nissen, V. (ed.) Advances in Consulting Research. CMS, pp. 385–403. Springer, Cham (2019). https://doi.org/10.1007/978-3-319-95999-3_19

Augenstein, F.: Consulting self-services—a multi-project management application. In: Nissen, V. (ed.) Digital Transformation of the Consulting Industry. PI, pp. 371–388. Springer, Cham (2018). https://doi.org/10.1007/978-3-319-70491-3_15

Bonabeau, E.: Decisions 2.0: the power of collective intelligence. MIT Sloan Manag. Rev. **50**(2), 45–52 (2009)

Crisan, E.L., Marincean, A.: The digital transformation of management consulting companies: a review. Inf. Syst. E-Bus. Manag. (2023)

Christensen, C.M., Wang, D., van Bever, D.: Consulting on the cusp of disruption. Harv. Bus. Rev. **91**(10), 106–114 (2013)

Deelmann, T.: Does digitization matter? Reflections on a possible transformation of the consulting business. In: Nissen, V. (ed.) Digital Transformation of the Consulting Industry. PI, pp. 75–99. Springer, Cham (2018). https://doi.org/10.1007/978-3-319-70491-3_3

Emrich, A., Sabine, K., Michael, F., Peter, F., Peter, L.: A platform for data-driven self-consulting to enable business transformation and technology innovation. Multikonferenz Wirtschaftsinformatik (2018)

Gatziu Grivas, S., Giovanoli, C., Grasshoff, G., Imhof, D.: Platform-based strategic consulting for digital transformation. In: Hinkelmann, K., Gerber, A. (eds.) Society 5.0 - 2022 EPiC Series in Computing, vol. 84, pp. 38–49 (2022)

Greff, T., Neu, C., Johann, D., Werth, D.: Digitization driven design – a guideline to initialize digital business model creation. In: Shishkov, B. (ed.) BMSD 2018. LNBIP, vol. 319, pp. 308–318. Springer, Cham (2018). https://doi.org/10.1007/978-3-319-94214-8_22

Guizzardi, G.: Ontological foundations for conceptual modeling with applications. In: Ralyté, J., Franch, X., Brinkkemper, S., Wrycza, S. (eds.) CAiSE 2012. LNCS, vol. 7328, pp. 695–696. Springer, Heidelberg (2012). https://doi.org/10.1007/978-3-642-31095-9_45

Heimann, S., Imhof, D., Gatziu Grivas, S.: Towards a leadership model focusing on mistakes making culture enhanced by collective intelligence. In: Proceedings of the 23rd European Academy of Management Conference EURAM. Ahead of publication (2023)

Hodler, A.E., Needam, M.: Graph Algorithms. O'Rilly Media, Inc. (2019)

Hogan, A., et al.: Knowledge graphs. Synth. Lect. Data Semant. Knowl. **12**(2) (2021)

Johann, D., Greff, T., Werth, D.: On the effect of digital frontstores on transforming business models concept and use-case from the consulting industry. In: Proceedings of the 6th International Symposium on Business Modeling and Software Design (BMSD 2016). Rhodes, Greece (2016)

Laurenzi, E., Hinkelmann, K., van der Merwe, A.: An agile and ontology-aided modeling environment. In: Buchmann, R.A., Karagiannis, D., Kirikova, M. (eds.) PoEM 2018. LNBIP, vol. 335, pp. 221–237. Springer, Cham (2018). https://doi.org/10.1007/978-3-030-02302-7_14

Löwer, T., Gärtner, C.: Consulting 4.0 – Kommt die digitale Disruption des Beratungsgeschäfts? In: Meinhardt, S., Pflaum, A. (eds.) Digitale Geschäftsmodelle – Band 2. EH, pp. 229–242. Springer, Wiesbaden (2019). https://doi.org/10.1007/978-3-658-26316-4_13

Lochbrunner, M., Witschel, H.F.: Combining machine learning with human knowledge for delivery time estimations. In: AAAI Spring Symposium: MAKE (2022)

Meyerson, G.: Effect of empowerment on employees performance. Adv. Res. Econ. Manag. Sci. (AREMS) (2012)

Nissen, V.: Plattformbasierte Geschäftsmodelle im Consulting. In: Bruhn, M., Hadwich, K. (eds.) Smart Services – Band 2: Geschäftsmodelle - Erlösmodelle - Kooperationsmodelle. Springer Gabler, Wiesbaden (2022). https://doi.org/10.1007/978-3-658-37346-7_4

Nissen, V., Füßl, A., Werth, D., Gugler, K., Neu, C.: On the current state of digital transformation in the German market for business consulting. In: Nissen, V. (ed.) Advances in Consulting Research. CMS, pp. 317–339. Springer, Cham (2019). https://doi.org/10.1007/978-3-319-95999-3_15

Nissen, V., Kuhl, J., Kräft, H., Seifert, H., Reiter, J., Eidmann, J.: ProMAT—a project management assessment tool for virtual consulting. In: Nissen, V. (ed.) Digital Transformation of the Consulting Industry. PI, pp. 351–369. Springer, Cham (2018). https://doi.org/10.1007/978-3-319-70491-3_14

Nissen, V., Seifert, H.: Evaluating the virtualization potential of consulting services. In: Nissen, V. (ed.) Digital Transformation of the Consulting Industry. PI, pp. 191–205. Springer, Cham (2018). https://doi.org/10.1007/978-3-319-70491-3_8

Petry, T.: Digital Leadership – Erfolgreiches Führen in Zeiten der Digital Economy. Haufe-Lexware GmbH & Co. KG, Freiburg (2019)

Sahoo, C.K.: Employee empowerment: a strategy towards workplace commitment. Eur. J. Bus. Manag. 3(11) (2011)

Van Harmelen, F., Ten Teije, A.: A boxology of design patterns for hybrid learning and reasoning systems. J. Web Eng. 18(1–3), 97–124 (2019)

Werth, D., Greff, T.: Scalability in consulting: insights into the scaling capabilities of business models by digital technologies in consulting industry. In: Nissen, V. (ed.) Digital Transformation of the Consulting Industry. PI, pp. 117–135. Springer, Cham (2018). https://doi.org/10.1007/978-3-319-70491-3_5

Developing a Maturity Assessment Tool to Enable the Management of Artificial Intelligence for Organizations

Philipp Fukas[1,2,3](✉) (iD), Aydin Bozkurt[1], Nora Lenz[1], and Oliver Thomas[1,2]

[1] Osnabrück University, Osnabrück, Lower Saxony, Germany
{philipp.fukas,abozkurt,nlenz,oliver.thomas}@uni-osnabrueck.de
[2] German Research Center for Artificial Intelligence, Osnabrück, Lower Saxony, Germany
{philipp.fukas,oliver.thomas}@dfki.de
[3] Strategion GmbH, Osnabrück, Lower Saxony, Germany
philipp.fukas@strategion.de

Abstract. Maturity Models (MMs) are a popular method to support Information Technology (IT) management. In recent years, several industry-specific Artificial Intelligence (AI) MMs were developed to support AI Management as part of the IT management in organizations. While the development of these AI MMs follows widely standardized procedures and therefore is sufficiently addressed in scientific discourse, a lack of attention toward their practical application can be seen. Therefore, this paper proposes a technical prototype for a generic web-based maturity assessment tool for AI management. Overall, a design science-oriented research procedure with a Systematic Literature Review, the design of Graphical User Interfaces (GUIs), the development of a web-based tool, and evaluations with Cognitive Walkthroughs and Personas are conducted. The results indicate that the development of a web tool is an innovative and promising way of applying AI MMs. This work contributes to the current body of knowledge in Information Systems Engineering research by providing a first technical prototype for a web-based maturity assessment tool for AI Management.

Keywords: Artificial Intelligence · Information Technology Management · Maturity Model · Graphical User Interface · Design Science

1 Introduction

To advance in today's business world, it is of paramount importance for a company to assess and continuously improve its current capabilities regarding the use of technologies. IT related Maturity Models (MMs) are commonly used for this purpose [1]. Due to the increasing application of Artificial Intelligence (AI) in business practice [2], AI MMs have also been increasingly developed in recent years to support the management of AI in companies. The developed MMs mostly represent abstract systems that are difficult to apply directly in business practice. However, these abstract models require application in an organizational context, because only the application and the resulting

© The Author(s), under exclusive license to Springer Nature Switzerland AG 2023
M. Ruiz and P. Soffer (Eds.): CAiSE 2023 Workshops, LNBIP 482, pp. 43–49, 2023.
https://doi.org/10.1007/978-3-031-34985-0_5

knowledge about organizational capabilities can achieve added value for a company [1]. Nevertheless, the practical application of MMs receives comparatively little attention in the scientific discourse. Ergo, MMs often must be applied manually and individually, which often requires external expertise. Therefore, the maturity assessment is conducted either by external consulting firms or in-house with significant effort [3]. The goal of our work is to overcome the "knowing-doing gap" by reducing the effort to apply AI MMs in practice [4, 5]. To achieve this, a technical prototype of a Maturity Assessment Tool (MAT) for the application of AI MMs is developed. The following Research Question (RQ) guides our overall research process: How can an Assessment Tool for the application of Artificial Intelligence Maturity Models be developed?

2 Research Approach

Our research follows the design science research (DSR) paradigm of Hevner et al. [6] as an overarching methodology. The artifact designed in this paper is a prototype of the AI MAT. For the further design of the artifact, the AI MM of Fukas et al. [7] is used as an example. The focus of this work can be assigned to the area of *"Conception of transfer and evaluation"* of the process model of Becker et al. [1].

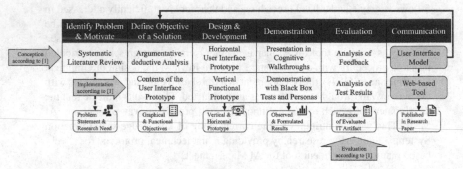

Fig. 1. Overall Research Design.

The overall research design follows the six distinctive steps proposed by Peffers et al. [8] (cf. Figure 1). In the beginning, the RQ is defined as a result of the *Problem Identification & Motivation (1)* step (cf. Sect. 1). In the *Objectives of a Solution (2)* step, relevant concepts used in the application of MMs are analyzed and objectives for designing an AI MAT are identified based on a SLR (cf. Sect. 3.1). The formulated objectives serve as the starting point for the *Design & Development (3)* step. In the first iteration (cf. *Conception* in Fig. 1), the objectives are mapped to a horizontal UI prototype (cf. Sect. 3.2). The UI prototype is conceptually designed as interactive mockups using Figma [9, 10]. In the *Demonstration (4)* and *Evaluation (5)* steps, the horizontal UI prototype is evaluated with Cognitive Walkthroughs (CWs) [10–12] (cf. Sect. 3.3). In the second iteration (*Implementation* in Fig. 1), the horizontal UI prototype is developed further into a vertical prototype. The previously designed horizontal UI prototype defines the objectives in the second iteration. In the *Design & Development (3)* step of the second iteration, the vertical prototype was implemented (cf. Sect. 3.4). Black box tests [13] were conducted in the *Demonstration (4)* and *Evaluation (5)* steps of the second iteration. In addition to the functionality of the web application, its usefulness is also to be evaluated. Three different personas [14, 15] are used for this purpose (cf. Sect. 3.5). Finally, the *Communication (6)* of the results is reached by publishing the entire documented research process including its results in this paper.

3   Development of the Maturity Assessment Tool

3.1   Objectives of the Maturity Assessment Tool

The results of the argumentative-deductive analysis based on the SLR are presented below. The main functionality of the AI MAT is the performance of maturity assessments. In 14 of 18 sources, data collection takes the form of a questionnaire. Furthermore, two articles explicitly mention the requirement for a survey-based assessment [16, 17]. Therefore, conducting an assessment by questionnaire is defined as an objective for the prototype. Since the tool is to be designed for a variety of industry-specific AI assessments, the user must be given the option to search for a suitable AI assessment. The evaluation of the questionnaire should be automatically displayed as a radar chart (8 sources) or bar chart (4 sources). The historical comparison of performed AI assessments should be also possible [17]. For user administration, the objectives of registration, login, and management of assessments should be realized [16, 17]. Finally, the GUI of the AI MAT emphasizes an intuitive and modern design.

3.2   Design of the Horizontal User Interface Prototype

At the top left of the navigation bar, the tool menu can be opened. The "Find Assessment" button starts a search for determining a suitable AI assessment. The user has to specify in which industry his company is active. When conducting an industry-specific AI assessment, the maturity level of the company is determined by a questionnaire. Subquestions are asked for each of the eight dimensions to determine the respective maturity level. At the end of the assessment, the results are presented automatically. The overall maturity level and the maturity level of individual dimensions are displayed with radar and bar charts. Under the "My assessments" tab, assessments that have already been completed can be viewed and managed. The buttons on the right of each assessment are used to display a company's historical development for a particular AI assessment (cf. Fig. 2).

3.3   Demonstration and Evaluation of the Horizontal User Interface Prototype

The horizontal UI prototype of the AI MAT is evaluated using CWs. The usability experts chosen for evaluation are prospective IS scientists and students. As in Wang [11], the evaluation is conducted with five people. The three use cases "Register/Login", "Find Assessment/Perform Assessment" and "Historical Comparison of Assessments" were tested. The individual tasks were run through with the participants and afterward, the

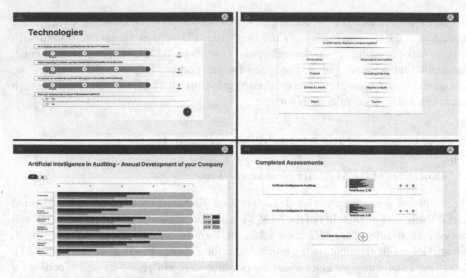

Fig. 2. Sample Graphical User Interfaces of the Artificial Intelligence Maturity Assessment Tool.

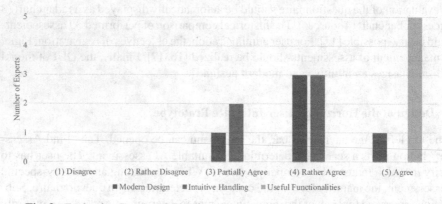

Fig. 3. Evaluation Results of the Likert Scales During the Cognitive Walkthroughs.

four questions of the CW method analogous to Moser [10], Paternò [12], and Wang [11] were answered by the participants.

In addition to the single use cases, the participants were finally asked questions about modernity, intuitiveness, and the presented functionalities. The functionalities presented are rated with five points by all participants (cf. Fig. 3). Intuitiveness and modernity also tend to be rated positively.

3.4 Development of the Vertical Prototype

Based on the evaluated concepts, a vertical prototype of the AI MAT was developed as a web-based software application in the second iteration (cf. Fig. 4). The core functionalities of the AI-MAT were implemented using HTML, CSS, and JavaScript. Based on a questionnaire, a scoring model automatically calculates the individual maturity scores of single dimensions and an overall AI Maturity score of the company (descriptive function). These scores are displayed in an interactive radar chart. Based on the individual maturity scores of the single dimensions, different recommendations for action are shown dynamically at the bottom of the web page (prescriptive function).

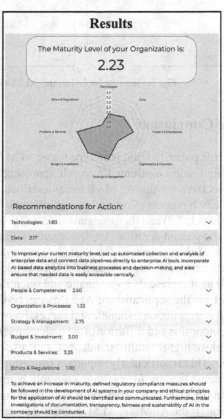

Fig. 4. Sample Screenshots of the Web-based Artificial Intelligence Maturity Assessment Tool.

3.5 Demonstration and Evaluation of the Vertical Prototype

In the second iteration (cf. Sect. 3), the vertical prototype was evaluated by conducting black box tests and by defining three personas [13–15]. The black box tests did not reveal any functional deficiencies in the vertical prototype whereas the evaluations with the personas confirmed the usefulness of the AI MAT. The automatically calculated maturity levels during the tests with the three different personas are shown in Fig. 5.

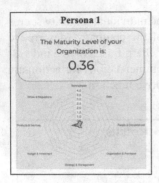 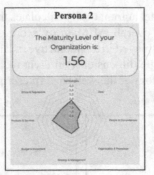 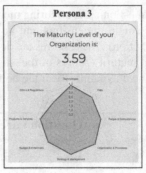

Fig. 5. Results by Using the AI MAT with the Three Different Personas.

4   Conclusion

In this paper, the first prototype for an AI MAT was developed by following a multi-step design science-oriented research approach. An SLR was conducted and the resulting objectives for the AI MAT were described (cf. Sect. 3.1). In the first iteration of our research process (*Conception*), a horizontal UI prototype of the AI MAT was developed (cf. Sect. 3.2) and then demonstrated and evaluated using the CW method (cf. Sect. 3.3). In the second iteration (*Implementation*), this horizontal UI prototype was implemented as a vertical prototype (cf. Sect. 3.4) and evaluated with black box tests as well as three different personas (cf. Sect. 3.5). The complete research process answers the overarching RQ as it represents a systematic and scientifically sound process, of how an assessment tool for the application of AI MMs can be developed. The AI MAT represents the first software solution to bundle and successively document management activities regarding the adoption and diffusion of AI technologies in companies. As a result, the AI MAT can achieve higher quality standards for the use of AI-related technologies in business practice. This is particularly important concerning potential certifications of AI management systems that are for example currently being developed by the International Organization for Standardization (ISO) [18]. Furthermore, time and cost savings are conceivable through the AI MAT. AI MMs must be entered once by the user and can then be used as often as desired for an assessment since an automated evaluation is performed by the software. This can minimize the coordination costs between the researcher and practitioner applying the respective model. The AI MAT can reduce the "knowing-doing gap" and promote the wide use of AI MMs as a tool for AI management. In the future, the technical prototype of the AI MAT should be launched as an open-access web application. With an open-access web application, practitioners can then evaluate the implemented AI MAT further by directly using it to assess and manage the organizational capabilities regarding the adoption and diffusion of AI in their companies.

References

1. Becker, J., Knackstedt, R., Pöppelbuß, J.: Developing maturity models for IT management. Bus. Inf. Syst. Eng. **1**(3), 213–222 (2009)

2. Zhang, D., et al..: The AI Index 2022 Annual Report (2022)
3. CMMI Product Team: CMMI® for Development, Version 1.3., Pittsburgh (2010)
4. Mettler, T.: Maturity assessment models: a design science research approach. Int. J. Soc. Syst. Sci. **3**(1/2), 81–98 (2011)
5. Fukas, P.: The management of artificial intelligence: developing a framework based on the artificial intelligence maturity principle. In: Van Looy, A., Weber, B., and Rosemann, M. (eds.) Doctoral Consortium Papers Presented at the 34th International Conference on Advanced Information Systems Engineering (CAiSE 2022), pp. 19–27. Leuven (2022)
6. Hevner, A.R., March, S.T., Park, J., Ram, S.: Design science in information systems research. Manag. Inf. Syst. Q. **28**, 75–105 (2004)
7. Fukas, P., Rebstadt, J., Remark, F., Thomas, O.: Developing an Artificial Intelligence Maturity Model for Auditing. In: ECIS 2021 Research Papers, 133. Marrakesch (online) (2021)
8. Peffers, K., Tuunanen, T., Rothenberger, M.A., Chatterjee, S.: A design science research methodology for information systems research. J. Manag. Inf. Syst. **24**(3), 45–77 (2007)
9. Figma: Figma: Nothing great is made alone. https://www.figma.com/. Accessed 2023/04/20
10. Moser, C.: User Experience Design. Springer, Berlin (2012)
11. Wang, X.: Design and evaluation of intelligent menu interface through cognitive walkthrough procedure and automated logging for management information system. In: Shen, W., Yong, J., Yang, Y., Barthès, J.-P., Luo, J. (eds.) CSCWD 2007. LNCS, vol. 5236, pp. 408–418. Springer, Heidelberg (2008). https://doi.org/10.1007/978-3-540-92719-8_37
12. Paternò, F.: Model-Based Design and Evaluation of Interactive Applications. Springer, London (2000)
13. Chauhan, R.K., Singh, I.: Latest research and development on software testing techniques and tools. Int. J. Curr. Eng. Technol. **4**(4), 2368–2372 (2014)
14. Friess, E.: Personas in heuristic evaluation: an exploratory study. IEEE Trans. Prof. Commun. **58**(2), 176–191 (2015)
15. Chisnell, D.E., Redish, J.C., Lee, A.: New heuristics for understanding older adults as web users. Tech. Commun. **53**(1), 39–59 (2006)
16. Frehe, V., Stiel, F., Teuteberg, F.: A Maturity model and web application for environmental management benchmarking. In: AMCIS 2014 Proceedings, pp. 1–14. Savannah (2014)
17. Krivograd, N., Fettke, P.: Development of a generic tool for the application of maturity models - results from a design science approach. In: Sprague, R.H. (eds.) Proceedings of the Annual Hawaii International Conference on System Sciences, pp. 4326–4335. IEEE, Washington, D.C. (2012)
18. ISO: ISO/IEC CD 42001. https://www.iso.org/standard/81230.html. Accessed 2023/04/20

Mapping Time-Series Data on Process Patterns to Generate Synthetic Data

Frederik Fonger[1]([✉]) [iD], Milda Aleknonytė-Resch[1] [iD], and Agnes Koschmider[2,3] [iD]

[1] Kiel University, Kiel, Germany
{ffo,mar}@informatik.uni-kiel.de
[2] Chair of Business Informatics and Process Analytics, University of Bayreuth,
Bayreuth, Germany
agnes.koschmider@uni-bayreuth.de
[3] Fraunhofer FIT, Bayreuth, Germany

Abstract. The combination of machine learning techniques with process analytics like process mining might significantly elevate novel insights into time-series data collections that are predominantly used in disciplines like life and natural science. To efficiently analyse time-series data by process mining requires bridging several challenges. For instance, time-series data need to be processed and represented in a useable form to turn into information. This paper provides: (1) A structured approach to map time-series data on control-flow patterns that we annotated for our purpose. (2) Based on the simulation of the patterns it is possible to generate synthetic data in varying quality, which is again a crucial step for accurate results from machine learning techniques. In this way, our approach contributes understanding novel insights in terms of causal-effects in time-series data, which could not be answered by traditional approaches used in the disciplines.

Keywords: time-series data · control-flow patterns · process mining

1 Introduction

In disciplines such as engineering as well as life and natural sciences, time-series are a common data format. To analyse these kinds of data, mostly correlation analysis is the first-class choice in these disciplines. Recently, the disciplines have applied machine learning techniques to advance the analysis in terms of understanding reasons behind the dataset. Additionally, the disciplines are highly interested in identifying causalities and cause-effect chains in time-series in order to identify anomalies and to understand new findings.

The combination of machine learning techniques with process analytics like process mining might even significantly elevate novel insights into time-series data collections. Process mining is concerned with automatic process analysis techniques based on event data. Such techniques include algorithms for the discovery of process models, for conformance checking between specifications and recorded events, and for predictive analytics. Thus, process mining is suitable

M. Ruiz and P. Soffer (Eds.): CAiSE 2023 Workshops, LNBIP 482, pp. 50–61, 2023.
https://doi.org/10.1007/978-3-031-34985-0_6

to advance the disciplines since it allows explaining new findings that previously could not be identified purely with machine learning. Applying process mining on time-series data, however, requires to bridge two challenges: (1) Virtually all techniques developed in the area of process mining assume as input discrete data, and, at a relatively high level (i.e., close to the business level). (2) Time-series data need form and meaning to be understandable. Time-series data need to be processed and represented in a useable form to turn into information.

To provide a solution, this paper presents an approach to map time-series data onto control-flow patterns that we annotated with additional values to suit our purpose. In this way, we aim to identify correlations and causal-effects within time-series data allowing to identify anomalies more accurate and providing a foundation to explain effects. By using a pattern-based approach to specify dependencies within time-series data, we provide a tool that generates synthetic time-series data for process mining from the pattern simulation. In this way, data varying in quality can be generated at any time. Figure 1 shows our approach for mapping time-series data onto control-flow patterns.

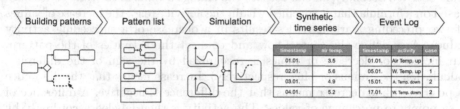

Fig. 1. Pipeline to map time-series data onto process patterns and generating synthetic event logs.

First, the user selects appropriate patterns for use. Possible patterns are: Sequence, XOR-split and XOR-join, AND-split and AND-join. Each pattern must fulfill specific conditions to be instantiated, as described below. The patterns are ordered in a list that is processed one after the other. The time axis of the time-series data is split into calculation segments depending on the data granularity to be considered and analysed like daily measurements that can be split into hourly measurements respectively. The simulation of the patterns generates synthetic data. Figure 1 shows the simulation of three time-series values, see the *Simulation* box. For instance, let's assume an AND-join pattern where the decrease of value 1 and a decrease of value 2 converge towards an increase of value 3. An example is later presented in Fig. 7 where different variables from marine research, such as water temperature or wave height, are aligned with a process model. Based on that model, a time series is generated for each variable.

This paper is structured as follows. Section 2 presents the pattern-based approach to map time-series data onto annotated control-flow patterns. Section 3 illustrates the application of the patterns on an use case. Section 4 describes the implementation of the approach and the generation of synthetic data. We review related work in Sect. 5, before Sect. 6 concludes this paper.

2 Formalization of Control-Flow Patterns for Time-Series Data

Our pattern-based approach relies on the basic control-flow patterns [4] as a foundation, which we extended for our purpose. The patterns are: Sequence, Exclusive Choice, Simple Merge, Parallel Split and Synchronization. A pattern consists of activities, arcs and gateways, which are formally introduced below. A formula is assigned to each activity that controls the instantiation of the activity.

2.1 Semantics of Activities

Activities describe what should happen or what is happening (e.g. increase, decrease or constancy of a value in time-series data). There are two different types of activities used in the patterns. Firstly, a *start activity* of a pattern determines the difference of observed values in the time-series data (e.g., the increase or decrease of value A). The assignment of observed values instantiates a start activity. Secondly, an *end activity* can change a value in the time-series data based on a formula that is specified within the activity (e.g., the increase of values of two preceding start activities results in a decrease of a succeeding activity value). Arcs define the control-flow and connect the activities of the pattern. An increase or decrease of values is recognized by the sign of the difference calculation (i.e., minus or plus, respectively). Increase means that the difference is positive, while decrease means that the difference is negative. A difference of zero points to no change of values. The activity is then labeled accordingly by the sign, i.e. + if wind increases, - if wind decreases. Arcs might have inscriptions in terms of individually assigned values by users. Finally, gateways are used to route the control-flow.

2.2 Sequence Pattern

Description: The *Sequence* pattern (see Fig. 2) connects two activities which execute in turn one after the other. The start activity is instantiated by assigning the difference of two observed data values at different points in time. The control-flow arc connecting both activities has a condition associated with it. The subsequent (end) activity is enabled after determining the difference of values of the previous activity multiplied with the condition assigned to the arc. The execution of the end activity results in a change of the value of the considered time-series point. It is possible to compose multiple *Sequence* patterns one after the other.

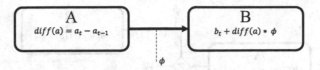

Fig. 2. Sequence pattern.

Calculation: Synthetic data can be generated based on the *Sequence* pattern as follows. Time-series data is parsed iteratively according to the following formula, where let $x_{a,t}$ be an observed value of activity a at t time $= 0$. Then, let $x_{a,t-1}$ be an observed value a at $t - 1$. An activity is instantiated by determining the difference of both values: $(x_{a,t} - x_{a,t-1})$. Furthermore, $\phi \in [0, \infty]$ is an individually assigned value by users or learned e.g. using machine-learning-based approaches on a training set. It is assigned to the arc directing the control-flow to activity b. Let $x_{b,t}$ be an observed value of activity b at t time $= 0$. The result of $(x_{a,t} - x_{a,t-1}) * \phi$ is either added or subtracted from $x_{b,t}$, depending of the observation of the value i.e., if the value increased or decreased. Then, let $x_{b,t+1}$ be the observed value of activity b at $t + 1$, which is calculated as follows:

$$x_{b,t+1} = x_{b,t} \pm (x_{a,t} - x_{a,t-1}) * \phi \tag{1}$$

$x_{y,t}$ — value of an activity y at time t, where $y \in A$ and A is the set of possible activities.

ϕ — value individually assigned prior by users.

t — point in time.

Example: We assume wind speed a at point in time t as the value $x_{a,t}$, while the value $x_{b,t}$ is wave height b at point in time t. The application of the Sequence pattern generates the following synthetic data: the wave height for t is 0.5 m and the user-defined value ϕ is 0.1. An increase of the wind speed from 5 $\frac{m}{s}$ to 10 $\frac{m}{s}$ was observed. According to Formula 1, wave length for time point *t+1* is determined by $x_{b,t+1} = x_{b,t} + (x_{a,t} - x_{a,t-1}) * \phi = 0.5 + (10 - 5) * 0.1 = 1$. Thus, the value of the wave height increased from 0.5 m to 1 m.

2.3 Exclusive Choice

Description: The Exclusive Choice pattern, see Fig. 3, consists of at least three activities. The start activity is instantiated by assigning the difference of two observed values at different points in time. The thread of control is passed to precisely one of the outgoing branches based on an individually assigned probability by users: W : $[0,1] \rightarrow B$, where B is the set of end activities.

Calculation: Synthetic data can be generated based on the Exclusive Choice pattern as follows: Let $x_{a,t}$ be an observed value a at t time $= 0$. Then, let $x_{a,t-1}$ be an observed value a at *t-1*. Furthermore, let ϕ_y be the condition of the

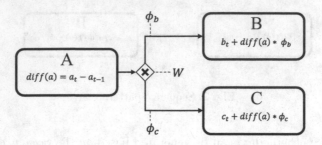

Fig. 3. Exclusive Choice pattern.

control-flow arc, where $y \in B$ and B is the set of end activities of the branches, where $B \subset A$ and A is the set of start activities. The condition ϕ_y is assigned by the user for each branch. Let $x_{y,t}$ be the observed value of activity y where $y \in B$ at t time $= 0$. The result of $(x_{a,t} - x_{a,t-1}) * \phi_y$ is either added or subtracted from $x_{y,t}$, depending on the users settings. Let $W : [0,1] \to B$ be a weighting function of probabilities w_y of the branches of activity y, defined by the user, with $\sum_{y \in B} w_y = 1$. Let p be a value with $p = random(0,1)$ where $random$: $\mathbb{R}^2 \to \mathbb{R}$ and selects a random value between two given values. Then $x_{y,t+1}$ where $y \in B$ and $W(p) = y$ be the observed value of activity y at $t+1$, which is calculated as follows:

$$x_{y,t+1} = x_{y,t} \pm (x_{a,t} - x_{a,t-1}) * \phi_y \tag{2}$$

$$y = W(p) \tag{3}$$

$$W : F \to B \tag{4}$$

$x_{y,t}$ — value of an activity y at time t, where $y \in B$.

ϕ_y — value individually assigned by the user for the branch of the activity y, where $y \in B$.

t — point in time

B — set of end activities of the pattern, where $B \subset A$ and A is the set of all activities.

W — $[0,1] \to B$

p — $p = random(0,1)$ where $random$ is $\mathbb{R}^2 \to \mathbb{R}$ and selects a random value between two given values.

Example: We assume the wind speed a at point in time t as the value $x_{a,t}$. An increase of the wind speed a from 8 kn to 15 kn was observed. We further assume that the sea level b is $x_{b,t}$ and the wave hight c is $x_{c,t}$, where $B = \{b, c\}$. We further assume that the user-defined value ϕ_b is 0,05, ϕ_c is 0,07 and the user-defined probability weighting w_b is 0.6, while w_c is 0.4. Given W, the control-flow passes to the first branch executing activity B. The value $x_{b,t}$ is the sea level b and implies an activity labeled "sea level increases". Based on

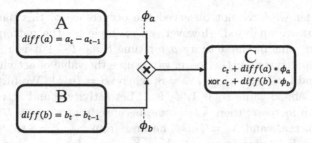

Fig. 4. Simple Merge pattern.

the application of this pattern, synthetic data is generated as follows: The sea
level b in time t is at $0{,}3\,\mathrm{m}$ below normal sea level and the user-defined value
ϕ_b is $0{,}05$. According to Formula 2, sea level b for point in time $t+1$ results in
$x_{b,t+1} = x_{b,t} + (x_{a,t} - x_{a,t-1}) * \phi_b = -0{,}3 - (15 - 8) * 0{,}05 = -0{,}65$. Thus,
the value of the sea level decreases from $0{,}3\,\mathrm{m}$ below normal sea level to $0{,}65\,\mathrm{m}$
below normal sea level.

2.4   Simple Merge

Description: In the Simple Merge pattern (or XOR-join pattern) (see Fig. 4)
two or more branches are converged to a single subsequent branch leading to
one activity. Therefore, the control-flow arcs connect each of the start activities
with the single end activity. The start activities are instantiated by assigning
the difference of two observed values at different points in time.

Calculation: Synthetic data can be generated based on the XOR-join pattern as
follows: Let B be the set of start activities of the pattern. Let $x_{y,t}$ be an observed
value of the activity y at time t, where $y \in B$. Then, let $x_{y,t-1}$ be an observed
value of the activity y at time $t - 1$. Then, let $x_{c,t+1}$ be the value of activity c
at $t + 1$, which is calculated using the formula 5, when $X_y \wedge \forall i : \overline{X_i} = true$ for
$y \in B, i \in B\backslash\{y\}$, where X_y is a logical value for every $y \in B$, that is $true$ if the
activity of the observed value is instantiated. The result of $(x_{y,t} - x_{y,t-1}) * \phi_y$ is
either added or subtracted from $x_{c,t}$, depending on the users settings. Then:

$$x_{c,t+1} = x_{c,t} \pm (x_{y,t} - x_{y,t-1}) * \phi_y \qquad (5)$$

where

$$y \in B, i \in B\backslash\{y\} \mid X_y \wedge \forall i : \overline{X_i} \qquad (6)$$

$x_{y,t}$ — value of an activity y at time t, where y $\in$ B.
ϕ_y — value individually assigned by the user for the branch of the activity y,
    where $y \in B$.
t — point in time.
B — set of start activities of the pattern, where B $\subset$ A and A is the set of
    possible activities.
X_y — The logical value for a activity y, where $y \in B$

Example: So far we have not observed the occurrence of this pattern in the time-series data we analysed. However, an example for the pattern might be: we assume the value of the activity a for time t and $t-1$ it is $x_{a,t} = 10$ and $x_{a,t-1} = 5$, respectively. Furthermore, we assume the value of activity b for time t is $x_{b,t} = 8$ and for $t-1$ are $x_{b,t-1} = 8$, where $B = \{a, b\}$. We further assume that the user-defined value ϕ_a is 1, ϕ_b is 2. Let activity a and activity b be an activity with an increase, then $X_a = true$, because from $x_{a,t-1} = 5$ to $x_{a,t} = 10$ there was an increase and $X_b = false$, because from $x_{b,t-1} = 8$ to $x_{b,t} = 8$ there was no increase. Following formula 6, $X_a \wedge \overline{X_b} = true$ for $y = a$. Let the value of the activity c be $x_{c,t} = 20$. Then the value for activity c in time $t+1$ is calculated with formula 5 as follows: $x_{c,t+1} = x_{c,t} \pm (x_{a,t} - x_{a,t-1}) * \phi_a = 20 + (10-5)*1 = 25$. Thus, we can state that activity c increased from 20 to 25.

2.5   Parallel Split

Description: The Parallel Split pattern or AND-split, see Fig. 5, consists of two or more branches. The start activity is instantiated by assigning the difference of two observed values at different points in time. The control-flow arcs direct the control-flow to branches of activities. When the start activity has been executed, all the subsequent activities are enabled.

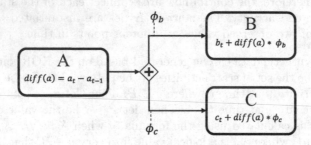

Fig. 5. Parallel Split pattern.

Calculation: Synthetic data can be generated based on the AND-split pattern as follows: Let A be the set of possible activities and B the set of end activities, thus $B \subset A$. Let $x_{a,t}$ be an observed value a at t time $= 0$. Then, let $x_{a,t-1}$ be an observed value a at $t-1$. Furthermore, $\phi_y \in [0, \infty]$ where $y \in B$ is an individually assigned value for each branch by users or learned e.g. using machine-learning-based approaches on a training set. Let $x_{y,t}$ be the observed value of activity y where $y \in B$ at t time $= 0$. The result of $(x_{a,t} - x_{a,t-1}) * \phi_y$ is either added or subtracted from $x_{y,t}$, depending on the users settings. Then, $x_{y,t+1}$ where $y \in B$ be the observed value of activity y at $t+1$, which is calculated separately for each branch of the pattern. The value of the start activity is determined following by the values of the outgoing branches:

$$\forall y \in B \mid x_{y,t+1} = x_{y,t} \pm (x_{a,t} - x_{a,t-1}) * \phi_y \qquad (7)$$

$x_{y,t}$ — Value of an activity y at time t, where $y \in B$.
 t — point in time.
 B — The set of end activities of the pattern, where $B \subset A$ and A is the set of possible activities.
 ϕ_y — value individually assigned by the user for the branch of the activity y, where $y \in B$.

Example: As explained above, the branches of the AND-split pattern are calculated separately. In the first calculation, we assume sea current a at point in time t as the value $x_{a,t}$, while the value $x_{b,t}$ where $b \in B$ is wave height b at point in time t and the value $x_{c,t}$, where $c \in B$ and c is the turbidity of the water. Based on the application of this pattern, synthetic data is generated as follows: The wave height b for t is $x_{b,t} = 0.3\,\mathrm{m}$ and the user-defined value ϕ_b is 0.2. An increase of the sea current from $2kn$ to $4kn$ was observed. According to Formula 7, the wave height for point in time $t+1$ is thus: $x_{b,t+1} = x_{b,t} + (x_{a,t} - x_{a,t-1}) * \phi_b = 0.3 + (4-2) * 0.2 = 0.7$. Therefore, we can state that the value of the wave height increased from $0.3\,\mathrm{m}$ to $0.7\,\mathrm{m}$.

For a second calculation we assume the turbidity of the water c for time t is $x_{c,t} = 3\,\mathrm{FNU}$ and the user-defined value ϕ_c is 0.5. Then, according to Formula 7, the turbidity of the water c for time $t+1$ is: $x_{c,t+1} = x_{c,t} + (x_{a,t} - x_{a,t-1}) * \phi_c = 3 + (4-2) * 0.5 = 4$. Thus, the value of the turbidity increased from 3 FNU to 4 FNU.

2.6 Synchronization

Description: The Synchronization pattern or AND-join (see Fig. 4) has two or more branches, which converge into one subsequent branch. The start activities are instantiated by assigning the difference of two observed values at different points in time. The control-flow arcs connecting the start activities to a single subsequent branch have conditions associated with them. The execution of the activity concurrently joining the start activity results in a value change in the time-series.

Calculation: Synthetic data can be generated based on the Synchronization pattern as follows. Let $x_{y,t}$ be the observed value of an activity y at time $t = 0$, where $y \in B$ and B is the set of start activities of the pattern. Then, let $x_{y,t-1}$ be an observed value at $t-1$. For each branch an activity is instantiated by determining the difference of both values from the same activity. There are two values individually assigned by users at each branch, where $\phi_y \in [0, \infty]$ and w_y is the user defined value for the other branch. The fraction is either added or subtracted from $x_{c,t}$, depending of the users settings. The setting depends on the increase or decrease of the value respectively. Then, let $x_{c,t}$ be the observed value of the joining activity c at t and $x_{c,t+1}$ be the value of activity c at $t+1$. Then the Synchronization pattern is calculated as follows:

$$x_{c,t+1} = x_{c,t} \pm \frac{\sum_{y \in B} |(x_{y,t} - x_{y,t-1}) * \phi_y * w_y|}{\sum_{y \in B} w_y} \qquad (8)$$

$x_{y,t}$ — value of an activity y at time t, where $y \in A$ and A is the set of possible activities.

c — subsequent activity c of y, where $y \in B$.

B — set of starting activities of the pattern, where $B \subset A$.

ϕ_y — value individually assigned by the user for the branch of the activity y, where $y \in B$.

w_y — Individually assigned weighting by the user for the branch of the activity y, where $y \in B$.

Example: We assume that the value $x_{a,t}$ of the start activity a is water temperature at time t and $x_{b,t}$ is the value of the second start activity b, which is salinity at time t, where $B = \{a, b\}$ and $x_{c,t}$ is the value of the chlorophyll in the water for time t. Based on the application of this pattern synthetic data is generated as follows: The chlorophyll in the water is $x_{c,t} = 0.25$ µg/L at point in time t. The water temperature for $t-1$ is $x_{a,t-1} = 10\,°C$ and for t is $x_{a,t} = 12\,°C$. ϕ_a is 0.02 and w_a is 3. The value of the salinity of activity b is $x_{b,t-1} = 30ppt$ in time $t-1$ and $x_{b,t}$ $35ppt$ in time t. ϕ_b and w_b are 0.02 and 1 respectively. According to the formula 8 the chlorophyll for $t+1$ results in $x_{c,t+1} = x_{c,t} + \frac{\sum_{i \in B} |(x_{i,t} - x_{i,t-1}) * \phi_i * w_i|}{\sum_{i \in B} w_i} = 0.25 + \frac{|2*0.02*3| + |4*0.02*1|}{3+1} = 0.3$. Thus, the value of the chlorophyll increases from 0.25 to 0.3 µg/L.

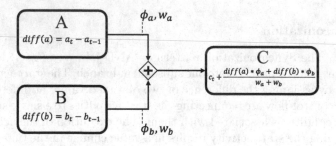

Fig. 6. Synchronization pattern.

Please note that a loop can be created by strongly connecting patterns. An example are two sequence patterns, that are strongly connected.

3   Application: Marine Time-Series Data

In the following, we apply the pattern-based approach to analyse marine time-series data. The purpose is to identify changes of algae, aiming to finally reduce

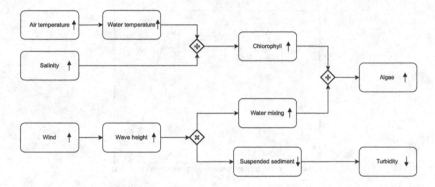

Fig. 7. Combination of patterns for a use case.

carbon usages. For this purpose, parameters such as the sea surface temperature or the salinity of the water are analysed. Figure 3 shows a process model composed from different control-flow patterns.

A Sequence pattern is used to link the increase of air temperature to the increase of water temperature. The water temperature and the salinity of the water are two branches of the AND-join. If both increase, the chlorophyll will increase as well. If the value of the wind increases, the Sequence pattern lead to an increase of wave height. This is the branch leading to the XOR-pattern, where, depending on the wind direction, the water mixing increases or the suspended sediment decreases. The decrease of the suspended sediment represents a Sequence pattern with decreasing turbidity values. Finally, an AND-join links the increase of water mixing and chlorophyll with the increase in algae. Based on the simulation of the process model, synthetic time-series is generated as shown in Table 1. For each measurement time point, a time stamp is generated with values of all simulated parameters. Figure 8 visualizes the generated time-series data, where the amount of algae is represented for the duration of one year.

Table 1. Example of time-series data from the marine use case.

Timestamp	Air Temperature	Salinity	...	Suspended Sediment
...	...	...	...	...
2020-03-18	6.507	32.363	...	1.643
2020-03-25	7.484	32.313	...	1.780
2020-04-01	8.461	32.263	...	2.000
2020-04-08	9.291	32.251	...	2.078
...	...	...	...	...

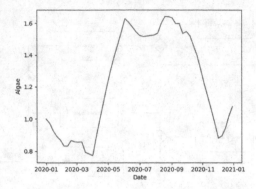

Fig. 8. Graph of the algae amount simulated in the time-series.

4 Implementation

The synthetic time-series data generator bases on the simulation engine presented in [6] and is implemented using python 3.10. The real time-series that serve as a base line is imported as a .csv-file. Then, the simulation results are stored in a .csv-file. The generated time-series data can then be downloaded. In the simulation, every time a measuring point in the time-series is generated, all patterns are checked for their input conditions. If all conditions for a pattern are fulfilled, the values are calculated according to the formula defined in Sect. 2. The measuring point of the time-series can vary according to different dimensions like weekly measuring points or daily calculations.

5 Related Work

Related approaches either provide a tool to generate synthetic time-series data [3] or to analyse time-series data with process mining [1,2,5]. Herbert et al. [3] present a tool for generating synthetic time-series data using neural networks. The purpose of their paper is to learn patterns from data and to generate synthetic data. However, it is neither possible to specify effects, nor define the order of effects by users. In this way, our approach allows more individual control when generating synthetic data, but without considering the control-flow aspect within data. The approach presented in [1] stores time-series data as an additional case attribute assuming that the case ID and process activity are given as high-level business process concepts. In this way, the approach presented in [1] cannot be applied for disciplines like engineering, natural and life science solely producing raw sensor data and preceding a matching of the data to events and activities. A further related approach is presented in [5], however, without any technical solution.

6   Conclusion

This paper presents an approach to generate synthetic time-series data based on annotated control-flow patterns. The benefits of the synthetic data are: (1) generation of data of varying quality, (2) a ground truth that might facilitate the use of machine learning techniques, and (3) a systematic approach that brings time-series data in a "behavior" control-flow perspective. Therefore, our approach aims at discovering causal-effects in time-series data that existing simulation techniques are not capable of. As future avenues, we aim to design an approach abstracting event logs from the synthetic time-series data. Also, we need to improve the AND-pattern, which produces in some cases unrealistic low values. This is done, when both inputs of an AND-join increase, but only one at a time. Then, the pattern will never be instantiated, even if both values are increasing over time.

Acknowledgment. This project has received funding from the Federal Ministry for Economic Affairs and Climate Action under the Marispace-X project grant no. 68GX21002E.

References

1. Dunkl, R., Rinderle-Ma, S., Grossmann, W., Anton Fröschl, K.: A Method for Analyzing Time Series Data in Process Mining: Application and Extension of Decision Point Analysis. In: Nurcan, S., Pimenidis, E. (eds.) CAiSE 2014. LNBIP, vol. 204, pp. 68–84. Springer, Cham (2015). https://doi.org/10.1007/978-3-319-19270-3_5
2. van Eck, M.L., Sidorova, N., van der Aalst, W.M.P.: Enabling process mining on sensor data from smart products. In: 2016 IEEE Tenth International Conference on Research Challenges in Information Science (RCIS). pp. 1–12. IEEE, Grenoble, France (2016). https://doi.org/10.1109/RCIS.2016.7549355
3. Herbert, T., Mangler, J., Rinderle-Ma, S.: Generating Reliable Process Event Streams and Time Series Data Based on Neural Networks. In: Augusto, A., Gill, A., Nurcan, S., Reinhartz-Berger, I., Schmidt, R., Zdravkovic, J. (eds.) BPMDS/EMMSAD -2021. LNBIP, vol. 421, pp. 81–95. Springer, Cham (2021). https://doi.org/10.1007/978-3-030-79186-5_6
4. Russell, N., Hofstede, ter, A., Aalst, van der, W., Mulyar, N.: Workflow control-flow patterns : a revised view. BPMcenter. org (2006). https://research.tue.nl/en/publications/5312cc11-e11d-466a-b9a4-0bee0fd9d25d
5. Valdés, J.J., Céspedes-González, Y., Tapping, K., Molero-Castillo, G.: A Process Mining Approach to the Analysis of the Structure of Time Series. In: Arai, K., Kapoor, S., Bhatia, R. (eds.) FTC 2020. AISC, vol. 1289, pp. 379–392. Springer, Cham (2021). https://doi.org/10.1007/978-3-030-63089-8_25
6. Zisgen, Y., Janssen, D., Koschmider, A.: Generating Synthetic Sensor Event Logs for Process Mining. In: De Weerdt, J., Polyvyanyy, A. (eds) Intelligent Information Systems. CAiSE 2022. Lecture Notes in Business Information Processing, vol 452. Springer (2022). https://doi.org/10.1007/978-3-031-07481-3_15

KG4SDSE

1st Workshop on Knowledge Graphs for Semantics-Driven Systems Engineering (KG4SDSE'23)

The 1st Workshop on Knowledge Graphs for Semantics-Driven Systems Engineering (KG4SDSE) was initiated with a desire to create a focus for CAiSE community members who are engaged in projects relying on Knowledge Graphs, their associated technologies (e.g. graph databases) or paradigms (e.g. knowledge engineering, conceptual modeling). The workshop aimed to highlight the role of semantics in information systems engineering, as emerging tools and methods - originating in research on the Semantic Web or Conceptual Modeling - can be operationalized for engineering or artifact-building research. We believe that Knowledge Graphs, recently positioned by Gartner's hype cycle at the "peak of expectations", will become a key ingredient for an emerging semantics-driven engineering paradigm, making this workshop a timely event that will grow as application ecosystems relying on machine-readable semantics diversify. The workshop received in total 17 submissions from 10 countries. Based on the constructive evaluations from the Program Committee, we accepted 5 full papers and 5 short papers, covering research in various stages of maturity - from advanced results to visions of early-stage research projects that will benefit from the workshop discussions. We are grateful to the keynote speaker who accepted the invitation to open this first KG4SDSE workshop - Nicolas Spyratos from University Paris-Saclay with the talk titled A Graph Data Model for Data Analytics and Information Integration. We hope this will become a recurring event and we are thankful that the CAiSE workshop chairs considered it relevant as a satellite event and committed to hosting it during the Workshops Days of the CAiSE 2023 Week. We are also thankful for the sponsorship of OMiLAB NPO, Germany, and FORTH-ICS Greece, as well as to our Web presence chair, Iulia Vaidian (University of Vienna).

June 2023

Robert Buchmann
Dimitris Karagiannis
Dimitris Plexousakis

Organization

KG4SDSE Workshop Co-chairs

Robert Buchmann   Babeş-Bolyai University, Romania
Dimitris Karagiannis   University of Vienna, Austria
Dimitris Plexousakis   Institute of Computer Science, FORTH and
                                  University of Crete, Greece

KG4SDSE Workshop Program Committee

Nick Bassiliades   Aristotle University of Thessaloniki,
                                  Greece
Sjaak Brinkkemper   Utrecht University, The Netherlands
Michael Fellmann   University of Rostock, Germany
Hans-Georg Fill   University of Fribourg, Switzerland
Aurona Gerber   University of Pretoria, South Africa
Ana-Maria Ghiran   Babeş-Bolyai University, Romania
Adrian Groza   Technical University of Cluj-Napoca,
                                  Romania
Marite Kirikova   Riga Technical University, Latvia
Dimitris Kiritsis   Swiss Federal Institute of Technology in
                                  Lausanne, Switzerland
Manolis Koubarakis   National and Kapodistrian University of
                                  Athens, Greece
Jose Emilio Labra Gayo   University of Oviedo, Spain
Ana León   Universitat Politècnica de València, Spain
Andreas Opdahl   University of Bergen, Norway
Axel Polleres   Vienna University of Economics and
                                  Business, Austria
Andrea Polini   University of Camerino, Italy
Achim Reiz   University of Rostock, Germany
Ben Roelens   Open University, The Netherlands
Anisa Rula   University of Brescia, Italy
Maribel Yasmina Santos   University of Minho, Portugal
Alberto Rodrigues da Silva   University of Lisbon, Portugal
Takahira Yamaguchi   Keio University, Japan

Towards Crisis Response and Intervention Using Knowledge Graphs - CRISP Case Study

Amin Anjomshoaa[1,2](✉)(iD), Hannah Schuster[1,2](iD), Johannes Wachs[2](iD), and Axel Polleres[1,2](iD)

[1] Vienna University of Economics and Business, 1020 Vienna, Austria
[2] Complexity Science Hub Vienna, 1080 Vienna, Austria
{Anjomshoaa,Schuster,Polleres,Wachs}@csh.ac.at

Abstract. Data plays a critical role in crisis response and intervention efforts by providing decision-makers with timely, accurate, and actionable information. During a crisis, data can help organizations and crisis managers identify the most affected populations, track the spread of the crisis, and monitor the effectiveness of their response efforts. We introduce the CRISP Knowledge Graph, constructed from various data resources provided by different stakeholders involved in crisis and disaster management, which presents a uniform view of infrastructure, networks, and services pertinent to crisis management use cases. We also present preliminary results for network and infrastructure analysis which demonstrate how the CRISP KG can address the requirements of crisis management and urban resilience scenarios.

Keywords: Knowledge graphs · Crisis management · Urban Resilience

1 Introduction

In recent years, it has become increasingly evident that the frequency and severity of crisis events have escalated, leading to extensive and severe consequences. During such events, decision-makers are presented with unprecedented volumes of data due to advances in information technology. This presents new challenges and increases the need for data mining and machine learning techniques that can support decision-making processes [3,10]. To effectively manage crisis events, it is essential to analyze the causes of events and understand their potential impacts. This includes simulating the effects of potential interventions to determine their effectiveness and identifying secondary effects, such as cascading effects of shocks and stresses. It is also important to assess the economic impact of crisis events and analyze the impact of interventions on specific indicators to offer protection

The authors acknowledge support from the Austrian Research Promotion Agency's ICT of the Future Program (FFG Project No. 887554.).

© The Author(s), under exclusive license to Springer Nature Switzerland AG 2023
M. Ruiz and P. Soffer (Eds.): CAiSE 2023 Workshops, LNBIP 482, pp. 67–73, 2023.
https://doi.org/10.1007/978-3-031-34985-0_7

against future shocks [5]. In addition, it is necessary to analyze the combined effect of shocks and stresses, including modeling the resilience profile and assessing the combined effect of events on infrastructure networks. Another important aspect is a city's ability to adapt or recover rapidly from a crisis [8]. By implementing comprehensive crisis management strategies, cities can effectively reduce the impact of a crisis and ensure the resilience of their urban infrastructure during critical times [4].

The CRISP Project (Crisis Response and Intervention Supported by Semantic Data Pooling) represents a data-driven approach to Crisis Management. It considers both the short-term management of disasters as well as long-term economic impact assessments at fine-grained regional and temporal granularity. For this purpose, CRISP ingests data from multiple heterogeneous sources and creates a comprehensive and continuously updated data pool, which represents a key asset for semantic modeling and impact forecasting. CRISP aims to increase the transparency of crisis response and intervention processes via a uniform and comprehensive knowledge graph that includes relevant information about infrastructure elements, service networks, and their vulnerability to different types of shock and stress. CRISP KG allows users to understand how interconnected systems react to crisis and shock situations by connecting data on population, medical services, weather, transport, and utilities. This paper introduces the fundamental elements of the CRISP KG and discusses how the infrastructure components and service networks are modeled to account for their interdependencies and vulnerability to shock and stress events. We also present the results of two real-world use cases to illustrate the versatility of the knowledge graph in addressing actual crisis situations.

2   CRISP Knowledge Graph

CRISP KG is specifically designed to gather pertinent information for crisis management purposes. It offers a comprehensive and collective view of urban infrastructure, service networks, and diverse environmental indicators. The knowledge graph is also useful in analyzing the impact of infrastructure failures on provided services and secondary effects on other systems. To construct the CRISP KG, we considered various conceptual aspects of crisis management to be included in the domain ontologies, as depicted in Fig. 1.

Grid Cells and Regions. To organize spatial concepts in a way that enables data processing and query, we use grid cells and regions. By assigning objects to grid cells, spatial data analysts can efficiently manage and analyze large datasets and gain insights into various phenomena related to the spatial distribution of objects. The selected grid cells in CRISP are one square kilometer cells defined by the Austrian Central Institute for Meteorology and Geodynamics [6]. All regions, including political regions (e.g. communities, districts, states) and service regions (e.g. hospital and fire-brigade care zones), are defined as spatial features and mapped to underlying grid cells. Depending on specific use cases

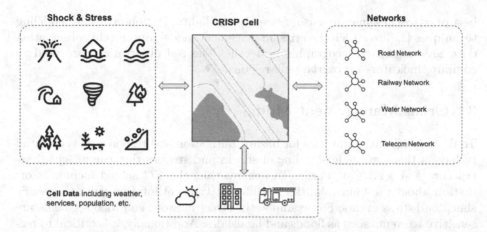

Fig. 1. Overview of CRISP information resources.

and their involved regions, infrastructure elements assigned to grid cells may be allocated to multiple overlaying regions.

Hazards. Hazards consist of two main components: shocks and stresses. Shocks are sudden, intense events typically associated with large-scale disasters such as earthquakes, hurricanes, or terrorist attacks. On the other hand, stresses are the gradual factors that can weaken a community's resilience and can be caused by various factors, such as climate change, population growth, urbanization, and economic instability. We use the INSPIRE categories introduced by the European Union spatial data infrastructure (SDI) initiative to classify hazards [1]. In the context of crisis management, the INSPIRE classification includes categories such as biological, epidemic, and fire hazards and corresponding subcategories.

Infrastructure and Networks. The physical elements of interconnected systems necessary to support, maintain, or improve the living conditions of society by providing essential goods and services are collectively known as urban infrastructure. In the CRISP KG, it refers to the collection of physical structures assigned to a specific grid cell that delivers essential services. We define two categories: those that are part of a network, like road segments of a street network, and those that operate independently, such as hospitals and fire stations. Many infrastructure elements are themselves dependent on each other. A malfunction in one infrastructure can cause disruptions to the services provided by dependent infrastructure and networks. For example, if the communication or transport network fails, the operation of a hospital can be impacted.

Spatio-Temporal Data. The CRISP domain ontology also includes concepts and properties describing observations and relevant spatio-temporal data, like weather and climate data, social media, and demographic information. It uses best practices in semantic sensor networks and lightweight observations modeling techniques [2, 7] to enrich the crisis management model. Specifically, observation data are assigned to geographic grid cells. The cell observations are used to compute indicators for overlapping regions.

3   Crisis Management Model

To develop effective strategies for hazard mitigation and response, it is essential to have a thorough understanding of shocks and stresses that can affect infrastructure and service networks. To achieve this, the KG should include information about the vulnerabilities of different types of infrastructure to specific shock and stress events. For example, the street network and road segments are sensitive to events such as floods and landslides. Additionally, it is critical to recognize that the failure of one service network may have far-reaching impacts on other infrastructure elements and networks. For instance, a flood-induced road blockage can impede access to a hospital, resulting in disruptions to its services. Such details are incorporated into the CRISP KG.

Figure 2 depicts the crisis management model of the CRISP project and shows the relationships between shocks, infrastructure elements, and service networks. To accurately assess the potential impact of a specific shock on infrastructure, it is necessary to investigate the infrastructure elements co-located in the affected cells that are sensitive to that particular type of shock. This analysis should include an evaluation of the potential disruption to services caused by the impacted infrastructure, both direct and indirect. For example, if a road segment is blocked, it can impact the routing and navigation in the street network, while the collapse of a railway bridge can affect crossing road segments.

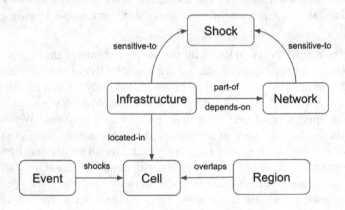

Fig. 2. CRISP Crisis management model.

4   Use Cases

In times of crisis, having access to comprehensive data about interconnected systems and services can be invaluable in helping key actors to make informed decisions and take effective actions to mitigate the impacts of the crisis. For instance, a road closure due to an avalanche or mudslide can block key transit corridors to important supplies or medical care centers. These second-order effects are often significant, and despite the deluge of data available to responders, it is rarely organized in a comprehensive way. This section showcases some potential applications, highlights the CRISP KG's effectiveness in addressing these real-world challenges, and shows how the CRISP KG can be used to build comprehensive models of network interdependencies and vulnerabilities.

4.1   Accessibility of Service Centers

The first use case we present focuses on ensuring accessibility via street or telecommunication networks of critical service centers like hospitals and fire stations during times of crisis. Given the potential for shock events to disrupt the network connectivity of vital infrastructure elements, identifying and rerouting service requests is crucial. The CRISP KG can capture the dependencies of infrastructure elements and service networks, providing valuable assistance in identifying vulnerable network parts. For example, the street network is crucial for the accessibility of service centers and the scene of the incident; disruptions like the flooding of streets can hinder fire stations from providing services.

4.2   Infrastructure Network Impact

The second use case illustrates a real-world crisis situation that highlights the interdependencies of multiple transportation networks. In June 1990, the Wildbichler (Kufstein) bridge in Tirol, Austria, was damaged due to the scour of the riverbed [9] impacting the European transport system. The bridge, which spans the Inn River, is part of a major international north-south autobahn heavily used for transportation and a key segment of the international railway system, as depicted in Fig. 3. Due to its collapse, the motorway link, federal highway, and local highways had to be closed to traffic, and all rail movement in the immediate region was suspended. This incident serves as a powerful reminder of the critical role that infrastructure plays in maintaining the functioning of society, as well as the potential for a single disruption to have cascading effects on a global scale.

Fig. 3. Wildbichler(Kufstein) bridge in Tirol, Austria, was blocked in June 1990 due to the danger of collapse. River transit and rail lines under the bridge were also closed.

5 Conclusions and Future Work

The complex interdependencies of infrastructure elements and service networks within the CRISP KG inform us about the potential impact of different types of shocks and stresses. They can help us develop more effective response strategies to mitigate the effects of future crises. We are currently enriching the CRISP KG based on the proposed modeling approach presented in this paper and address the technical challenges of big data integration. The next step towards achieving semantic interoperability in crisis management use cases is the integration of relevant crisis management processes and including access control to secure sensitive data and processes in the knowledge graph.

References

1. Bartha, G., Kocsis, S.: Standardization of geographic data: The european inspire directive. Eur. J. Geog. **2**(2), 79–89 (2011)
2. Bereta, K., Xiao, G., Koubarakis, M.: Ontop-spatial: Ontop of geospatial databases. J. Web Seman. **58**, 100514 (2019)
3. Cao, L.: Ai and data science for smart emergency, crisis and disaster resilience. Int. J. Data Sci. Anal. **15**, 231–246 (2023)
4. Desouza, K.C., Flanery, T.H.: Designing, planning, and managing resilient cities: a conceptual framework. Cities **35**, 89–99 (2013)
5. Drobniak, A.: The urban resilience-economic perspective. J. Econ. Manag. **10**, 5–20 (2012)
6. Haiden, T., Kann, A., Wittmann, C., Pistotnik, G., Bica, B., Gruber, C.: The integrated nowcasting through comprehensive analysis (INCA) system and its validation over the eastern alpine region. Weather Forecast. **26**(2), 166–183 (2011)
7. Janowicz, K., Haller, A., Cox, S.J., Le Phuoc, D., Lefrançois, M.: Sosa: A lightweight ontology for sensors, observations, samples, and actuators. Journal of Web Semantics **56**, 1–10 (2019)

8. Ribeiro, P.J.G., Gonçalves, L.A.P.J.: Urban resilience: a conceptual framework. Sustain. Cities Soc. **50**, 101625 (2019)
9. Wicke, M.: Damage incurred at the bridges over the inn river at kufstein (austria), and their repair. Struct. Eng. Int. **1**(1), 28–34 (1991)
10. Zagorecki, A.T., Johnson, D.E., Ristvej, J.: Data mining and machine learning in the context of disaster and crisis management. Int. J. Emerg. Manag. **9**(4), 351–365 (2013)

The RAI Way: A Technical Analysis and Design Method for Building Enterprise Semantic Layers

R. E. K. Stirewalt[(✉)] and Márton Búr[ID]

RelationalAI Inc., Berkeley, USA
{kurt.stirewalt,marton.bur}@relational.ai
https://relational.ai

Abstract. The enterprise-wide semantic layer is the Holy Grail of data management. Unlike a data lake or data warehouse, semantic layers promise to democratize access across an organization. Traditional implementations tailor to specific application domains and require significant upfront investment and development to associate semantics to the underlying data. In this paper, we present a new technical analysis and design method that standardizes and simplifies the development of enterprise semantic layers. Our approach provides semantics via an ontology that is modeled in the Object-Role Modeling language. The layer then conforms to this ontology and is populated by weaving source data from physical data assets into the ontology using a relational knowledge graph.

Keywords: Knowledge graphs · Semantic layer · Data landscape · Development methodology

1 Introduction

Data analysts working for large organizations are expected to understand the meaning of stored data, but the sheer number and size of data stores and the general inadequacy of documentation and provenance make this a very challenging task. One solution to this problem is to weave these data into a *semantic layer* that provides a common vocabulary and structure for access, analysis, and management. While not a new idea (cf. [8]) semantic layers are only now becoming practical thanks to the advent of knowledge-graph management systems and the scalability of the modern data stack. Even so, implementing a semantic layer remains a challenging task that will require rigorous methods to manage and measure. We contribute a novel analysis and design method for repeatably and predictably building semantic layers at scale using a relational knowledge-graph management system.

This paper describes a new method called the *RAI Way* to design and implement semantic layers at scale. RAI Way is a technical analysis and design method that standardizes and simplifies the development process in the same way that traditional methods [6,7] do for the development of more general software systems. Methods clarify what it means to solve a problem and explain how to go about doing so in a structured and predictable way.

Because semantic layers are meant to democratize access to data, their constructs must be intuitive and familiar to anyone who works in a given domain. What will be familiar are the concepts, relationships, and business rules that domain experts use to think about their work. That collection of constructs is called an *ontology*. Our method begins by explicitly modeling that ontology and then uses this model to build out the full implementation. RAI Way patterns and techniques assist in the systematic *refinement* of an ontology and in the *weaving of source data* into the layer. In addition to explaining how to build a layer, RAI Way provides tools and metrics for assessing the completeness and progress of an effort, thereby enabling rigorous project management.

2   The RAI Way Method

Our method makes the following assumptions:

- There exists an ontology that domain experts will recognize by virtue of their knowledge of the domain;
- The schema of a semantic layer must conform to that ontology;
- Conceptual-modeling methods can elicit a model of that ontology; and
- A data architect must decide how to reify the ontology into implementation structures and must do so by weaving in the underlying source data.

A semantic layer constructed in the RAI Way is a materialized and incrementally-maintained view of the heterogeneous data sources in an enterprise. To conform to an ontology, the view's schema must be in *graph normal form* (GNF) [5], which implies the technology used to materialize and maintain it must be able to efficiently process the multi-way joins that arise from querying such a schema.

We use a relational knowledge graph management system (RKGMS) that declares and incrementally maintains views consisting of GNF relations using rules written in a declarative modeling language called Rel [9]. A GNF relation is simply a narrow table with set semantics, no nulls, and at most one functional dependency. Rel is an extension of Datalog that naturally expresses recursion and the graph queries that are needed to weave data into an ontology. An RKGMS offers scalable evaluation for such graph queries by offering separation between storage and compute as well as supporting worst-case optimal join algorithms.

The method starts with a model of the ontology created using the Object-Role Modeling (ORM) method and language [2]. We find that our customers are willing to adopt ORM as the ontology modeling language, mostly because it has good tool support. We then iteratively reify each construct from the model by:

1. designing one or more GNF relations that conform to it (refinement); and
2. writing Rel rules that declare how to populate each relation from GNF views of the source data (weaving).

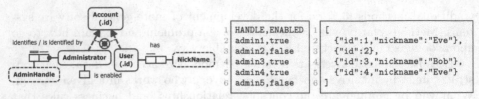

Fig. 1. Sample ontology in ORM   **Listing 1.1.** CSV and JSON data sources

GNF relations are fundamental to this method because they naturally encode both ontological structures and source data. A unary relation naturally implements a concept, while an n-ary relation naturally implements some *reading* of a relationship.[1] Our RKGMS provides primitives that expose both tabular and structured data sources as modular collections of GNF relations, as we explain below. The method completes when one has fully refined the ORM model by weaving all of the source data. The resulting view—the collection of relations that reify the various constructs of the ontology— *is* the semantic layer. It may be directly queried and searched by writing Rel queries that refer to its relations.

How to design those relations and rules can be thought of as a top-down refinement process or a bottom-up weaving process, though in truth it is never entirely one or the other. Refinement decisions provide the structure required to write the weaving logic, while weaving concerns that refer to the low-level details of source data influence refinement decisions. Both perspectives are necessary: The RAI Way defines refinement patterns and weaving metrics that are applied together to flesh out an implementation.

2.1 Example of Use

We illustrate the method via a small ontology whose ORM model appears in Fig. 1 and two example data sources shown in Listing 1.1. The model declares a supertype concept Account with two (exclusive) subtypes, Administrator and User. Each Administrator is identified by a unique AdminHandle, while Users are identified by unique ids. Each Administrator might be enabled, and each User might have up to one NickName which may not be unique to that User.

The data sources—one in CSV format, the other in JSON—serve as source of record for Administrator and User data, respectively. These must be woven to populate the semantic layer that conforms to this example ontology. The following sections demonstrate how the RAI Way method directs the weave of these sources into the semantic layer.

2.2 Concept Reification

There are many ways to reify the concepts and relationships of an ontology. One strategy is the *entity pattern*, which reifies an entity concept C and the relationship that connects C to the concept used to identify it using three constructs:

---

[1] Relationships can have multiple readings, e.g., the relationship between Administrator and AdminHandle in Fig. 1.

```
 1  entity type Administrator = AdminHandle
 2  def admin_handle:identifies(h, a) {
 3    h = ^AdminHandle[admin_csv:HANDLE[_]] and
 4    a = ^Administrator[h] }
 5  def administrator:identified_by {
 6      transpose[admin_handle:identifies] }
 7  def Administrator = admin_handle:identifies[_]
 8
 9  entity type User = UserId
10  def user_id:identifies(id, u) {
11    id = ^UserId[user_value:id[_]] and
12    u = ^User[id] }
13  def User = user_id:identifies[_]
14  def user:nickname(u, n) {
15    exists(o: n = user_value:nickname[o] and
16    u = user_id:identifies[
17      ^UserId[user_value:id[o]]]) }
18  def Account { Administrator ; User }
19
20  value type AdminHandle = String
21  value type UserId = Int
22
23  /* Data sources */
24  def admin_csv = load_csv[...]
25
26  def user_json = load_json_general[...]
27
28  def user_object(n, x, z) {
29    exists(y: user_json:child(x, y, z) and
30    n = #(user_json:value[y])) }
31
32  def user_value(n, o, v) {
33    exists(t: user_object(n, o, t) and
34    user_json:value(t, v)) }
```

Listing 1.2. Concept reifications and data source weaving in Rel

- A new Rel *entity type* called C that will serve as the unique type for every instance of C in the semantic layer;
- One or more n-ary ($n \geq 2$) *reference relations* that map $n-1$ objects (key components) that we use to refer to a given instance of C; and
- A unary *existence relation*, also called C, that materializes in one place all instances of C in the semantic layer.

Lines 1–7 of Listing 1.2 reify Administrator and its identifying relationship. Line 1 declares Administrator to be an entity type [5] that, consistent with Fig. 1, is identified by a value-type concept[2] called AdminHandle (line 20). Lines 2–4 declare a binary reference relation that implements the identifies reading of Administrator's identifying relationship. Line 5 declares the other reading as a relation that is the transpose of admin_handle:identifies. Line 7 defines the existence relation that maintains the population of Administrator. Lines 9–13 reify the User concept and its identifying relationship following the same pattern. Finally, line 18 reifies the Account concept as the relational union (;) of the existence relations for the two subtypes.

2.3 Data Weaving

The RAI Way approach for weaving data leverages the ability of an RKGMS to treat each source as a collection of GNF relations. The load_csv primitive derives such a collection from tabular data sources, generating one relation per source column where each relation maps a row identifier to the value of that column in that row. Line 24 of Listing 1.2 defines a *module* called admin_csv by applying load_csv to the URI of the CSV source in Listing 1.1. A module in Rel is an n-ary relation whose first column contains relation names that allow the module to *specialize* into a collection of one or more $(n-1)$-ary relations. We can refer to

---

[2] Value types in Rel are nominal types. We elide for brevity, but see [5] for details.

value v in row r of the HANDLE column in Listing 1.1 as admin_csv(:HANDLE, r, v) or equivalently by its specialized form admin_csv:HANDLE(r, v). The rule in lines 2–4 creates Administrator instances by weaving data from this source, specifically from any HANDLE-column value from any row of the source.[3]

Similarly, lines 26–34 of Listing 1.2 derive from a JSON source a collection of GNF relations—one per field (key). This is done in two steps. The user_json module specializes to relations that provide a general tree-schema view of any JSON source, with unary relations user_json:root and user_json:array populated with root and array nodes respectively, a binary user_json:value relation that maps a tree node to a simple value like an integer or a string, and a ternary relation user_json:child for navigating edges in the tree. The rules in lines 28–34 then further specialize this general schema into two modules that specialize to relations whose names correspond to the names of fields (keys) in the JSON source. When loaded with the JSON source in Listing 1.1, the user_value module specializes to two relations—user_value:id and user_value:nickname that map from a node representing a JSON message to an integer and a string respectively. An important conversion happens in line 30, as the string JSON keys are converted to relation names through the specialize operator (#). This provides a convenient access to the members of a JSON object in Rel that is very similar to accessing values in a CSV.

Having reduced various kinds of data sources to a set of GNF relations, weaving then reduces to writing rules that reference those relations. A source is fully woven into a semantic layer once each of these relations is used by rules that derive one or more constructs in the ontology. We can therefore measure the completeness of a weave by analyzing the Rel program (currently manually but via program analysis tools in the future) and manage projects along a timeline that incrementally weaves in any unwoven fields or columns. For instance, the analysis of the example Rel code in Listing 1.2 concludes that the is enabled flag in Fig. 1 is not reified, and the ENABLED column from Listing 1.1 is not woven into the semantic layer.

3   Related Work

Associating semantics to data has been a topic of interest data management for decades. Approaches inspired by the Semantic Web (cf. Szilagyi and Wira [10]) use ontologies to prescribe the schemas of physical data representations. By contrast, our method relies on a separate weaving step between the conceptual model (i.e., ontology) and the physical model (i.e., database schema) of the data.

Other approaches use language models and machine learning to automate the enrichment of data with semantics [1,3,4]. These approaches weave data into an ontology but in a way that is at once more general and less precise than in the RAI Way. On one hand, they can extract meaning from a wider variety of data sources (including unstructured data like images) and they can be used to

---

[3]   The square-bracket notation denotes relational-projection, in the case of line 3 of Listing 1.2 it projects away the row-identifier, leaving only the values.

facilitate information retrieval and knowledge discovery. However, due to their heuristic nature, they cannot automatically produce rules that weave source data into an ontology. One open problem is the extent to which such approaches could assist a data architect in applying a method like the RAI Way.

Finally, Song et al. [8] proposed an ontology-driven framework for building semantic layers for enterprises. This work federates queries over heterogeneous sources rather than materializing a view of the ontology. We materialize such a view using a novel data weaving approach that utilizes knowledge graphs.

4 Summary and Future Work

This paper introduces the RAI Way, an analysis and design method that offers a systematic approach to implement semantic layers. The method relies on connecting domain ontology models with source data using knowledge graphs. We are currently using the method to implement semantic layers for tier-1 enterprise clients in the telecom and tax accounting spaces. Going forward, we expect to extend our collection of reification patterns and are developing tools to provide immediate and quantified feedback about the development of the semantic layer.

References

1. Costa, R., Figueiras, P., Jardim-Gonçalves, R., Ramos-Filho, J., Lima, C.: Semantic enrichment of product data supported by machine learning techniques. In: 2017 International Conference on Engineering, Technology and Innovation (ICE/ITMC), pp. 1472–1479. IEEE (2017)
2. Halpin, T.A.: Object-role modeling (ORM/NIAM). In: Handbook on Architectures of Information Systems, pp. 81–103 (2006)
3. van Luijt, B., Verhagen, M.: Bringing semantic knowledge graph technology to your data. IEEE Softw. **37**(2), 89–94 (2020)
4. Özcan, F., Lei, C., Quamar, A., Efthymiou, V.: Semantic enrichment of data for AI applications. In: Proceedings of the Fifth Workshop on Data Management for End-To-End Machine Learning. DEEM '21, Association for Computing Machinery, New York, NY, USA (2021)
5. RelationalAI: RAI knowledge graph management system documentation. https://docs.relational.ai/rel/concepts/overview (2022). Accessed 13 Mar 2023
6. Ross, D.: Structured analysis and design technique (SADT): a language for communicating idea. IEEE Trans. Softw. Eng. **3**(1) (1977)
7. Rumbaugh, J., Blaha, M., Premerlani, W., Eddy, F., Lorensen, W.E., et al.: Object-Oriented Modeling and Design, vol. 199. Prentice-Hall Englewood Cliffs, New Jersey (1991)
8. Song, F., Zacharewicz, G., Chen, D.: An ontology driven framework towards building enterprise semantic information layer. Adv. Eng. Inf. **27**(1), 38–50 (2013)
9. Stirewalt, K.: Experience report: building enterprise applications using LogiQL and Rel (2022). https://www.hytradboi.com/2022/experience-report-building-enterprise-applications-using-logiql-and-rel
10. Szilagyi, I., Wira, P.: Ontologies and semantic web for the internet of things - a survey. In: IECON 2016–42nd Annual Conference of the IEEE Industrial Electronics Society, pp. 6949–6954 (2016)

Towards Recommendations for Knowledge-Graph-Based Requirements Management in Construction: A Report on the EU DigiChecks Project

Bram Bazuin[1]([⊠]) [iD], Sander Stolk[1] [iD], and Marco Stevens[2] [iD]

[1] Semmtech, Scorpius 124, 2132 LR Hoofddorp, The Netherlands
{brambazuin,sanderstolk}@semmtech.nl
[2] Neanex Technologies, Klokstraat 12,2600 Antwerpen, Belgium
marco.stevens@neanex.com

Abstract. This paper positions the work of the EU DigiChecks project, presenting its approach and preliminary findings for standardizing and automating the Verification & Validation (V&V) process of permit requirements in construction projects. For the context of Permit Requirements Management (PRM), we formulate and explore four levels of explicitness for modelling requirements, ranging from document-based to model-based, and discuss how higher levels increase automation capabilities. Our early findings indicate that while model-based requirements offer the highest potential for automation, their explicitness is incompatible with current PRM processes and poses challenges for human understanding. By adopting the intermediate level of enriched text as level of explicitness for PRM instead, enabled by knowledge-graph technology, benefits of existing document-based processes are maintained. This level also offers an increased level of machine-interpretability compared to document-based permits and traceable proof of permit compliance across contexts. First explorations of these two levels suggest that enriched text is more feasible for use by non-technical users, also in terms of software solutions already available, than alternative, model-based solutions.

Keywords: Model-based · Knowledge Graph · Linked Data · Requirements management · DigiChecks

1 Introduction

The construction industry is characterized by a project-based way of working, where multiple stakeholders need to collaborate and share information in a fast and accurate fashion. Often, such a particular combination of client, engineer, contractor and specific governing bodies only collaborate on a single project [4]. This characteristic results in a lack of organic standardization of information

M. Ruiz and P. Soffer (Eds.): CAiSE 2023 Workshops, LNBIP 482, pp. 80–91, 2023.
https://doi.org/10.1007/978-3-031-34985-0_9

management processes within the industry. Therefore, there is a need for standardization developed outside the scope of individual projects. Ensuring quality and satisfaction of project demands depends heavily on accurate requirements processing. This processing, often referred to as the Verification & Validation (V&V) process, is therefore a key component that standardization of Permit Requirements Management (PRM) should take into account. A special case of the V&V process is the process which deals with *permit* requirements. The EU Horizon research project DigiChecks aims to standardize and automate the V&V process for such requirements and to ensure a compliance trail [5].

This paper introduces and explains knowledge-graph-based approaches to Requirements Management (RM) and its application to PRM, specifically within the DigiChecks project. The paper shares preliminary findings of the DigiChecks project and suggests a manner in which a transition could be achieved from document-based PRM – which tends to be the current state of affairs – to knowledge-graph-based PRM. The remainder of this paper is structured as follows. Section 2 offers background information and related work. Section 3 provides an overview of the DigiChecks framework. Section 4 contains a detailed description of our approach to RM. Finally, Sect. 5 concludes and suggests future areas of research.

2   Background and Related Work

Information management maturity varies greatly within the construction industry, from organizations that work with traditional means to early adapters of highly digitized and/or standardized methods. In this section, we first consider the methods of the majority of organizations within the industry; findings of which have been obtained by the DigiChecks consortium for PRM, specifically. Subsequently, the efforts of early adapters are considered, including the use of knowledge graphs. As a result, this section can be seen as indicating both the current state as well as the goal of standardization in the construction industry.

2.1   Current PRM Methods in the Construction Industry

As indicated above, (permit) requirements management is necessary for ensuring quality and satisfaction of demands on construction projects. For PRM, compliance with these requirements results in the granting of a permit by governing bodies. Engineering and construction teams prepare the necessary project data and carry out their own review of compliance with the requirements. Through the process of permit application, information is transmitted from the project organization to the governing body. The governing body then performs their own V&V process to decide whether the requested permit will be issued.

The majority of the information transmittals during this process is document-based [13]. This statement is also supported by the literature review and analysis of the DigiChecks consortium[1]: preliminary results reveal significant variation

---

[1] Countries currently included in the analysis are Austria, Belgium, France, the Netherlands, Spain, and the United Kingdom.

in information, formats, and information structures across countries, regions, municipalities, and projects. The majority of cases still rely on document-based formats, either digitally-born or scans of handwritten documents, while occasionally information is recorded through online forms and presented as text.

Although software applications can aid in PRM and V&V, the lack of information standardization and mechanisms for exchanging information is a burden on replacing document-based communication. As a result, human interpretation of documents is often necessary, and traceability between sources relies on implicit references between complete documents. An additional consequence is that permit request handling is currently often a manual process, leading to slow processing times, potential errors, and reliability issues. Such issues hinder effective collaboration and knowledge sharing among supply chain partners [21]. Recent research, such as Noardo's study on the use of Building Information Modeling (BIM) in the context of building permits [9], has explored opportunities and challenges of using more advanced digital methods for permit management, highlighting the potential for more automated and efficient approaches using BIM and knowledge graphs.

2.2   Usage of Knowledge Graphs in Construction

The construction industry is exploring the potential of automation using knowledge graphs. This is shown through the development of core ontologies for information exchange, such as CEN 17632 [8]. Additionally, domain-specific ontologies have been developed, such as the CEDR Road OTL by INTERLINK [3] and the BOT ontology on buildings by W3C's Linked Building Data group [14]. To illustrate, the Netherlands has emerged as a leading country in Europe for implementing knowledge graphs in RM. Notably, TenneT, the energy transmission systems operator, has achieved success using knowledge graphs for EU-303 asset information exchange and project requirements management, V&V based on physical asset information against SHACL shapes and organization-specific domain ontologies [18].

Despite the potential of knowledge graphs to enable more automated and efficient approaches, the construction industry has yet to adopt them for PRM [15]. Additional research and development is needed to extend the use of knowledge graphs in this area.

3   The DigiChecks Framework Overview

The previous section highlighted the significant role of V&V in PRM, emphasizing its function in comparing project information against requirement data to guarantee precise permit requirement processing. The DigiChecks framework is conceived as a federated, modular, and scalable ecosystem that underscores the importance of the V&V process and aims to optimize and automate its operations.

To do so, the DigiChecks project consists of several phases; (1) a comprehensive literature review and analysis; (2) defining the requirements for the DigiChecks framework; (3) designing the framework, encompassing system architecture, interoperability and data sovereignty; (4) implementing the core components, including application to pre-selected business cases and the validation of the replicability of the solution; and (5) dissemination. The first phase has been completed, and the second and third phase are ongoing at the moment of writing. A key principle of the DigiChecks consortium is allowing third parties to develop additional components once the dissemination has occurred, enabling the solution to be utilized and further developed outside the project's scope.

The remainder of this section is organized as follows: Sect. 3.1 provides a high-level description of the DigiChecks architecture, while Sect. 3.2 discusses the requirements for automation in PRM, building on the findings of the completed first research phase of the DigiChecks project. Afterwards, Sect. 4 will further explore the methodologies and tools involved in managing requirements within the DigiChecks framework, ensuring that the designed ecosystem effectively addresses the challenges and demands of the PRM process.

3.1   The DigiChecks Architecture

In the ongoing third research phase, the DigiChecks consortium is developing a knowledge-graph-based PRM system architecture, consisting on the highest abstraction level of three primary functions performed by various stakeholders. Figure 1 presents an overview of these three primary functions within the permitting process and the roles of their associated stakeholders.

The first function, requirements management, is carried out by a wide range of parties, including governing authorities, standardization bodies, and engineers. The total set of requirements for permit eligibility depends on the permit type and can combine requirements from multiple sources. A competent authority may, but is not required to, act as a requirements manager in a permitting process instance. Engineering and construction stakeholders may serve as applicants, submitting a permit request based on project data to the competent authority. The authority subsequently needs a V&V function to perform compliance checks based on this project data and the permit requirements. In case all requirements are met, a permit may be granted to the applicant.

Considering that distinct stakeholders perform each function, the DigiChecks framework incorporates *modular, interchangeable components* tailored to each function. Interoperability is ensured through a set of agreements for information sharing. This design enables stakeholders to substitute dependent components with their preferred alternatives without compromising compatibility. The next section further elaborates on the necessary conditions to provide these functions within the DigiChecks framework effectively.

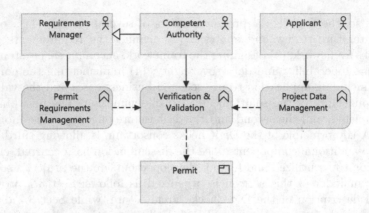

Fig. 1. ArchiMate 3.2 diagram of the DigiChecks PRM Architecture, showing the different roles involved and their functions [1].

3.2   Requirements for Automation in PRM

In order for a solution to be adopted in the industry, that solution will need to have a realistic expectation of its use and adoption. For automated compliancy checking, specifically, a solution must be able to interpret and compare PRM information with which it is supplied. The following three high-level requirements have been formulated thus far, based on the first research phase:

1. PRM must be able to process pre-existing document-based requirements to avoid creating barriers for parties to use DigiChecks.
2. Data exchange must be based on open and widely-accepted structured data formats to enable PRM to be implemented as a federated framework.
3. Non-technical users must be able to execute PRM, utilising current processes that are already in place for document-based PRM.

   The system architecture of the DigiChecks solution encompasses these three high-level requirements. The first requirement ensures that the solution can be immediately used, whereas the second enables further development in the future. Lastly, the third requirement focuses on continuous usability. The application of these requirements will be discussed in the next section.

4   Requirements Management in DigiChecks

In addition to designing a system architecture, the ongoing third research phase of the DigiChecks consortium involves formulating a set of recommendations for knowledge-graph-based PRM. This process encompasses two primary activities. The first activity aims to examine different levels of requirement expressivity and their impact on automation in V&V (Sect. 4.1). The second activity investigates methods and tools that can be utilized to attain higher levels of the framework (Sect. 4.2).

4.1   Requirements Explicitness and Automation Potential

This section outlines the various levels of explicitness in expressing requirements and their automation potential, based on the 5-star Linked Data frame principle by Tim Berners-Lee [19]. We present them below and in Fig. 2: (1) document-based requirements, (2a) text-based requirements, (2b) enriched text-based requirements, and (3) model-based requirements. Levels 2b and 3 are at least partly model-based, and therefore knowledge graphs are suitable for their implementation. Indeed, the use of persistent, Web-based identifiers in such graph structures (URIs) allows information on individual requirements to be traced throughout exchange in distributed PRM and V&V processes, both among stakeholders and across software components.

In general, higher levels of explicitness enable finer-grained compositions of information, which in turn facilitate computer-interpretability. As a result, higher levels of explicitness are more suitable for automating processes than lower levels. Furthermore, information stored with higher levels of explicitness can be combined into representations that conform to levels of lower granularity such as a document, in case this is demanded by stakeholders. In contrast, adding explicitness to information often necessitates interpreting the implicit information to correctly decompose it into its constituents. In the following paragraphs, we will examine each level in more detail, including their distinctive characteristics and automation potential.

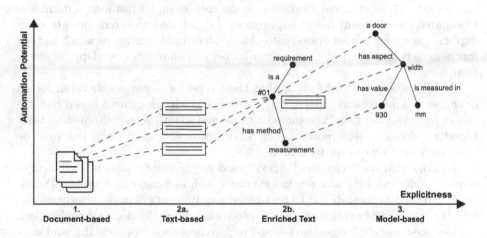

Fig. 2. Explicitness versus automation potential in PRM.

(1) Document-Based Requirements. In the majority of the cases, requirements in the construction industry are exchanged in the form of **documents**. Documents are human-readable collections of information, often textual, but may also include images or tabular data. Document structure arises from the way words, phrases and styling are combined. Examples of documents include leaflets, digital documents such as PDFs, and books.

Writer and reader are granted some interpretational freedom: the writer may omit information or leave it up to the reader to deduce from context, and the reader may choose how to interpret information. This requires the reader to access a document in full to obtain a precise understanding of the intended meaning of requirements contained by it.

This is a potential conflict for a construction project where responsibilities are distributed. Namely, distribution of parts of a holistically written of documents results in an approximation of the intended meaning, which can make it challenging to convey precise messages. This possibly leads to permit applications that do not fully align with the intended permit requirements, which in turn might result in compliance issues, rework, and delays in project timelines. Additionally, the ambiguity in document-based requirements poses a challenge for machine interpretation, as the lack of explicitness can make it difficult for algorithms to accurately interpret and understand the requirements [22].

Despite these challenges, document-based requirements offer a useful starting point for capturing requirements and remain valuable for their ease of use in reading and writing. In fact, this ease is the precise reason why requirement exchange in the industry is still largely document-based.

(2a) Text-Based Requirements. Text-based requirements are requirements that are stored, in a textual form, as separate entities in, for instance, a database. Compared to document-based requirements, text-based requirements are more explicit since they are separated into clearly identifiable instances which in turn forces each requirement to have a clear scope, and eliminates overlapping specifications.

A disadvantage of this form is that these types of requirements often forego of contextual information that is commonly found with document-based requirements (e.g., chapter headings, introductions, and so on). As a consequence, text-based requirements are more explicit than document-based ones, but may be more difficult to interpret by humans.

Existing RM tools can handle text-based requirements, although challenges remain in dealing with non-textual elements such as images and tables. Transitioning from document-based to text-based requirements requires interpretation and the addition of explicit statements to make up for the decontextualization.

Despite these challenges, text-based requirements are more scalable and suitable for non-linear information structures, such as permitting processes or structured V&V where individual compliancy can be answered by a binary response.

(2b) Enriched Text Requirements. Enriched text requirements build on the advantages of text-based requirements by incorporating more explicit model-based statements as relations with other elements. Examples of such relations are the type of requirement, its subject matter, a standardized plan for V&V, or its relation to other requirements in different sets, such as national standards.

Non-textual elements, such as images and tables, can also be related to these statements to enhance human interpretation.

Enriched text requirements enable software to query requirements based on their additions, improving requirements filtering, and providing relevant information to those responsible for specific permitting steps. The addition of enrichments aids machine interpretability, allowing software applications to understand the context of requirements and provide users with the right information. By adding interrelationships between requirements, sparse knowledge graphs are created for traceable proof of permit compliance across contexts.

However, enriched text requirements are unsuitable for making precise mathematical or logical statements and complete interpretation still relies on an understanding of human language. Nevertheless, the combination of text-based and model-based information improves scalability and automatability, and enables derivation from lower-level requirements and assembly into document-based requirements.

(3) Model-Based Requirements. Model-based requirements represent the need in a machine-readable format without relying on human-readable texts, allowing for precise description, transmission, and perception of information. These characteristics make these requirements highly scalable and capable of offering the highest level of automation.

Because model-based requirements lack a representation in natural language, they are more challenging for humans to understand, as they necessitate more precise statements. Deriving model-based requirements from text-based requirements requires interpretation and therefore potentially a change in meaning. Assembling model-based requirements into human-readable text is still feasible in cases where such a presentation is beneficial.

4.2   First Explorations of Solutions

In this section, we investigate two distinct approaches to address the challenges posed by a concrete example. For this, we have chosen an accessibility requirement that is formulated in the context of public building permits in Spain [17]. Specifically, regulations stipulate specific maximum slopes for access ramps. The translated specification outlines these constraints:

> The ramps will have a slope of maximum 12%, except those belonging to accessible routes, whose slope will be maximum 10% when their length is less than 3 m, 8% when the length is less than 6 m, and 6% in all other cases.

First Explorations of an Enriched Text Solution. The accessibility requirement mentioned above can be expressed in a knowledge graph in an enriched text form adopting the CEN 17632 ontology. [16]. To enable the implementation of enriched text requirements in permitting and engineering processes, three steps are required: (1) expressing requirements as individual text strings; (2) enriching them by linking additional elements and related requirements; and (3) sharing them with other stakeholders. Notably, the example incorporates a plan for V&V related to the requirement, ensuring a comprehensive approach to RM. As the management of requirements requires domain expertise, it should be possible to execute these steps without specific IT skills. To facilitate such utilization by non-technical users, we are exploring the integration of Permit Requirements Management Tooling (PRMT) into the DigiChecks framework. In our investigations we tested an existing solution, the Laces Suite, which offers capabilities that meet the three requirements outlined in Sect. 3.2, and leverages knowledge graph technology [10].[2]

Our investigation shows that the evaluated PRMT enables non-technical users to create and manage PRM knowledge graphs that conform to Linked Data standards. The solution supports document extraction and software-based management of individual requirements, which can be positioned in a hierarchy to support model-based organization and navigation. To add context to the requirements, explicit relationships are established with model entities and related ontologies. Furthermore, a flexible schema allows the publication of a versioned dataset on a Linked Data Platform, enabling easy access, querying, and distribution of requirements and associated information across contexts, making them available to all stakeholders through Web-based mechanisms [12]. The Laces web application, along with a set of enriched text requirements, is shown in Fig. 3.

First Explorations of a Model-Based Solution. In the construction industry, open and distributed standards for information exchange are necessary due to the highly collaborative nature of the industry. Linked data and knowledge graphs provide a promising solution for PRM, but numerical information requires mathematical extensions to achieve full coverage and explicitness.

The DigiChecks consortium has explored two solutions for mathematical coverage thus far: the MINDS Translator [6], and the Numerate Web [20]. MINDS approximates mathematical formulates in SPARQL, which is fast and uses widely-accepted formats. However, it requires a higher level of mathematical understanding than to be expected of non-technical users in the construction industry. In contrast, the Numerate Web is easy to use by this group of users and can evaluate and express equations in OpenMath-RDF [2].

The accessibility requirement quoted earlier can be expressed in a model-based form using this solution, as demonstrated in [16]. Unfortunately, Numerate Web currently relies on a specific set of separate but interdependent tooling. Both solutions therefore require further support and improvements in order to ensure realistic applicability in PRMT.

---

[2] Such solutions also offer the means for applicants to split requirements into distinctive parts that they can cover separately for easier management. See [16].

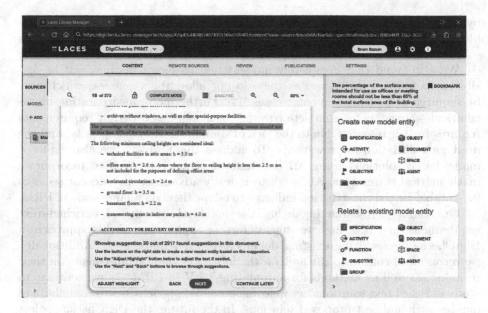

Fig. 3. Extracting requirements from a document, in Laces.

As the nature of engineering in early design phases often deals with imprecise and vague steps, fully formal or model-based approaches may not be feasible. While they can reduce ambiguity in natural language requirements, vagueness may be required or beneficial in these cases, making a fully model-based approach impractical [7]. Consequentially, a hybrid approach, combining natural language requirements and model-based representations, may be the most practical and effective solution for PRM in the construction industry [11].

5 Conclusion and Future Work

This paper presented a research approach to Permit Requirements Management (PRM) in the construction industry, developed as part of the DigiChecks project. We investigated the challenges associated with a document-based approach to PRM and the potential benefits of using a knowledge-graph-based approach in construction projects. Our early explorations suggest that enriched text solutions is a promising direction to pursue, using PRMT to support non-technical users in managing knowledge graphs [10].

Enriched text-based requirements represent a significant step towards more explicit Requirements Management (RM). This increased level of explicitness compared to document-based solutions allows for the leveraging of Linked Data technology capabilities, such as querying, conjunct use, and application in software, leading to explicit V&V, possibly facilitated by the sharing mechanisms of a Linked Data Platform [12]. Text extraction and enrichment can be done by users without necessarily requiring IT expertise, while remaining compatible with current PRM processes and human interaction. As a consequence, this solution satisfies the requirements for automation in PRM set in Sect. 3.2.

We also found that completely model-based requirements may not be feasible in permitting processes, as they do not allow the vagueness which may be required or beneficial in some cases [11]. Furthermore, incorporating mathematical statements for complete coverage of model-based permit requirements requires further research due to the lack of standardization, complexity, and the need for calculation improvements. To address this problem, we also explored model-based solutions using MINDS and the Numerate Web to incorporate mathematical statements. Although technically advanced, they do not seem to be suitable for the construction industry to adopt them on a large scale in PRM.

Our ongoing research highlights the potential benefits of enriched text requirements in PRM, and we suggest further exploration of this approach in DigiChecks by rewriting existing document-based requirements. Additionally, we recommend continued research on the impact of these requirements on their meaning, as well as methods for automating V&V in PRM. As we continue to study enriched text solutions, we welcome potential participants to contribute to our research and test proposed solutions. In the future, the DigiChecks project will focus on designing a solution for automated compliancy checking based on PRM and relevant information from projects.

Acknowledgements. This project has received funding from the European Union's Horizon Europe research and innovation programme - Project 101058541 - DigiChecks. Additionally, we would like to thank Ani Mkheidze for her assistance with the initial explorations of our model-based solution.

References

1. ArchiMate 3.2 Specification, https://pubs.opengroup.org/architecture/archimate32-doc/. Accessed 19 Apr 2023
2. Buswell, S., Caprotti, O., Carlisle, D., Dewar, M., Gaetano, M., Kohlhase, M.: The open math standard (2004)
3. CEDR Road OTL, https://www.roadotl.eu/. Accessed 28 Feb 2023
4. Curry, E., O'Donnell, J., Corry, E., Hasan, S., Keane, M., O'Riain, S.: Linking building data in the cloud: integrating cross-domain building data using linked data. Adv. Eng. Inf. **27**(2), 206–219 (2013)
5. Digital permits and compliance checks for buildings and infrastructure (IA), https://ec.europa.eu/info/funding-tenders/opportunities/portal/screen/opportunities/topic-details/horizon-cl4-2021-twin-transition-01-10. Accessed 27 Feb 2023
6. Graux, D., Sejdiu, G., Stadler, C., Napolitano, G., Lehmann, J.: MINDS: A Translator to Embed Mathematical Expressions Inside SPARQL Queries. In: Blomqvist, E., et al. (eds.) SEMANTICS 2020. LNCS, vol. 12378, pp. 104–117. Springer, Cham (2020). https://doi.org/10.1007/978-3-030-59833-4_7

7. INCOSE Guide to Writing Requirements V3.1 - Summary Sheet, https://www.incose.org/docs/default-source/working-groups/requirements-wg/rwg_products/incose_rwg_gtwr_summary_sheet_2022.pdf. Accessed 6 Mar 2023
8. NEN-EN 17632:2022. Building Information Modelling (BIM) - Semantic Modelling and Linking (SML) - Part 1: Generic modelling patterns, https://www.nen.nl/nen-en-17632-1-2022-en-304869. Accessed 20 Apr 2023
9. Noardo, F., Ellul, C., Harrie, L., Overland, I., Shariat, M., Arroyo Ohori, K., Stoter, J.: Opportunities and challenges for GeoBIM in Europe: developing a building permits use-case to raise awareness and examine technical interoperability challenges. J. Spatial Sci. 62(2), 209–233 (2020)
10. Laces Suite https://laceshub.com/laces-suite/. Accessed 1 March 2023
11. Lebeaupin, B., Rauzy, A.: Toward a better integration of requirements and model-based specifications. Syst. Eng. 23(6), 751–769 (2020)
12. Linked Data Platform 1.0, https://www.w3.org/TR/ldp/. Accessed 27 Feb 2023
13. Patacas, J., Dawood, N., Kassem, M.: BIM for facilities management: a framework and a common data environment using open standards. Autom. Constr. 120, 103366 (2020)
14. Rasmussen, M.H., Lefrançois, M., Schneider, G.F., Pauwels, P.: BOT: the building topology ontology of the W3C linked building data group. Seman. Web 12(1), 143–161 (2021)
15. Rasmussen, M. H., Lefrançois, M., Pauwels, P., Hviid, C. A., Karlshøj, J.: Managing interrelated project information in AEC knowledge graphs. Autom. Constr. 108, 102956 (2019)
16. Repository KG4SDSE, https://github.com/semmtech/kg4sdse2023/. Accessed 20 April 2023
17. Seguridad de utilización y accesibilidad, https://www.codigotecnico.org/pdf/Documentos/SUA/DccSUA.pdf. Accessed 17 April 2023
18. Stolk, S., Lubbers, W., Braakman, F., Weitkamp, S.: Ontologies and JSON-LD at TenneT: The use of linked data on EU-303 projects. In: Proceedings of LDAC 2022 Workshop at the 19th European Semantic Web Conference. https://linkedbuildingdata.net/ldac2022/files/papers/paper02.pdf. Hersonissos (2022)
19. W3.org - Linked Data, https://www.w3.org/DesignIssues/LinkedData.html. Accessed 6 Mar 2023
20. Wenzel, K.: The Numerate Web: Mathematical Formulas and Computations on the Web of Data. Pre-print (2022)
21. Zhang, J., & El-Gohary, N. M.: Semantic NLP-based information extraction from construction regulatory documents for automated compliance checking. J. Comput. Civil Eng. 30(2), 141013064441000 (2016)
22. Zhang, R., El-Gohary, N.: Building information modeling, natural language processing, and artificial intelligence for automated compliance checking. Research Companion to Building Information Modeling. Edward Elgar Publishing, 248–267 (2022)

Semantic Matching Through Knowledge Graphs: A Smart City Case

Alexander Voelz[1]([⊠]), Danial M. Amlashi[1], and Moonkun Lee[2]

[1] Research Group Knowledge Engineering, University of Vienna, Vienna, Austria
`alexander.voelz@univie.ac.at`
[2] Department of Computer Science and Engineering, Jeonbuk National University,
Jeonju, Jeonbuk 561-756, Republic of Korea
`moonkun@jbnu.ac.kr`

Abstract. Using selected building blocks of the Semantic Web vision to enhance domain-specific modeling methods is advancing as a new research area. The study at hand aims to contribute to this novel area of research by proposing a *Semantic Matching Model* that serves as a foundation for matching the purpose of a certain modeling method with the intention of future users. Within this matching model, Linked Open Data is utilized to semantically align user inputs in the form of words or phrases with resources from the Semantic Web, which can then form the basis for semantic enrichment of model instances. An experimental proof-of-concept is provided in the form of a smart city-related implementation scenario. In this scenario, tour models are first matched with relevant information from the Semantic Web and then translated into semantic-rich knowledge graphs that enable the publication of the enriched models.

Keywords: Conceptual Modeling · Domain-Specific Modeling Methods · Knowledge Graph · Semantic Matching · Linked Open Data

1 Introduction

Conceptual modeling is a powerful tool for reducing the complexity in a domain under study, enabling stakeholders with different interests to better understand and communicate the underlying concepts and mechanisms of the respective domain. Consequently, the development of dedicated modeling languages and their implementation in the form of a complete modeling method have gained increasing attention in research and industry. The available modeling languages vary in their degree of specificity, thus forming the basis for the separation between general-purpose and domain-specific languages. However, more extensive classifications based on specificity and purpose have been proposed [4].

Domain-specific modeling methods offer advanced functionalities that enhance the value of models beyond visual representations by leveraging underlying domain semantics. Recent efforts in research have explored how such functionalities can be leveraged by incorporating certain aspects of the Semantic Web

M. Ruiz and P. Soffer (Eds.): CAiSE 2023 Workshops, LNBIP 482, pp. 92–104, 2023.
https://doi.org/10.1007/978-3-031-34985-0_10

vision. Among these efforts are the serialization of diagrammatic models according to Semantic Web standards [3], their linking in the manner advocated by the linked data vision [15], and their deployment as hybrid knowledge base [14].

In this paper, we aim to match modeling methods with the intent of expected users by building upon existing research in the field. With this goal in mind, we elaborate on how modeling methods can be matched with suitable Semantic Web knowledge graphs based on the respective method purpose. Through this matching, models can be enriched with domain-specific information from suitable graphs. The presented ideas are finally applied in an experimental smart city implementation scenario of a domain-specific modeling method.

The remainder of the contribution is structured as follows: To begin with, the broader theoretical background on conceptual modeling and knowledge graphs is presented before more detailed elaborations on related work follow. Afterwards, the *Semantic Matching Model* is presented and showcased in the context of a specific smart city implementation scenario. Finally, we conclude with a summary and evaluate the idea of this study based on a SWOT analysis.

2   Theoretical Background and Related Work

The following chapter introduces the theoretical background relevant to this study before related works on existing semantic approaches and their current use within conceptual modeling are discussed.

2.1   Conceptual Modeling and Domain-Specific Modeling Languages

Conceptual modeling is a long-standing topic in scientific literature and was early defined as the process of formally describing aspects of the physical and social world with the goal of improving understanding and communication [25]. The conceptual modeling approaches that emerged since then have been widely applied in the field of computer science to simplify complex information systems, for instance by representing their underlying concepts and structures as diagrammatic models. In order to achieve such a reduction in complexity and foster comprehension among the involved stakeholders, abstraction is commonly employed [21]. Accordingly, the essence of conceptual modeling comprises the *"use of abstraction to reduce complexity for a specific purpose."* [30, p.244]

Compared to so-called general-purpose modeling languages, Domain-Specific Modeling Languages (DSMLs) allow for customizations that aim at achieving a desired level of simplification [2]. As a result, such specified languages have several benefits over their general-purpose counterparts [9], leading to DSMLs being widely adopted across various disciplines [17,18]. To create a DSML, the corresponding notation, syntax, and semantics need to be specified. This underlying structure is captured in the form of a metamodel, which itself is created using a modeling language, referred to as the metamodeling language [16].

The customization of modeling languages for a specific domain extends the value of models created with them beyond comprehensible representations [2,9].

Consequently, DSMLs are commonly implemented as complete methods, including advanced functionalities and specifications on how to apply the respective language. The resulting components are captured in the Generic Modeling Method Framework (GMMF), in which the modeling language is supported through a corresponding modeling procedure and through mechanisms and algorithms that enable generic, specific, or hybrid functionalities [16].

Beyond the functionality-based value, the process of creating model value through co-creation needs to be considered in the context of modeling methods. The co-creation of model value is based on the interaction of two key roles: the *modeler* designing model artifacts, and the *method engineer* creating the modeling method [2,30]. This study focuses on how functionalities implemented by the method engineer can create value for the modeler. Future works are intended to derive additional value through the co-creation process by utilizing the created models to derive further functionalities during the iterative process of the Agile Modeling Method Engineering (AMME) life cycle [13].

2.2   Knowledge Graphs, RDF and Linked Open Data

In today's research, knowledge graphs are commonly understood as graph-based data structures that capture knowledge by explicitly representing concepts and the relationship between them. At the same time, it remains a rather undefined term [8] that has gained a lot of its popularity after Google announced the launch of its knowledge graph in 2012, with the corresponding blog entry regularly being cited in the literature as a seemingly valid definition of the term.

Graph-based data representation gained traction in the early days of the Semantic Web vision, prompting the development of the Resource Description Framework (RDF) by the W3C as a standard to represent web data in a machine-processable way [32]. Further, graph-based data structures ensure a seamless extension and linking to other data sources. Some authors argue that knowledge graphs not only consist of the represented data but are also characterized by an integrated reasoning engine used to make inferences [8].

Finally, the prevalence of Linked Open Data (LOD)[1] is emphasized. LOD can be described as the last of five data openness levels that were proposed by Tim Berners-Lee [1]. According to these openness levels, RDF data representations already fulfill the requirements of machine-readability, non-proprietary, and the use of an open standard. If such data representations are enriched by contextual linking to other resources, it fulfills all requirements to be considered LOD.

2.3   Related Work

The related work section shortly delimits semantic approaches used in literature, before comparable applications in the field of conceptual modeling are discussed.

---

[1] e.g., see the history of linked data sets in the Linked Open Data Cloud [22].

Delimitation of Semantic Approaches. Various semantic approaches related to this study are often used interchangeably in the literature. Namely, *Semantic Matching*, *Semantic Alignment*, and *Semantic Enrichment* are discussed in the following due to their relevance for this research.

Semantic Matching is concerned with comparing concepts from different graph-like data sources to align them based on shared semantic properties [11]. This process of identifying related concepts typically involves *ontology matching*, which employs various semantic similarity measures to determine concepts from different database schemas, such as ontologies, that can be matched [12].

Semantic Alignment, on the other hand, originates from linguistics and is an important concept when comparing how the grammatical structures of languages differ. Within computer science, it is prominently employed for text or image generation [19], natural language processing [26], and other areas that rely on the alignment of words or phrases with corresponding concepts.

Further, *Semantic Enrichment* builds upon the extensible graph-based data structure of RDF and has the goal of adding contextual semantics to existing data by integrating links to other LOD sources. This approach is increasingly discussed in the literature, encompassing the domains of cultural heritage [7], bibliographic records [31], and information retrieval [28]. Among the resulting benefits are advanced data integration and reasoning mechanisms.

In the context of this research, we deemed the term semantic matching to be most suitable for describing the identification of relevant knowledge graphs that can be matched with concepts of a DSML based on shared semantic meaning, while semantic alignment forms one specific approach to how such matching mechanisms can be performed. Finally, semantic enrichment is understood as any effort to integrate links to or information from LOD sources.

Semantic Approaches Within Conceptual Modeling. For several years, researchers have investigated how the benefits of conceptual modeling and the Semantic Web vision can be combined. As a result, mechanisms that enable an automated RDF-based serialization of conceptual diagrammatic models have been established. One such example is the RDFizer, which is designed as method-independent functionality for the ADOxx[2] metamodeling platform [3]. The representation as RDF triples enables advanced querying and inferencing procedures, as was shown in a corresponding proof-of-concept study [5] and through the deployment of translated models as knowledge base on GraphDB [14].

In addition, the transformation of conceptual models into knowledge graphs based on a generic cloud platform has been discussed in the literature [29]. The implementation of the platform was tested on a set of 5.000 UML models, thus demonstrating the capability of processing large volumes of models.

Still, the use of semantic approaches within conceptual modeling is still in its infancy. First efforts have contributed to making the semantics contained in conceptual diagrammatic models accessible through linked data enrichment by building upon Semantic Web conform model transformations [3,6].

---

[2] BOC-Group, ADOxx tool. http://www.adoxx.org/live/ (accessed 04.03.23).

Further, the notion of *Linked Open Models* has been brought forward, requiring to match and align models with resources outside of the respective modeling environment [15]. For this purpose, an RDF serialization of models is utilized to ensure their conformance with the linked data paradigm.

3 Semantic Matching Between Domain-Specific Modeling Methods and Linked Open Data

This contribution aims at providing an approach for matching semantically relevant knowledge graphs from the LOD cloud with domain-specific modeling methods to enable advanced functionalities and increase the value of created models. For this purpose, we propose a *Semantic Matching Model*, which is later instantiated to a concrete implementation scenario in the smart city context.

3.1 Semantic Matching Model

In the *Semantic Matching Model* displayed in Fig. 1, we differentiate between the generic version and a LOD-based instance of it. The *Generic Semantic Matching Model* emphasizes the fundamental requirement of matching the *purpose* of a modeling method with the anticipated *user intent* in a semantically relevant manner. The respective method purpose and user intent, as well as the resulting process of semantic matching, are specific to each instance.

The *LOD-based instance of the Semantic Matching Model* is closely related to the underlying principles of model value co-creation (cf. section 2.1), as both put an emphasis on the interaction between modeler and method engineer. This interaction is guided by the semantic matching between the methods purpose and the anticipated *user intent* with the goal of increasing model value. At this point, we have to emphasize that our understanding of semantic matching differs from the common approach of ontology matching used in this context. While ontology matching is concerned with comparing and aligning entire schemas or concepts, our semantic matching process is focused on identifying knowledge graphs that can be matched with concepts of a DSML based on shared semantic meaning.

In Fig. 1, this matching of purpose and anticipated intent is performed by the *method engineer* who defines a *domain structure* during the creation of a *Domain-Specific Modeling Method* (DSMM). The domain structure refers to a collection of knowledge graphs from the LOD cloud that have been selected based on their semantic relevance to the domain under study. Subsequently, this selection is used to establish permanent access between the DSMM and the chosen graphs, ensuring seamless integration of relevant data. In order to ultimately increase the value of created models, the established access has to be utilized in such a way that advanced functionalities supporting the anticipated user intent can be offered within the modeling environment. The actual intent is determined by the modeler's final decision of which subset of the domain structure to retrieve during the use of the respective DSMM.

3.2 A Smart City Implementation Scenario

Finally, the described Semantic Matching Model is applied in the context of an implementation scenario, which is based on the tour guide case presented as part of our previous work on a citizen development approach for smart cities [24]. The scenario is used to showcase how smart city tour models can be matched with a selection of knowledge graphs to retrieve semantically relevant information.

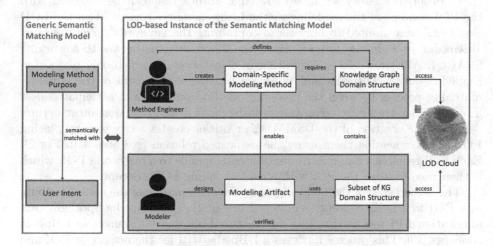

Fig. 1. Semantic Matching Model (LOD cloud diagram taken from [22]).

Tour Guide Case in the Vienna Smart City Setting. The tour guide scenario presented in [24] is located in the smart city of Vienna and builds upon the idea of citizen development. According to this idea, a person with little to no skills in software engineering or coding can still be enabled to develop their own applications by utilizing dedicated low-code, or no-code platforms [27]. This principle was applied in the smart city context to provide citizens with an easy solution to develop their own services through conceptual modeling.

In the specific scenario, a citizen of Vienna makes use of a dedicated platform that provides microservices relevant to the design of a city tour. Besides selecting and integrating suitable services (e.g., routing, payment, etc.), the citizen also has to design the actual city tour using a conceptual modeling environment. The work at hand aims to support this specific aspect of the city tour design process that is enabled through a dedicated modeling method.

Matching Smart City Tour Models with LOD. The matching of knowledge graphs with smart city tour models is assessed using the setting described previously. The corresponding city tour modeling method allows users to create simple city tours centered around points of interest (POIs) they wish to include.

During the creation of the DSMM, the method engineer defines the domain structure containing several knowledge graphs that are determined by the matching between modeling method purpose and anticipated user intent (cf. section 3.1). The resulting domain structure is represented as *structure of touristic information* in Fig. 2. Within the context of the implementation scenario, the modeling method purpose is to enable the design of city tours using POIs, while the anticipated user intent is to enrich these POIs with relevant information.

In order to identify suitable knowledge graphs that can be matched with the POI concept of the modeling method, the instances registered on the LOD cloud [22] were limited to only those containing the keywords *travel*, *tourism*, *Wikipedia*, or *Points_of_interest*. From the 20 results, the ones with a working SPARQL API were selected, resulting in 8 instances, of which only two are in English. Namely, DBpedia and Wikidata constitute the result of the semantic matching process between the modeling method purpose and anticipated user intent, and are thus selected as most suitable knowledge graph domain structure.

After the creation of the DSMM, the modeler creates a city tour by placing POIs and connecting them using the dedicated relation (see Step 1 in Fig 2). Each POI requires a name attribute that corresponds to a real-world POI, which is then used to align the POI with a corresponding LOD concept.

The second step of the LOD alignment involves matching the name attribute of a POI to a LOD concept (see Step 2 in Fig 2). The DBpedia Spotlight text annotation API was used to link unstructured information sources to DBpedia concepts [23]. This process retrieves a DBpedia URI for the respective POI and displays it in the POI notebook. This step of the alignment process is guided by the user intent that determines which domain-specific information to retrieve.

In the third step, the user verifies which information should be ultimately retrieved. In our scenario, the decision is between the description available on DBpedia or Wikidata, as these two knowledge graphs were selected as the domain structure (see Step 3 in Fig 2). For the retrieval of the DBpedia description, the URI from the previous step is combined with a SPARQL query to request the abstract of the POI from DBpedia. Retrieving the description from Wikidata requires two separate API calls. First, the Wikidata URI of the POI is retrieved through the "owl:sameAs" predicated on DBpedia, which links the two LOD instances. The received URI can then be used to request the description of the POI from Wikidata. In both cases, the received description is imported as the value of the "POIDescription" attribute in the POI notebook of the model.

To summarize, we call the output of the Semantic Matching Model instance a *linked model artifact*, which is aligned with and enriched by resources from the Semantic Web. Accordingly, such model artifacts follow the notion of linked and open models (cf. [15], or Sect. 2.3) while also enabling their RDF-based serialization. Building upon this notion, we propose the utilization of open government data to further leverage the capabilities of the Semantic Matching Model.

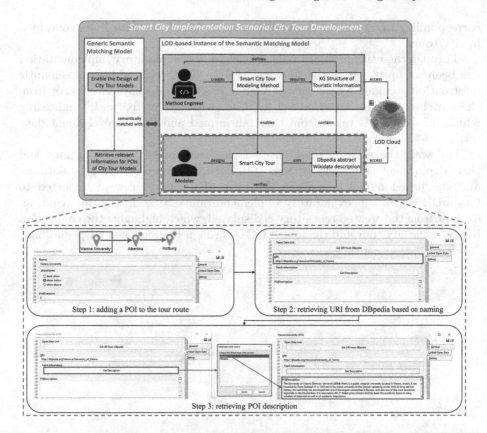

Fig. 2. Execution of information retrieval within the smart city implementation scenario of the Semantic Matching Model implemented on the ADOxx platform.

Utilizing Open Government Data for Semantic Matching. Combining RDF-based conceptual model serializations with LOD and Open Government Data (OGD) opens up interesting future research opportunities, especially in the smart city context. While LOD can be defined as RDF data sources linked to each other, OGD describes structured but not linked data made publicly available by governmental institutions on a country or city level [20].

Currently, we are investigating an interconnected process that utilizes the benefits resulting from the combination of conceptual model serializations, LOD and OGD. This process requires the identification of OGD relevant for the domain under study, which in our case is the "Sehenswürdigkeiten Standorte Wien" data set[3] containing information about more than 2700 POIs in Vienna. Through semantic approaches discussed in this paper (cf. section 2.3, 3.2), it is possible to first align the OGD (after its translation into RDF) with links to

---

[3] Original data set in JSON format is available at https://www.data.gv.at/katalog/en/dataset/stadt-wien_sehenswrdigkeitenstandortewien (accessed 04.03.23).

corresponding LOD resources and then match these links with POIs contained in city tours.

Through the utilization of this approach, a first exploratory implementation has been set up to enrich the tour model from Fig. 2 with additional semantic information provided by the city of Vienna. Figure 3a displays an excerpt from the enriched tour model serialized as RDF, with the prefix *"ns1:"* indicating which information is taken from the transformed and linked government data set.

Following the existing research on conceptual model transformations and their deployment as knowledge base [14], both the linked government data set and the linked model artifact in the form of a city tour were imported to GraphDB within this exploratory implementation setting. In Fig. 3b, again, an excerpt from the created repository is displayed, which highlights the connection between the city tour and the linked OGD through the retrieved DBpedia links.

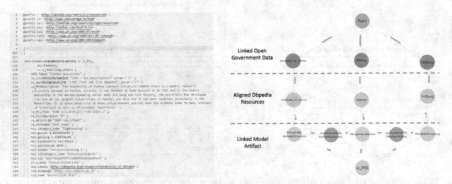

(a) Excerpt of city tour POI "Vienna University" enriched by OGD

(b) Model artifact and OGD linked through DBpedia and deployed on GraphDB

Fig. 3. Semantic Matching of open government data and city tour models.

4   Conclusion and Evaluation

4.1   Summary

The main contribution of this paper consists of the Semantic Matching Model, which aims to contribute to the research efforts investigating how to combine the benefits of conceptual modeling and the Semantic Web vision. Within this model, the purpose of designing a DSMM guides the selection of a suitable graph-based domain structure. The resulting matching process determines the permanent access established between the modeling method and the selected knowledge graphs that constitute the domain structure. Subsequently, the modeler designing a modeling artifact verifies the information to retrieve from the selected domain structure. The information retrieval is guided by the modelers' intent, which together with the modeling method purpose forms the major influence within the proposed Semantic Matching Model. To showcase the proof-of-concept, an implementation scenario within a smart city setting was provided as an instance of the Semantic Matching Model to illustrate its application.

4.2   SWOT Evaluation

Conclusively, a SWOT analysis is presented in order to evaluate the proposed Semantic Matching Model while incorporating future research possibilities.

Strengths. Even though the realization of the Semantic Web vision as a whole is still a long way ahead, the presented Semantic Matching Model still benefits from the wide range of data available through the LOD cloud. As future extensions to the LOD cloud can be expected, the prospect of matching a wider range of relevant knowledge graphs due to their increased availability forms the main strength. Nevertheless, if such extensions fail to materialize in the future, this strength can transform into a threat, as will be addressed subsequently.

Weaknesses. The current focus on the process guided by the modeling method purpose within the implementation scenario forms the main weaknesses of the contribution. Future efforts must be invested so that the finalized DSMM in the form of a packaged tool can be applied to a greater extent. Only under these conditions can a collection of modeling artifacts be accumulated to form the basis for iterative improvements within the AMME life cycle [13]. Further, it must be acknowledged that the domains covered in the LOD cloud are often too specific to be utilized across the variety of available DSMLs [17,18].

Opportunities. Future research directions include exploring the use of RDF-based serialization of conceptual diagrammatic models with both LOD and OGD, as discussed in Sect. 3.2. The resulting representation of these components as interconnected knowledge graph bears the potential to become a LOD cloud instance (e.g., see [10]), and thereby serves as domain-specific structure for future touristic applications in the city of Vienna. Additionally, future research efforts are aimed at identifying suitable machine learning techniques that can be utilized to analyze the collection of city tour models and derive semantically relevant recommendations, as soon as such a collection has been accumulated.

Threats. As future extensions to the LOD cloud are expected, but not certain, the prospect of matching a wider range of relevant knowledge graphs may not materialize, thus limiting further advancements of the Semantic Matching Model. One indication of this threat is the lack of working APIs from the knowledge graphs identified during the definition of the domain structure (cf. section 3.2). Although 20 relevant instances were identified during this step, more than half had to be excluded because no working SPARQL API was available. Further, the reliance on semantic matching through knowledge graphs may not be sufficient to meet the dynamic demands of tourists, and integration with multiple web services may be necessary in the future to ensure adaptability.

References

1. Berners-Lee, T.: Up to design issues - linked data (2006), https://www.w3.org/DesignIssues/LinkedData.html. Accessed 04 Mar2023
2. Bork, D., Buchmann, R., Karagiannis, D., Lee, M., Miron, E.T.: An open platform for modeling method conceptualization: the omilab digital ecosystem. Commun. Assoc. Inf. Syst. **34**, 555–579 (2019). https://doi.org/10.17705/1CAIS.04432
3. Buchmann, R.A., Karagiannis, D.: Enriching linked data with semantics from domain-specific diagrammatic models. Bus. Inf. Syst. Eng. **5**(58), 341–353 (2016). https://doi.org/10.1007/s12599-016-0445-1
4. Buchmann, R.A.: The purpose-specificity framework for domain-specific conceptual modeling. In: Karagiannis, D., Lee, M., Hinkelmann, K., Utz, W. (eds.) Domain-Specific Conceptual Modeling: Concepts, Methods and ADOxx Tools, pp. 67–92. Springer International Publishing, Cham (2022). https://doi.org/10.1007/978-3-030-93547-4_4
5. Buchmann, R.A., Karagiannis, D.: Agile Modelling Method Engineering: Lessons Learned in the ComVantage Research Project. In: Ralyté, J., España, S., Pastor, Ó. (eds.) PoEM 2015. LNBIP, vol. 235, pp. 356–373. Springer, Cham (2015). https://doi.org/10.1007/978-3-319-25897-3_23
6. Buchmann, R.A., Karagiannis, D.: Pattern-based transformation of diagrammatic conceptual models for semantic enrichment in the web of data. Procedia Comput. Sci. **60**, 150–159 (2015). https://doi.org/10.1016/j.procs.2015.08.114
7. Candela, G., Escobar, P., Carrasco, R.C., Marco-Such, M.: A linked open data framework to enhance the discoverability and impact of culture heritage. J. Inf. Sci. **45**(6), 756–766 (2019). https://doi.org/10.1177/0165551518812658
8. Ehrlinger, L., Wöß, W.: Towards a definition of knowledge graphs. SEMANTiCS (Posters, Demos, SuCCESS) **48**(2), 1–4 (2016)
9. Frank, U.: Domain-specific modeling languages: Requirements analysis and design guidelines. In: Reinhartz-Berger, I., Sturm, A., Clark, T., Cohen, S., Bettin, J. (eds.) Domain Engineering: Product Lines, Languages, and Conceptual Models, pp. 133–157. Springer, Berlin Heidelberg, Berlin, Heidelberg (2013). https://doi.org/10.1007/978-3-642-36654-3_6
10. Garijo, D., Villazón-Terrazas, B., Corcho, O.: A provenance-aware linked data application for trip management and organization. In: Proceedings of the 7th International Conference on Semantic Systems. p. 224–226. I-Semantics '11, Association for Computing Machinery, New York, NY, USA (2011). https://doi.org/10.1145/2063518.2063554
11. Giunchiglia, F., Shvaiko, P.: Semantic matching. Knowl. Eng. Rev. **18**(3), 265–280 (2003). https://doi.org/10.1017/S0269888904000074
12. Jean-Mary, Y.R., Shironoshita, E.P., Kabuka, M.R.: Ontology matching with semantic verification. J. Web Semant. **7**(3), 235–251 (2009). https://doi.org/10.1016/j.websem.2009.04.001

13. Karagiannis, D.: Agile modeling method engineering. In: Proceedings of the 19th Panhellenic Conference on Informatics. p. 5–10. PCI '15, Association for Computing Machinery, New York, NY, USA (2015). https://doi.org/10.1145/2801948. 2802040

14. Karagiannis, D., Buchmann, R.A.: A proposal for deploying hybrid knowledge bases: the adoxx-to-graphdb interoperability case. In: Proceedings of the 51st Hawaii International Conference on System Sciences. pp. 4055–4064 (2018)

15. Karagiannis, D., Buchmann, R.A.: Linked open models: Extending linked open data with conceptual model information. Inf. Syst. **56**, 174–197 (2016). https://doi.org/10.1016/j.is.2015.10.001

16. Karagiannis, D., Kühn, H.: Metamodelling Platforms. In: Bauknecht, K., Tjoa, A.M., Quirchmayr, G. (eds.) EC-Web 2002. LNCS, vol. 2455, pp. 182–182. Springer, Heidelberg (2002). https://doi.org/10.1007/3-540-45705-4_19

17. Buchmann, R.A.: The Purpose-Specificity Framework for Domain-Specific Conceptual Modeling. In: Karagiannis, D., Lee, M., Hinkelmann, K., Utz, W. (eds) Domain-Specific Conceptual Modeling. Springer, Cham. (2022). https://doi.org/10.1007/978-3-030-93547-4_4

18. Karagiannis, D., Mayr, H.C., Mylopoulos, J. (eds.): Domain-Specific Conceptual Modeling: Concepts, Methods and Tools. Springer Cham, 1 edn. (2016). https://doi.org/10.1007/978-3-319-39417-6

19. Karpathy, A., Fei-Fei, L.: Deep visual-semantic alignments for generating image descriptions. IEEE Trans. Pattern Anal. Mach. Intel. **39**(4), 664–676 (2017). https://doi.org/10.1109/TPAMI.2016.2598339

20. Lnenicka, M., et al.: Transparency of open data ecosystems in smart cities: definition and assessment of the maturity of transparency in 22 smart cities. Sustain. Cities Soc. **82**, 103906 (2022). https://doi.org/10.1016/j.scs.2022.103906

21. Mayr, H.C., Thalheim, B.: The triptych of conceptual modeling. Softw. Syst. Model. **20**, 7–24 (2021). https://doi.org/10.1007/s10270-020-00836-z

22. McCrae, J., et al.: The linked open data cloud (2020). http://lod-cloud.net/. Accessed 04 Mar 2023

23. Mendes, P.N., Jakob, M., García-Silva, A., Bizer, C.: Dbpedia spotlight: Shedding light on the web of documents. In: Proceedings of the 7th International Conference on Semantic Systems. pp. 1–8. I-Semantics '11, Association for Computing Machinery, New York, NY, USA (2011). https://doi.org/10.1145/2063518.2063519

24. Muck, C., Voelz, A., Amlashi, D.M., Karagiannis, D.: Citizens as developers and consumers of smart city services: A drone tour guide case. In: Companion Proceedings of the Web Conference 2022. p. 1228–1236. WWW '22, Association for Computing Machinery, New York, NY, USA (2022). https://doi.org/10.1145/3487553. 3524848

25. Mylopoulos, J.: Conceptual modelling and telos. In: Loucopoulos P. and Zicari R. (eds.). Conceptual modelling, databases, and CASE: An integrated view of information system development pp. 49–68. Wiley Publishers, New York (1992)

26. Deepak, G N.K.: Knowsum: knowledge inclusive approach for text summarization using semantic alignment. In: 2021 7th International Conference on Web Research (ICWR). pp. 227–231. IEEE (2021). https://doi.org/10.1109/ICWR51868.2021. 9443149

27. Sahay, A., Indamutsa, A., Di Ruscio, D., Pierantonio, A.: Supporting the understanding and comparison of low-code development platforms. In: 2020 46th Euromicro Conference on Software Engineering and Advanced Applications (SEAA). pp. 171–178. IEEE, New York, NY (2020). https://doi.org/10.1109/SEAA51224.2020. 00036

28. Silvello, G., Bordea, G., Ferro, N., Buitelaar, P., Bogers, T.: Semantic representation and enrichment of information retrieval experimental data. Int. J. Digital Libr. **18**(2), 145–172 (2017). https://doi.org/10.1007/s00799-016-0172-8

29. Smajevic, M., Bork, D.: From conceptual models to knowledge graphs: A generic model transformation platform. In: 2021 ACM/IEEE International Conference on Model Driven Engineering Languages and Systems Companion (MODELS-C). pp. 610–614 (2021). https://doi.org/10.1109/MODELS-C53483.2021.00093

30. Strecker, S., Baumöl, U., Karagiannis, D., Koschmider, A., Snoeck, M., Zarnekow, R.: Five inspiring course (re-)designs. Bus. Inf. Syst. Eng. **61**, 241–252 (2019). https://doi.org/10.1007/s12599-019-00584-5

31. Takhirov, N., Duchateau, F., Aalberg, T.: Linking FRBR Entities to LOD through Semantic Matching. In: Gradmann, S., Borri, F., Meghini, C., Schuldt, H. (eds.) TPDL 2011. LNCS, vol. 6966, pp. 284–295. Springer, Heidelberg (2011). https://doi.org/10.1007/978-3-642-24469-8_30

32. W3C: Rdf - resource description framework (2014). https://www.w3.org/RDF/. Accessed 04 Mar 2023

A Linked Data Based Advanced Credit Rationale

Newres Al Haider(✉), Keng Ng, Ali Hashmi, Lauma Veidemane,
and Diederik Schut

ING, Amsterdam, The Netherlands
{Newres.Al.Haider,Keng.Ng,Ali.Hashmi,Lauma.Veidemane,
Diederik.Schut}@ing.com
http://www.ing.com

Abstract. A credit rationale forms an integral part of the credit granting and credit decision making process. Historically such credit rationales
were written as a natural language document. This meant that automated
handling of the meaning, i.e.: semantics, of such documents by machines
was too complex to be done with sufficient accuracy. As a consequence,
the creation and verification of a credit rationale is a time consuming and
manual process. The solution that we propose is to create a Linked Data
based credit rationale that we call the Advanced Credit Rationale (AdCR).
Linked Data can ensure that the semantics in the credit rationale are both
human and machine understandable. This enables the automated checking
of the credit rationale for potential regulatory issues, as well as semantic
based querying over a whole portfolio of such credit rationales. An issue
that often hinders the use of a Linked Data based approach is that the creation of the knowledge graph can be challenging for domain experts. In this
work we propose an approach that facilitates the creation of a credit rationale that is based on a Linked Data knowledge graph. We evaluate this
approach with a prototype. We also demonstrate that with this approach
the creation of a Linked Data based credit rationale should not take more
time than a natural language based credit rationale. In addition we show
that the structures that a Linked Data based credit rationale provides are
generally seen as helpful.

Keywords: Finance · Lending · Linked Data · Knowledge Graph ·
FinTech · RegTech

1 Introduction

The credit rationale, i.e. the reasoning why a particular lending facility is acceptable to the lender, is a key element in the credit origination and credit monitoring processes. The credit rationale has to demonstrate that lender has fulfilled
its regulatory obligations, which is necessary to ensure that institutions have
appropriate standards for credit risk taking and monitoring. Examples of such
regulatory obligations are described within the European Banking Authority's
"Guidelines on loan origination and monitoring" (EBA LOM) [5].

© The Author(s), under exclusive license to Springer Nature Switzerland AG 2023
M. Ruiz and P. Soffer (Eds.): CAiSE 2023 Workshops, LNBIP 482, pp. 105–111, 2023.
https://doi.org/10.1007/978-3-031-34985-0_11

Traditionally, the credit rationale is denoted as a natural language document created using a word processor. In this document the required elements are analyzed and described by lending transaction managers and reviewed by credit risk managers and other stakeholders. However, given that processes such as credit origination are time sensitive and require significant expert input [3], technological methods need to be devised to reduce the time spent on validating, documenting and checking the elements of the credit rationale [1]. It is essential that this is done in a way that upholds the required quality of the credit origination and monitoring processes.

In this paper we propose an approach in which the information within the credit rationale is described as a Linked Data knowledge graph. Linked Data provides a way to make knowledge both human and machine understandable [11]. It has been successfully used in various domains to represent and utilize information about geographic locations, companies, clinical trials and more [2]. Linked Data allows for a more accurate way of searching for information, such as using queries based on the represented structures and semantics, as opposed to just the natural language text of the credit rationale [8]. Furthermore, it gives a possibility to allow for automated compliance checking using the Linked Data representation as a model.

An important challenge with a Linked Data based credit rationale is the authoring process of the credit rationale as a knowledge graph, which can be difficult for non-technical end users [4]. This is especially true as it is currently expected that the credit rationale is a natural language document. To ensure that the Linked Data based approach is useful in providing the previously highlighted benefits, we must demonstrate that these benefits are not negated by the time and effort required to author and use the Linked Data based credit rationale.

In this work we aim to provide an approach with a Linked Data based credit rationale. In this approach we formalize the guidelines in a Linked Data based light weight ontology that we call the input ontology. This Linked Data knowledge graph is used as a template to generate a user interface and other parts of a software system. With this software the domain experts, e.g. lending transaction managers, can fill in the required information and analysis. From this representation we are able to generate document outputs, such as reports, as required by other processes and credit risk managers. We do this while maintaining and saving the Linked Data representation of the credit rationale. We will also demonstrate that using this approach the creation of a credit rationale will not take more time than authoring it as a natural language text document.

The rest of the paper is structured as follows: in Sect. 2 we describe our approach to help create a Linked Data based credit rationale in detail. Afterwards in Sect. 3 we show how our approach was implemented in a prototype version of the Advanced Credit Rationale (AdCR), a software system aimed at enabling the creation and use of a Linked Data based credit rationale. The results of evaluating this system we will show in Sect. 4. Finally, we give our conclusions and outline future work in Sect. 5.

2 Approach to Create a Linked Data Based Credit Rationale

The main aim of the approach described here is to create a system in which a Linked Data based credit rationale could be drafted that is compliant with all the required regulations. We intend to achieve this in a way that minimizes the effort from the lending transaction managers in drafting the credit rationale, while upholding its quality. We also want to ensure that the resulting system is compatible with processes and software systems that still expect a natural language document.

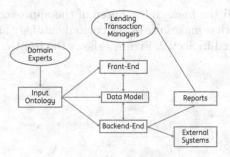

Fig. 1. An overview of the approach.

Figure 1 shows the steps taken with the proposed approach, notably that an input ontology is created by domain experts and how that ontology, and the data model derived from it, are used as the basis of a software system.

In order to be compliant with the regulations various aspects of the deal need to be analyzed, such as information on the borrower, the purpose of (credit) application, etc. The input ontology is a formalization of the required regulations related to the credit rationale as a series of inputs. It is defined as a Linked Data (JSON-LD) knowledge graph that makes use of a RDFS [9] vocabulary. It represents the properties of the input, such as the title (i.e. a short label), the type of inputs required (e.g. text, table, etc.) and the guidance text. It also orders the inputs into sections and subsections.

The data model of the application is a JSON-LD graph that links the inputs in the ontology with the information the user interacts with. This information can come through the user's input from the front-end and/or can be filled from external systems.

These two graphs combined allow for a user interface to be generated for the user as a template that can greatly reduce the effort required to create the knowledge graph [4]. It also forms the basis on which reports, in which the knowledge graphs can be embedded, could be generated as required for other users and processes.

3   Evaluation Methodology

We evaluate the approach presented in Sect. 2 by applying a Design Science methodology [6,10]. To do this we implement a prototype application, titled "Advanced Credit Rationale" (AdCR), that uses the approach.

For the prototype, two domain experts have formalized regulations relating to credit origination and monitoring to the input ontology, notably the European Banking Authority's "Guidelines on loan origination and monitoring" (EBA LOM) [5], as well to other policies applicable. There are 93 inputs in the input ontology of the prototype organized into 9 sections and 28 subsections. In the prototype the types of inputs were limited to texts, lists of events and tables.

The front-end and the back-end required of the approach were implemented as a web-application that makes use of the created ontology as well as the derived data model, as outlined in Sect. 2. Figure 2 shows the front-end generated for the prototype.

Fig. 2. The UI of the front-end generated based on the input ontology.

To evaluate the prototype we have presented it to a number of people who could be potential users of such an application and its reports, notably lending transaction managers and credit risk managers. Through a survey and a subsequent interview, we have aimed to capture both quantitative and qualitative feedback from these users.

In the prototype that we describe in this paper we do not use other (external) sources to prefill information in the credit rationale although the Linked Data graph representation would be highly conductive to it. We aim to compare the creation of the knowledge graph backed credit rationale through the prototype AdCR application versus the former scenario of creating it as a text document purely through the user's input. We hypothesize that even without features such as prefills, the system would already bring benefits through the structures defined and that the creation of the credit rationale with the AdCR would not require additional time compared to a natural language version.

4   Results of the Evaluation

In this section we detail the results of our evaluation. A total of 24 experts were surveyed and interviewed that were presented with the prototype application.

Table 1. Perceived time savings.

Difference in Perceived Time Spent	Nr. of Responses
> 5 h Saved	2
3–5 h Saved	3
1–2 h Saved	8
0 h Saved	3
1–2 h Extra Spent	7
3–5 h Extra Spent	1
> 5 h Extra Spent	0

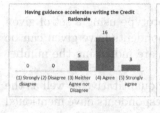

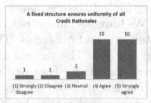

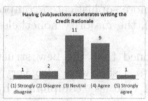
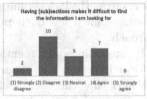
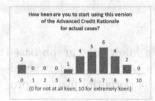

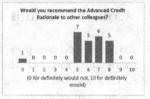

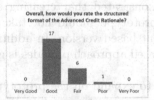
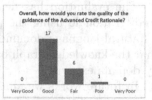

Fig. 3. Shows the number of respondents and their answers for the given statement or question.

A key aspect that we aimed to measure was time savings compared to the natural language document based version of the credit rationale. The perceived time savings are listed in Table 1 where the difference of perceived time spent on the AdCR is compared to the previous, document based, version of the credit rationale. The results verify our hypothesis that given the prototype implementation creating a Linked Data knowledge graph backed credit rationale does not take more time than a pure natural language based document version. An argument could be made that there is even a slight reduced time spent, but the overall effect is minor. This is understandable as in the experiment we explicitly did not measure the likely key features for large time savings, such as prefills using Linked Data semantics.

We have also measured various aspects of the prototype using a set of given statements and questions. The answers that the respondents have given can be seen in Fig. 3. The vertical axes on each of the charts are indicating the number of respondents for that particular answer.

The majority of feedback was positive in both the quantitative as well as the qualitative part of the survey. Although a number of respondents have mentioned that some big time saving features such prefills are missing in the prototype and it currently lacks some more sophisticated components for input (these are the causes for a few outliers), the majority nonetheless see the potential of the approach.

It was commonly mentioned that the new structure enables a clean and uniform interface and reports. Users were also very positive on the guidance text and how the tool itself enables "compliance by design" [7], due to the formalization of regulations mentioned in Sect. 3.

5   Conclusion and Future Work

In this work we have presented an approach to create a knowledge graph based credit rationale we call the Advanced Credit Rationale (AdCR). We have evaluated this approach by surveying domain experts on the potential use of a prototype implementation.

The evaluation has demonstrated that creating a knowledge graph based credit rationale using the prototype should not take more time than creating a natural language document based version. In addition, the explicit structure that the knowledge graph based approach provides is generally seen as beneficial by domain experts.

In future works we aim to expand on the prototype and evaluate its use in the context of time saving features such as prefills. We also hope to integrate the input ontology with other (external) ontologies. Finally, we believe the approach could be extended and generalized to other use cases where information for regulations or guidelines needs to be captured and utilized in a similar fashion.

References

1. Bedayo, M., Jimenez, G., Peydró, J.L., Vegas Sánchez, R.: Screening and loan origination time: lending standards, loan defaults and bank failures (2020)
2. Bizer, C., Heath, T., Berners-Lee, T.: Linked data: the story so far. In: Semantic Services, Interoperability and Web Applications: Emerging Concepts, pp. 205–227. IGI Global (2011)
3. Cornelli, G., Frost, J., Gambacorta, L., Rau, P.R., Wardrop, R., Ziegler, T.: Fintech and big tech credit: drivers of the growth of digital lending. J. Bank. Finance **148**, 106742 (2023). https://doi.org/10.1016/j.jbankfin.2022. 106742, https://www.sciencedirect.com/science/article/pii/S0378426622003223
4. Davies, S., Hatfield, J., Donaher, C., Zeitz, J.: User interface design considerations for linked data authoring environments. LDOW **628** (2010)
5. European Banking Authority: Final report - guidelines on loan origination and monitoring (2020)
6. Hevner, A.R., March, S.T., Park, J., Ram, S.: Design science in information systems research. Manag. Inf. Syst. Q. **28**(1), 6 (2008)
7. Lohmann, N.: Compliance by design for artifact-centric business processes. Inf. Syst. **38**(4), 606–618 (2013)
8. Lopez, V., Unger, C., Cimiano, P., Motta, E.: Evaluating question answering over linked data. J. Web Semant. **21**, 3–13 (2013)
9. McBride, B.: The resource description framework (RDF) and its vocabulary description language RDFs. In: Handbook on Ontologies, pp. 51–65 (2004)
10. Peffers, K., Tuunanen, T., Rothenberger, M.A., Chatterjee, S.: A design science research methodology for information systems research. J. Manag. Inf. Syst. **24**(3), 45–77 (2007)
11. W3C: Linked data (2023). https://www.w3.org/standards/semanticweb/data. Accessed 02 Mar 2023

Interactive Machine Learning of Knowledge Graph-Based Explainable Process Analysis

Anne Füßl[✉], Volker Nissen, and Stefan Horst Heringklee

Technische Universität Ilmenau, Institute of Business and Information Systems
Engineering, Helmholtzplatz 3, 98693 Ilmenau, Germany
anne.fuessl@tu-ilmenau.de
https://www.tu-ilmenau.de/wid

Abstract. The core idea behind combining knowledge graph-based AI
and machine learning is to formalize explicit knowledge as a knowledge
base, which does not need to be learned, and to consider it in machine
learning. Interactive machine learning provides an alternative to explicit
knowledge modeling to include feedback from human experts in order
to adapt and improve learned models. For semantic process analysis, we
have developed an explainable AI approach based on a specific knowledge
graph that delivers interpretable results about weaknesses and improvement potentials in business processes. In the present paper we show
how interactive machine learning can extend the knowledge graph with
human implicit knowledge. The knowledge graph does not solely rely
on the initially created knowledge elements and defined calculation formulas, but learns incrementally at the time of user feedback by making
small adjustments in the graph.

Keywords: Knowledge graph · Interactive machine learning ·
Explainable artificial intelligence · Process analysis · Consulting
self-service

1 Introduction

Besides the well-known restrictions of high performance Artificial Intelligence
(AI) systems, the need for large training data and intransparency, challenges
to broad democratization of AI systems also include the lack of generalizability
of AI results and the lack of causal reasoning capabilities (analogous to human
reasoning) [20]. The use of expert knowledge and Interactive Machine Learning
(IML) helps to counteract this data engineering bottleneck by allowing human
experts to confirm results or make corrections [11].

An promising concept of semantic web technologies are Knowledge Graphs
(KG) that formalize explicit knowledge elements hierarchically in terms of linked
entities and their properties, and enable causal reasoning [10]. The use of machine

M. Ruiz and P. Soffer (Eds.): CAiSE 2023 Workshops, LNBIP 482, pp. 112–124, 2023.
https://doi.org/10.1007/978-3-031-34985-0_12

learning refines KGs inferences to retrieve information and provide meaningful answers to queries in the form of language-like structured statements [4,10]. Exploiting the respective complementary strengths of each approach supports the design of so-called Knowledge-Based eXplainable AI (KBXAI) systems that produce user-understandable results [17]. In order to not only passively receive explanations, but also to enable mutual explanations and to consider implicit human knowledge in machine learning, the creation of IML models seems to be a convenient approach [18].

Process analysis is an essential part of a consultant's daily work. Established consulting companies become increasingly data-driven and deploy fully auto-mated solutions, such as consulting self-services in some application areas [8,15], e.g., for analyzing the current state of business processes. However, most anal-ysis tools, such as process mining, require expert knowledge to interpret results in a client-oriented manner as well as to incorporate implicit knowledge. Only when AI-based technologies are extended by KBXAI and IML approaches can understandable results be generated for customers and machine learning mod-els be improved interactively based on user feedback. In this way, self-services in the consulting context can provide human-centered AI results tailored to an individual industry.

Based on an inferential KG architecture with machine learning methods [7] we developed a KBXAI approach for semantic analysis of business processes [5,6] in several design cycles, following the Design Science Research (DSR) method-ology of Peffers et al. [16]. Using different data sources, complex analysis ques-tions can be answered to identify weaknesses in processes and recommend suit-able improvement measures. Deduction algorithms perform the process analy-sis depending on defined association classes in the graph and machine learning methods extend the KG [6]. The traceability and interpretation of process anal-ysis results is enabled by generating interpretable models based on stochastic decision trees, which was elaborated in a recent design cycle [5]. In order to actively involve people in the learning process and to adapt learned models in a human-centered way, the consideration of implicit knowledge in the form of user feedback is required.

The aim of the present design cycle according to DSR [16] is to integrate user feedback in an IML model contributing to human-centered improvement of the KG. For this purpose, we first define relevant terms and provide an overview of previous work on our KBXAI-PA approach. In Sect. 3, we present an IML model to consider user feedback in the machine learning process and demonstrate the applicability of the developed approach using a case study and expert interviews. Finally, Sect. 4 summarizes the findings and outline research perspectives.

2   Terms, Definitions and Previous Work

2.1   Terms and Definitions

Explainable Artificial Intelligence (XAI) focuses on developing methods that better explain AI results to users, thus addressing the compromise between AI performance and its explainability [9]. Explainability is an active feature to reveal internal functionality, while interpretability is more a passive feature to make the meaning of results understandable to humans [1]. With the time at which explainability starts, three generic XAI approaches can be distinguished: ante-hoc approaches include exploratory data analyses using mathematical-statistical methods, XAI by Design approaches aim to develop intrinsically interpretable models, and post-hoc explanations are applied to black-box models [3,14].

IML assumes explainability of AI systems and aims to optimize the learning behavior of an algorithm through user interactions (both explicit and implicit knowledge) [11]. Compared to classical machine learning, IML is faster (directly at the time of user feedback), more focused (a specific aspect of the model is adapted), and incremental (small adaptations that do not fundamentally change the model) [2]. Such model adaptations include label corrections, adaptation of features and feature weights, and corrections of symbolic explanations [18]. IML research includes different concepts on how to interactively drive models towards the desired behavior without changing them in a purely data-driven way, often only under lack of traceability [2]. One of the most prominent human-XAI interactions is based on question-answering dialogs [12]. IML can be implemented based on KBXAI approaches and benefits from their interpretable approaches.

KBXAI systems integrate symbolic approaches of formal knowledge and interpretable machine learning approaches that can be assigned to XAI by Design, where the learned models are in principle inherent and directly trace-able [18,20]. Formal knowledge of KGs comprise domain as well as factual knowl-edge, is machine readable and linked across domains. Logic-based component structures of TBox (terminological, for abstract descriptions of classes and prop-erties of knowledge objects) and ABox (assertional, for concrete descriptions of attributes of knowledge instances) allow knowledge elements a semantic descrip-tion [10].

For generating knowledge-based explanations, rule- or tree-based subsym-bolic methods as well as neural networks are used. Table data, images or text data serve as input to perform various tasks, such as classification, prediction or regression. Explanations are provided in textual form, in natural language, or visually via images, and can refer to the output model, system behavior, or both. [14,17,20]

One fundamental limitation of KG-based explanations is the restricted use of knowledge elements according to the nearest neighborhood principle. Path-based semantic encodings may be lost and are not available for interpreting the results. However, striving for the explanatory goals of transparency and verifiability of generated explanations, and improving a model interactively based on user feedback [12], will require inherently interpretable models that enable path-based explanations in KGs, and use both explicit and implicit knowledge for human understandable interpretations.

2.2   Knowledge Graph-Based Explainable Process Analysis

Design. The Knowledge graph-Based eXplainable Process Analysis (KBXAI-PA) supports the identification of weak points and suitable improvement measures in business processes based on expert knowledge in a KG. In consulting practice, such reasoning cannot be automatically derived from process models without the necessary semantic context. Even process mining only analyzes log data from IT systems and neglects manual tasks and implicit process knowledge.

According to Morelli et al. [14] and Tiddi and Schlobach [20], our KBXAI-PA approach can be classified as XAI by Design approach. KBXAI-PA's design is based on a directed, edge-labeled graph with deduction algorithms and inductive learning mechanisms [7]. Defined element (node) and association (edge) classes allow a standardized representation of knowledge considering semantic relations. Analogous to the empirical knowledge of a consultant, the KG comprises both factual knowledge about analysis criteria, potential weaknesses, suitable improvement measures, and domain knowledge from the area of the process to be analyzed. In terms of its edge types, the architecture most resembles the multilingual KG ConceptNet [19] compared to other KGs. However, ConceptNet does not allow customizable calculation formulas that relate knowledge elements to a concrete semantic context.

Deduction algorithms execute the inference mechanisms in the KG depending on their association classes, representing the analysis procedure of business process models [6]. Regarding rule-based node calculations, classification answers in the form of weaknesses and improvement measures are generated. Reconstruction of activated node elements of their result paths enables the derivation of intrinsically interpretable models that generate human-understandable explanations [5]. These explanations are textual, in near-natural language and refer to the analysis path leading to the result as well as to semantic background knowledge associated with the result.

With each process analysis, a reusable KG is refined and extended through inductive learning approaches. The KG expands with new knowledge elements from the input data of the process model (e.g., new IT systems as "tools" of "improvement measures") [6]. Furthermore, concrete knowledge elements inherit their attributes to abstract knowledge elements at a higher level (e.g., the abstract Item "process" inherit an element "analogue document" as has-association of the concrete element "manual process") [6]. The learning of the KG through implicit knowledge and the verification of reasoning results based on user feedback represents another inductive learning approach introduced in the present design cycle.

Architecture and Analysis Procedure. The architecture of the KG is structured in five layers [7]: a data input layer L4, a data transfer layer L3, L2 and L1 for information processing and knowledge representation, as well as a solution layer L0 that contains all activated nodes as result paths. Except for L0, the layers consist of different element classes that fulfil the respective layer function, see Fig. 1.

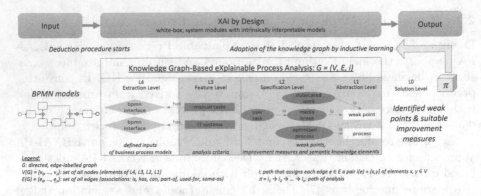

Fig. 1. Concept of KBXAI-PA with example nodes.

The "Data Source" element class (L4) is used to connect external data sources that represent the input of an analysis. Process models in the XML-based BPMN style are read out by interfaces. In addition to interfaces, data source elements can also be used for user questions to enable user interactions for process analysis. Each Data Source element requires at least one "Feature" element of level L3. The Feature element class is used for the data transfer from level L4 in the necessary format and semantic context to activate knowledge elements of level L2. Features represent process analysis criteria, such as number of manual tasks or synonymous tasks, which identify potential weaknesses in process models, such as media breaks or duplicated work. Weaknesses and improvement measures are modeled in the information processing levels L2 and L1 (comparable to A- and TBox). The element types "Cell", "Combining" and "Activity" (L2), and the type "Item" of the abstraction level L1 are used for the knowledge representation. The basic association classes "is, has, can, part-of, used-for" and "same-as" enable semantic relationships between the elements. Nodes of the levels L2 and L1 are provided with calculation formulas ("Result Expressions") to obtain the Boolean values true (1) or false (0). A Result Expression $r(v_x)$ is defined for the conditional activation of an element v_x and are indicated by "Constraints" (dashed line in Fig. 1). The node "user task" as type of a media break (see Fig. 1) can be identified, if a process has a manual task and an IT system at the same time. The related Result Expression of the node $v_{userTask}$: $r(v_{userTask}) = true \leftarrow r(v_{manualTask}) > 0$ && $r(v_{ITSystem}) > 0$ can activate this node, which in turn leads to the activation of all "is"-successor nodes (here: $v_{mediaBreak}$ and $v_{weakPoint}$). The Constraint between $v_{weakPoint}$ and $v_{optimizedProcess}$ indicates that an optimized process exists as long as no weak points have been identified. Consequently, $v_{optimizedProcess}$ represents the entry node of a process analysis and thus the first analysis step, see Fig. 2.

The analysis procedure is generically executed by deduction algorithms that are divided into abstraction (Isn't-it, Kind-of) and concretization algorithms (Characterize, Parts, Like, Find). Abstraction algorithms check knowledge elements of the association class "is" for their Boolean values, activate linked issuccessor elements of an entry node and serve the identification of weak points. During the analysis, concretization algorithms are triggered depending on their respective association class. For example, if a same-as-association of an element to be analyzed is triggered, the Like-algorithm is called to identify existing synonyms in the KG. In this way, semantic descriptions are generated and suitable improvement measures that are related to an identified weakness are identified (exemplary analysis results are shown in the example of Fig. 2). All activated elements of a process analysis ultimately become part of a result path, which enables the derivation of an associated interpretable model to track the generation of results and generate textual, near-natural language and understandable interpretations [5]. In the following, we enhance our approach by integrating mutual explanations via human-in-the-loop verification of the results.

3   Interactive Machine Learning for a Knowledge Graph

3.1   Design

The analysis procedure of business processes consists of four generic analysis steps triggered by deduction algorithms, see Fig. 2, Q1-Q4 (algorithm sequence simplified below KBXAI-PA). The first analysis step Q1 is the entrance into the analysis of a process model, such as for stationary travel bookings, see Fig. 2. Within analysis step (2), further concretization algorithms are called depending on associated and activated nodes in the graph for semantic contexts, which are subsequently used to determine suitable improvement measures in steps (3) and (4). Weaknesses identified include user tasks (e.g., enter date of departure) and an improvement tool is suggested (online booking engine). All steps are calculated as soon as a process model is selected as input for analysis. However, displaying the answers is done with the selection of the questions by the user. A question-answering dialog (QAD) represents the explanation interface of the result interpretations to the user. Within the interaction concept QAD, interaction is considered as a cycle of communication phases based on input and output with the system and perception or action by the human [12].

The goal of QAD is to achieve the best possible match between analysis results and user intention by improving analysis results through obtaining user

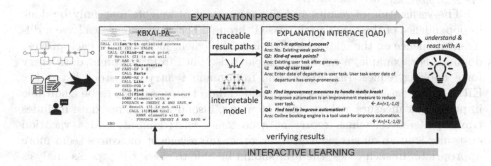

Fig. 2. IML for KBXAI-PA by assessing results with A and assigning weights w.

feedback [11]. Here, a natural dialog supports user interaction to verify identified improvement measures (e.g., online booking engine is a tool used-for improve automation). Verification of the results can be done in different ways. In the following, we focus on assigning weights by confirming or rejecting system decisions and correcting labels and calculation formulas.

3.2 Assigning Weights by Verifying Results

According to a process analysis, a suggestion for improvement measures is given for each identification of a weakness. However, not all improvement measures always apply to a particular process. Here, the user should have the possibility to evaluate the system-generated improvement suggestions.

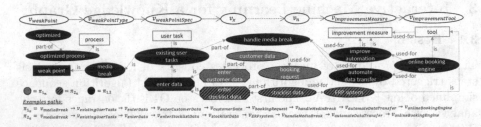

Fig. 3. Result paths π following activated knowledge elements.

Considering the example in Fig. 2, along the analysis procedure (1–4) generated result paths can be structured into generic aggregations, see Fig. 3 (arrow directions in the KG show semantic context, not the analysis direction). All weak point nodes are first analyzed, starting at the abstraction level (e.g., media break as $v_{weakPointType}$) up to the specification level (e.g., existing user task as $v_{weakPointSpec}$). All nodes that have semantic relationships through their associations serve to describe a weakness in more detail and also become part of the result path (e.g., enter customer data, booking request as v_x). Subsequently, the nodes of improvement measures (e.g., improve automation as $v_{improvementMeasure}$) and tools/options (e.g., online booking engine as $v_{improvementTool}$) are analyzed.

The verification of results and the assignment of weights may only be done in dependence of the result path passed through, because weaknesses have a different influence on the relevance of their improvement measures for each process domain. For example, a media break can arise both from customer data entry for a booking request (π_1, Fig. 3) and from manual entry of a stock list in the ERP system (π_2). In both cases, automated data transfer seems to be a suitable improvement measure at first sight. However, insofar as customer data includes travel preferences, which represent a customer-related input, and a vacation customer is in an on-site consultation, other improvement measures seem more appropriate. In such cases, the user should be able to check the process analysis results.

For each result path of an identified weakness, the user has the option of confirming (+1) or rejecting (-1) an identified improvement measure. If the user has no experience with the suggested output, the result is evaluated as zero (0), thus the passed analysis path is still included in the assignment of result weights. Accordingly, the weighting w of a result node ($v_{improvementMeasure/Tools}$) learned through interaction can be calculated via the mean value of all assessments A of a respective result path of a weak point specification ($\pi_{v_{weakPointSpec}}$) as follows:

$$\bar{A} = w(v_{improvementMeasure/Tool}|\pi_{v_{weakPointSpec}}) = \frac{1}{n_\pi}\sum_{i=1}^{n} A_i \qquad (1)$$

$$\text{with } A = \begin{cases} +1 = confirmed, \\ -1 = rejected, \\ 0 = neutral. \end{cases} \qquad (2)$$

Considering the result paths (π_1, π_2) from the example in Fig. 3, the weightings of each improvement measure per result path are calculated for three assumed assessment cycles as shown in Table 1. In result path π_1 of the improvement measure $v_{automateDataTransfer}$ (column three), it is assumed that only in the first run is appropriate. In the second and third path run, the customer's individual travel preferences also count towards the input of customer data, which cannot be automated in these cases. Consequently, after three assessment cycles, the target node $v_{automateDataTransfer}$ receives a weighting of $0,\bar{3}$ for the next path run of π_1. Similarly, this target node was assessed not fully as a suitable improvement measure in result path π_2 and receives a weighting of $0,\bar{67}$.

Table 1. Assignment of weights per result path by user feedback.

Result path of a weak point	Improvement measure or tool		
	$v_{improveAutomation}$	$v_{automateDataTransfer}$	$v_{onlineBookingEngine}$
$\pi_1(v_{enterCustomerData})$	$A = [1,1,1]\|w = 1$	$A = [1,0,0]\|w = 0,\bar{3}$	$A = [1,1,1]\|w = 1$
$\pi_2(v_{enterStocklistData})$	$A = [1,1,1]\|w = 1$	$A = [1,0,1]\|w = 0,\bar{67}$	$A = [-1,-1,-1]\|w = -1$

For demonstration purposes, there is a faulty link between weak point and suitable improvement measure in the presented example. For the identified weakness of the result path π_{2_a} (Fig. 3), the node $v_{onlineBookingEngine}$ is incorrectly suggested as an improvement tool. In each of the three assessment cycles, this result was rejected, resulting in a weighting of -1 (see Table 1, last column, last row). If the value of the weighting of a target node takes on the value -1 after three assessment cycles, the calculation formula (Result Expression) stored in the target node must be checked for correctness. By a user question, the system requires correcting the rejected reasoning. Here, the Result Expression of the node $v_{onlineBookingEngine}$ needs the specification about the type of data to be entered (customer data used-for booking request) and has to be changed as follows (additions in bold): $r(v_{onlineBookingEngine}) = true \leftarrow (r(v_{enterData})$ **&&** $\boldsymbol{r(v_{customerData})}$ **&&** $\boldsymbol{r(v_{bookingRequest})}) == true$.

In the analysis procedure, weightings and label or formula corrections are considered in the third and fourth analysis steps, see Fig. 2. Higher weighted nodes can be analyzed by the deduction algorithm prioritized and lead to more specific improvement measures.

3.3 Demonstration and Evaluation by a Case Study

Case Description. The case study represents an ex-post evaluation, which is part of a separate design cycle currently in progress that focuses on the development of explanation user interfaces for KBXAI. A process model in BPMN style is analyzed by six independent participants using the prototype of the KBXAI-PA approach, followed by expert interviews. The participants work primarily as SAP consultants, in project management or logistics, and record between five and 15 years of professional experience. As analysis input, a typical order-to-cash process was chosen, since this process is familiar to many process analysts and consultants. A section of the order-to-cash process as BPMN model is shown in Fig. 4, where user tasks, data transfer of analog documents and duplicated work can be identified as weak points.

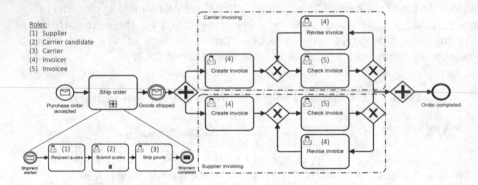

Fig. 4. Excerpt of the order-to-cash BPMN model.

Case Implementation. The KG used to perform the process analysis includes standardized weak points (e.g., media breaks, IT system breaks, duplicated work) and suitable improvement measures, as well as knowledge elements that are semantically related to the order-to-cash process model, such as "ship goods reduce inventory" or "user task create invoice has error-proneness". Each case study participant analyzes the process model using the C# based prototype of KBXAI-PA in the same way under the supervision of a case study advisor. Therefore, the four analysis steps were performed according to the deduction procedure (see Fig. 2), during which all result paths were traced for interpretation and assessment of the results. Different weaknesses and improvement measures are identified, which were assessed subsequently by each participant in turn on the basis of the interactive learning approach.

Table 2. Process analysis results and their weightings after six assessment cycles.

Result path of a weak point	Improvement measure or tool		
	$v_{reduceDuplicatedWork}$	$v_{automateInvoicing}$	$v_{automateCarrierSelection}$
$\pi_1(v_{duplicatedWork})$	$w = 0,\bar{6}7$	$w = 1$	$w = -0,\bar{6}7$
$\pi_2(v_{mediaBreak})$	$w = 0,5$	$w = 0,8\bar{3}$	$w = 0,\bar{3}$
$\pi_3(v_{userTask})$	$w = 0,\bar{1}6$	$w = 0,\bar{6}7$	$w = 0,\bar{6}7$
$\sum w(v_x\|\pi_{weakPoint})$	$1,28$	$2,56$	$0,\bar{3}$

Table 2 shows three suggested improvement measures for each of the three weaknesses including weightings w after submission and calculation of user interactions. A sample result interpretation of a result path π_1 for the improvement measure $v_{automateInvoicing}$ is shown below (bold highlights refer to association classes in the graph that help to convert the knowledge elements on the result path into natural language):

- Automate invoicing **is used** to handle duplicated work.
- The user tasks create invoice, check invoice and revise invoice **are** duplicated work and **have** error-proneness.
- User task check invoice **has** potential for automation.
- User tasks and manual activities **have** error-proneness.
- Create invoice, check invoice and revise invoice **are** user tasks.
- An Invoicer **can** create and revise invoices.
- An Invoicee **can** check invoices.

Case Analysis and Expert Interviews. Table 2 illustrates the weighted results of different user interactions for the analyzed process. It becomes apparent that from different user perspectives, the improvement measures also appear to have different suitability in view of a process model. The summation of all weights per improvement measure indicates the relevance of the improvement measures in terms of user interaction. The higher the summed weights of an improvement measure, the more relevant the improvement measure appears. Overall, after running through six evaluation cycles, the improvement measure $v_{automateInvoicing}$ seems to be the most suitable. In result path π_1, only the result of automating invoicing was confirmed in each of the six evaluation cycles. Reducing duplication of work seems to be the least suitable in identifying user tasks as weak points. This may be due to the large number of user tasks in the process model, which do not represent all duplicated work. On the other hand, automating carrier selection seems to be a less suitable improvement measure for identified duplicated work ($w = -0.\bar{6}7$). According to expert interviews, carrier selection is often dependent on free vacancy and project-specific carrier costs. Such user justifications can be used to specify knowledge modeling in the graph. Thus, the element $v_{carrierSelection}$ receives new has-associations to the nodes "vacancy" and "cost" in the KG to be considered in subsequent analysis.

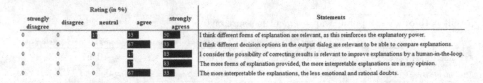

strongly disagree	disagree	Rating (in %) neutral	agree	strongly agress	Statements
0	0	17	33	50	I think different forms of explanation are relevant, as this reinforces the explanatory power.
0	0	0	67	33	I think different decision options in the output dialog are relevant to be able to compare explanations.
0	0	0	17	83	I consider the possibility of correcting results is relevant to improve explanations by a human-in-the-loop.
0	0	0	17	83	The more forms of explanation provided, the more interpretable explanations are in my opinion.
0	0	0	67	33	The more interpretable the explanations, the less emotional and rational doubts.

Fig. 5. Rating of key statements made in expert interviews.

An abstract of the expert interview results is presented in Fig. 5. The following key findings are worth highlighting: More than 80% of case study participants consider correcting results by a human-in-the-loop relevant to improve suggested improvement measures. 83% agree with the statement that multiple forms of explanations contribute to a higher interpretability of the results. A slightly lower level of agreement was achieved with the statement: the more interpretable explanations are, the fewer doubts exist towards the generated explanations.

4   Résumé and Perspectives

The Knowledge graph-Based eXplainable Process Analysis (KBXAI-PA) approach represents a hybrid AI approach that relies on knowledge representation combined with deduction algorithms to generate user-driven, interpretable results considering human interaction. Interpretable models allow the origin of solution elements can be made readable, understandable and even plausible for the user. The presented IML approach enriches the analytical KG by user feedback, which, besides automatic reasoning, continuously refines the KG. Verified results are considered and prioritized by deduction algorithms. If the plausibility is validated by feedback from outside, the acceptance of the interpreted results and their use in decision-making processes increases [13].

With respect to existing XAI approaches, the generation of interpretable models from the KG architecture [7] combined with IML can achieve mutual explainability between human-AI system and interactively improve both the understandability of analysis results and analysis capabilities our KBXAI approach. Considering the evaluation of XAI approaches, it seems worthwhile to observe the verification of analysis results depending on different user perspectives.

The design of an appropriate explanation user interface has a significant impact on how analysis results and their interpretations are communicated and understood to users, and how users can respond to system outputs by verification and feedback. Recent research results on this issue are still pending.

Compared to other KGs, the KBXAI graph is characterized by its individual architecture that enables the generation of intrinsically interpretable models. Nevertheless, the KG ConceptNet, which is similar in its basic structure, might be suitable for knowledge implementation in the KBXAI graph.

In the context of consulting research, mutual explanations between KBXAI systems and customers can boost the acceptance and practical added value of consulting self-services insofar as resources can be steered in a targeted manner and, consequently, consultants can focus on other tasks, such as social aspects of processes.

References

1. Adadi, A., Berrada, M.: Peeking inside the black-box: a survey on explainable artificial intelligence (XAI). IEEE Access **6**, 52138–52160 (2018)
2. Amershi, S., Cakmak, M., Knox, W.B., Kulesza, T.: Power to the people: the role of humans in interactive machine learning. AI Mag. **35**(4), 105–120 (2015)
3. Bauckhage, C., Fürnkranz, J., Paaß, G.: Vertrauenswürdiges, transparentes und robustes Maschinelles Lernen. In: Görz, G., Schmid, U., Braun, T. (eds.) Handbuch der Künstlichen Intelligenz, pp. 571–600. Walter de Gruyter GmbH, Berlin (2021)
4. Dessì, D., Osborne, F., Reforgiato Recupero, D., Buscaldi, D., Motta, E., Sack, H.: AI-KG: An Automatically Generated Knowledge Graph of Artificial Intelligence. In: Pan, J.Z., et al. (eds.) ISWC 2020. LNCS, vol. 12507, pp. 127–143. Springer, Cham (2020). https://doi.org/10.1007/978-3-030-62466-8_9
5. Füßl, A., Nissen, V.: Interpretability of knowledge graph-based explainable process analysis. In: IEEE 5th AIKE. pp. 9–17 (2022). https://doi.org/10.1109/AIKE55402.2022.00008
6. Füßl, A., Nissen, V., Dopf, S., Füßl, F.F.: An inferential knowledge model for the digitalisation and automation of business process analysis. In: Gronau, N., Heine, M., Poustcchi, K., Krasnova, H. (eds.) Proc. WI2020 Community Tracks, pp. 185–200. GITO Verlag (2020). https://doi.org/10.30844/wi_2020_w1-fuessl
7. Füßl, F.F.: Entwicklung eines Modells zur Anwendung inferenzfähiger Ontologien im Software Engineering. Doctoral dissertation, TU Ilmenau (2016)
8. Göpel, F., Nissen, V.: Eine Methode zur Bestimmung der Self-Service-Eignung von Leistungen der Unternehmensberatung. In: Bruhn, M., Hadwich, K. (eds) Smart Services. Forum Dienstleistungsmanagement. Springer Gabler, Wiesbaden (2022). https://doi.org/10.1007/978-3-658-37344-3_5
9. Gunning, D.: Explainable artificial intelligence (XAI). DARPA, 2 edn. (2017)
10. Hogan, A., et al.: Knowledge graphs. ACM Comput. Sur. **54**(4), 1–37 (2022)
11. Holzinger, A.: Interactive machine learning. Informatik-Spektrum **39**(1), 64–68 (2016). https://doi.org/10.1007/s00287-015-0941-6
12. Hornbæk, K., Oulasvirta, A.: What is interaction? In: Mark, G. (ed.) CHI. pp. 5040–5052. ACM, New York (2017). DOI: 10.1145/3025453.3025765
13. Meske, C., Bunde, E., Schneider, J., Gersch, M.: Explainable artificial intelligence: Objectives, stakeholders, and future research opportunities. ISM pp. 1–11 (2020)
14. Morelli, F., Geschwill, S., Zerr, K., Lossos, C.: Rationalität maschineller Entscheidungen im Unternehmen durch die Einbindung von Explainable Artificial Intelligence (XAI). Tagungsband 33th AKWI pp. 8–17 (2020)

15. Nissen, V.: Digital transformation of the consulting industry – introduction and overview. In: Nissen, V. (ed.) Digital Transformation of the Consulting Industry - Extending the Traditional Delivery Model, pp. 1–58. Springer (2018). https://doi.org/10.1007/978-3-319-70491-3_1
16. Peffers, K., Tuunanen, T., Rothenberger, M.A., Chatterjee, S.: A design science research methodology for information systems research. JMIS **24**(3), 45–77 (2007)
17. Rajabi, E., Etminani, K.: Knowledge-graph-based explainable AI: a systematic review. J. Inf. Sci. (2022). https://doi.org/10.1177/01655515221112844
18. Schmid, U., Finzel, B.: Mutual explanations for cooperative decision making in medicine. KI - Künstliche Intelligenz **34**(2), 227–233 (2020)
19. Speer, R., Chin, J., Havasi, C.: Conceptnet 5.5: an open multilingual graph of general knowledge. AAAI **31**(1), 4444–4451 (2017)
20. Tiddi, I., Schlobach, S.: Knowledge graphs as tools for explainable machine learning: a survey. Artificial Intel. **302**, 103627 (2022)

A Weighted Knowledge Graph for Representing the Results of a Systematic Literature Review

Jolanta Graudone(✉) and Marite Kirikova

Department of Artificial Intelligence and Systems Engineering, Riga Technical University, Kipsalas iela 6A, Riga 1048, Latvia
{jolanta.graudone,marite.kirikova}@rtu.lv

Abstract. In information systems engineering, one of the most important success factors is understanding the latest scientific research on the use of IT solutions in the enterprise's field of activity. For this purpose, systemic literature reviews are often used to identify the most important concepts and their relationships in a respective domain. This paper illustrates how a knowledge graph can help to visualize and analyze the results of a systemic literature review. A simplified weighted knowledge graph, in which weights are assigned to its nodes, is constructed using the results of a systematic literature review on the application of the agile approach to the development of information systems in the public sector. The graph reflects and, also, helps to analyze the collected information on the state of the art of agile information systems engineering in public organizations.

Keywords: Knowledge Graph · Knowledge Management · Public Sector · Agile

1 Introduction

Systematic literature reviews are performed for different purposes and in different types of projects. These can be innovation-driven projects, student thesis projects, and other types of projects, including "ordinary" information systems engineering projects. The results of the structured literature reviews may be published in scientific papers, however, in many cases, knowledge gained in this activity is not further reused. At the same time, respecting recent developments in knowledge graphs and other areas of artificial knowledge processing, new reuse scenarios can be envisioned, for instance, the reuse of scientific information, amalgamated by university students, in industry.

Therefore, the goal of this paper is to show how the literature review knowledge amalgamated in a student project can be illustrated and analyzed using a simplified knowledge graph to enhance the reusability of the review results. The systemic literature review, the results of which are used as an example in this paper, was performed to investigate the use of the agile approach in the public sector to address the challenges and obtain the benefits that agile approach (further in the text abbreviated as Agile) can bring to the public organizations. The results were amalgamated in a simplified knowledge graph that illustrates and helps to analyze the domain of interest and can be used to transfer the obtained knowledge to a larger audience.

© The Author(s), under exclusive license to Springer Nature Switzerland AG 2023
M. Ruiz and P. Soffer (Eds.): CAiSE 2023 Workshops, LNBIP 482, pp. 125–131, 2023.
https://doi.org/10.1007/978-3-031-34985-0_13

Section 2 of the paper briefly represents the initial results of the literature review in the form of table, showing the various aspects of Agile discussed in in the literature in the context of the public sector. In Sect. 3, the detected aspects are organized in a simplified weighted knowledge graph, where weights are assigned to the nodes, and graph analysis is performed. Section 4 discusses the related work. Conclusions are provided in Sect. 5.

2   Literature Review as the Basis of a Knowledge Graph

The literature review, which, in this paper, is used to demonstrate the proposed approach, was performed on papers published in 2016–22. The search by keyword combinations "application of agile in public sector" and "challenges with Agile in public sector", in the Scopus database, brought 34 and 56 results respectively. From these, 10 articles that provided validated knowledge on the use of Agile in the public sector were selected. The review results from the 10 sources are illustrated in Table 1.

Table 1. Mapping of Agile application aspect to project lifecycle phases

Project phase	Aspect	Reference										Count
		[1]	[2]	[3]	[4]	[5]	[6]	[7]	[8]	[9]	[10]	
Initiation	Organizational hierarchy		x							x		2
	Innovation						x	x				2
	Business case									x		1
	Contracting	x	x	x				x	x		x	6
	Evaluation of potential contractor		x						x	x		3
Planning	Scope and price	x		x			x		x			4
	Project plan	x	x	x	x		x				x	6
	Roles and responsibilities			x			x	x				3
	Risk management			x		x				x		3
Execution	Scrum	x	x				x	x				4
	Practices	x	x			x			x		x	5
	Collaboration and communication		x		x	x	x	x				5

(continued)

Table 1. (*continued*)

Project phase	Aspect	Reference										Count
		[1]	[2]	[3]	[4]	[5]	[6]	[7]	[8]	[9]	[10]	
	Business and IT team alignment	x	x	x	x				x	x		6
	Knowledge and skills			x				x	x	x	x	5
Moni-toring and control	Progress monitoring	x					x					2
	Feedback		x		x				x			3
	Change management	x	x	x	x	x	x	x			x	8
Close	Delivery		x		x	x						3
	Documentation						x	x				2
	Evaluation of project	x										1

In Table 1, the revealed aspects of the use of Agile in the public sector (shown in the second column) are organized in groups by project phases [11] shown in the first column of the table. Further columns refer to the literature sources analyzed. If a particular aspect *i* was discussed in a particular referred article *j*, the "x" mark is displayed in the table cell that corresponds to the aspect *i* and reference *j*. The last column in the table shows how many titles refered to one and the same aspect discussed in the related work. More details about the literature review are available in [12].

Table 1 is a traditional way of representing the results of a literature review. In Sect. 3, the table will be transferred into the knowledge graph, which can show more information and helps to visualize and analyze the results of the literature review.

3 The Results of the Literature Review as a Knowledge Graph

The literature results were manually transferred into a simplified weighted knowledge graph shown in Fig. 1.

The graph reflects not only the objects (aspects from Table 1), the links between the objects and their meaning, but also, by the size (weight) of the nodes, the commonality of inclusion in the articles. The node's diameter is proportional to the percentage of the articles where a respective aspect is highlighted and elaborated. The color of the node relates to the project lifecycle phase. In addition to the aspects listed in Table 1, the law of public procurement in the public sector was identified as highly influential in the initiation phase of the project lifecycle [12] and was therefore also included in the graph. Navigating through the graph helps to better understand the relationships between the aspects and their significance. For instance, if we start at "Organizational hierarchy", it

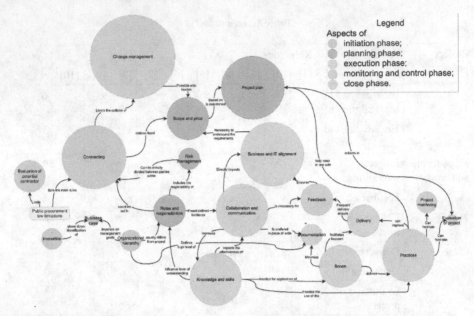

Fig. 1. Simplified weighted knowledge graph representing literature review results.

influences "Roles and responsibilities"; and, if they are well defined, "Collaboration and communication" should improve which, in turn, is important for "Feedback". This path in the graph passes through three different project phases, and other variations of the paths exist. The knowledge graph shows how strongly linked the aspects are and how one aspect in a one phase of the project can indirectly or directly influence aspects in other project phases. Therefore, it is possible to evaluate the influence of each aspect. In addition, the knowledge graph gives an insight into how the changes in one aspect can lead to different outcomes of the project.

For further analysis, the nodes were numbered, and the directed graph analysis algorithms were applied. The node numbers corresponding to each analyzed aspect are shown in the second column of Table 2. With the application of algorithms, graph analysis shifts the focus from specific aspects to systems thinking. The basis of such analysis is methods used for systems structure analysis in systems theory (such as calculation of the number of outgoing and incoming links of the nodes, analyzing directed paths between the nodes, etc.). Table 2 shows the results of graph analysis, it is assumed that the aspects that have more direct and indirect links with other aspects are more

important for being considered and respected in Agile information systems development in the public sector.

To determine the impact of specific aspects represented in the knowledge graph, the following activities were performed: (i) the adjacency matrix of the graph was created, (ii) the reachability matrix was calculated, (iii) the sum of links for each object was calculated, (iv) the degree of structural impact was calculated, and (v) ranking was done based on calculated results. By this approach, the most impactful aspects were identified analytically by qualitative measures. In Table 2 they are shown in italics. The comparison

Table 2. Results of qualitative and topological analysis.

Aspect	Node No.	Number of out-going links	Number of incom-ing links	Sum of links	Rank (by links)	Degree of struc-tural impact (DS impact)	Rank (by DS im-pact)	Summary Rank
Organizational hierarchy	1	3	0	3	4	0.857	1	3
Innovation	2	1	0	1	6	0.095	10	10
Business case	3	0	2	2	5	0.048	11	10
Contracting	4	2	3	5	3	0.238	7	5
Evaluation of potential contractor	5	0	1	1	7	0.048	11	12
Scope and price	6	1	3	4	3	0.143	9	7
Project plan	7	1	2	3	4	0.095	10	8
Roles and responsibilities	8	3	2	5	2	0.762	2	2
Risk management	9	1	1	2	5	0.286	6	6
Scrum	10	3	1	4	3	0.476	3	4
Practices	11	4	2	6	1	0.381	4	3
Collaboration and communication	12	4	2	6	1	0.762	2	1
Business and IT team alignment	13	1	2	3	4	0.190	8	7
Knowledge and skills	14	4	1	5	2	0.762	2	2
Progress monitoring	15	0	1	1	6	0.048	11	11
Feedback	16	1	2	3	4	0.238	7	6
Change management	17	1	1	2	5	0.190	8	7
Delivery	18	1	2	3	4	0.286	6	5
Documentation	19	0	3	3	4	0.048	11	9
Evaluation of project	20	0	2	2	5	0.048	11	10
Public procurement law	21	2	0	2	5	0.333	5	5

of the results with the opinions in the literature about the Agile confirmed the obtained results [12].

4 Related Work and Discussion

The standard for a framework of knowledge graphs has been introduced in 2022 [14]. It provides a conceptual model of a knowledge graph and defines the knowledge graph supplier, integrator, user, and ecosystem partner. In this paper, the knowledge graph is considered from the supplier's point of view. It is a simplified weighted knowledge graph that, in its current version, is discussed at the instance level, but has the potential to be moved to the ontology level for amalgamating knowledge about related works in the domain of the use of Agile in information systems development in the public sector.

Different knowledge graph-based approaches, in analyzing related work, are used for relating publications which consider specific topics, e.g., [15]. There is also research work devoted specifically to using knowledge graphs as a basis for literature reviews. For instance, [16] presents an approach to partly automate the conduction of a systematic literature review by designing interfaces to digital libraries and embedding search criteria as well as using natural language processing to further filter and classify results. The publication is presented as a knowledge graph thus enabling an enhancing analysis by querying the graphs. But also, this method is devoted rather to searching for the publications than analyzing already obtained results. The approach discussed in this paper could benefit from the approaches such as in [15] and [16]; and could combine the publication-oriented knowledge graphs with the domain-oriented graphs that are based on the literature review results. This combination and the possibility to extend the initial domain-oriented knowledge graph with new nodes and move it to the ontology level [14] are the aims of further research.

5 Conclusion

This work in progress applied a simplified weighted knowledge graph for representing and analyzing the results of a structured literature review about agile information systems development practices in the public sector. The graph was constructed manually. The first results of its use showed its potential in the analysis of the domain in terms of visual representation, navigation, and applying graph analysis algorithms. Further work is intended towards the improvement and elaboration of graph formation and analysis methods in order to move towards the possible use of controlled automatic graph generation and navigation through the graph-based and tabular forms of representation of knowledge of a specific domain.

At this stage of research, the results obtained were just crosschecked with the opinions available in the related work. In the next iterations, the use of this knowledge graph in public organizations is intended to validate the usefulness of knowledge graphs for promoting Agile practices in the public sector.

References

1. Russo, D., Taccogna, G., Ciancarini, P., Messina, A., Succi, G.: Contracting agile developments for mission critical systems in the public sector. In: Proceedings of the 40th International Conference on Software Engineering: Software Engineering in Society, pp. 47–56 (2018)
2. Fontana, R.M., Marczak, S.: Characteristics and challenges of agile software development adoption in Brazilian government. J. Technol. Manag. Innov. 15(2), 3–10 (2020)
3. Kaczorowska, A.: Traditional versus agile project management in public sector in Poland. In: Scientific Papers of Silesian University of Technology. Organization and Management Series, vol. 2020, no. 149, pp. 287–302 (2020)
4. Mohagheghi, P., Jørgensen, M.: What contributes to the success of IT projects? success factors, challenges and lessons learned from an empirical study of software projects in the norwegian public sector. In: 2017 IEEE/ACM 39th International Conference on Software Engineering Companion (ICSE-C), pp. 371–373 (2017)
5. Elbanna, A., Sarker, S.: The risks of agile software development: learning from adopters. IEEE Softw 33(5), 72–79 (2016)
6. Ribeiro, A., Domingues, L.: Acceptance of an agile methodology in the public sector. Procedia Comput. Sci. 138, 621–629 (2018)
7. Nuottila, J., Aaltonen, K., Kujala, J.: Challenges of adopting agile methods in a public organization. Int. J. Inf. Syst. Proj. Manag. 4(3), 65–85 (2016)

8. Lindsjørn, Y., Moustafa, R.: Challenges with lack of trust in agile projects with autonomous teams and fixed-priced contracts. In: ACM International Conference Proceeding Series, vol. 147763, pp. 1–5 (2018)

9. Shahzad, B., Awan, K.M., Ikram-Ullah Lali, M., Aslam, W.: Identification of patterns in failure of software projects. J. Inf. Sci. Eng. **33**(6), 1465–1480 (2017).

10. Mergel, I., Gong, Y., Bertot, J.: Agile government: systematic literature review and future research. Gov Inf Q. **35**(2), 291–298 (2018)

11. The standard for project management and a guide to the project management body of knowledge (PMBOK guide), Seventh edition. 2021. PMI Homepage. https://www.pmi.org/pmbok-guide-standards/foundational/pmbok

12. Graudone, J., Kirikova, M.: Systematic literature review of agile framework application for IT system development in public sector. Accepted for publishing in the Proceeding of the 2nd International Workshop on Agile Methods for Information Systems Engineering (Agil-ISE), which will be held in conjunction with the CAiSE'23 conference, CEUR (2023)

13. Directive 2014/24/EU of the European Parliament and of the Council of 26 February 2014 on public procurement and repealing Directive 2004/18/EC. European Parliament, An official website of the European Union. https://eur-lex.europa.eu/legal-content/EN/TXT/?uri=celex%3A32014L0024. Accessed 2022/01/01

14. IEEE standard for framework of knowledge graphs, IEEE Computer Society (2022)

15. Connected papers. https://www.connectedpapers.com/

16. Sahlab, N., Kahoul, H., Jazdi, N., Weyrich, M.: A knowledge graph-based method for automating systemic literature reviews. Preprint (2022). https://doi.org/10.48550/arXiv.2208.02334

Knowledge Engineering Formalizing *DECENT* Meta Model

Angelo Fiorentino[1]([⊠]), Fadime Kaya[2], and Paul Johannesson[3]

[1] University of Trento, Trento, Italy
angelo.fiorentino@studenti.unitn.it
[2] Vrije Universiteit Amsterdam, Amsterdam, The Netherlands
f.kaya@vu.nl
[3] Stockholm University, Stockholm, Sweden
pajo@dsv.su.se

Abstract. Blockchain governance has emerged as a research topic with the introduction of blockchain technology that allows for collaboration without a centralized actor. This offers a unique opportunity to examine alternative structures for platform governance and to develop a theory around governance structures for disruptive ecosystems. In the past years, we have been working on developing *DECENT* a domain specific language (DSL) that allows for designing decentralized governance from a conceptual modeling perspective. An important subset of the DSL is the *DECENT* meta model. In this paper, we explore if we can formalize the *DECENT* meta model from a mathematical perspective. The formalization of *DECENT* meta model will contribute to our long-term research goal to develop a graphical visualization of the *DECENT* meta model by using ADOxx and to work towards computational governance.

Keywords: Blockchain Governance · *DECENT* · Knowledge Engineering · Decentralization · Conceptual Modeling

1 Introduction

Decentralized forms of governance have become increasingly popular, partly due to the emergence of peer-to-peer (P2P) and blockchain technology. Governance is about the process and system of decision-making as well as policy and regulation implementation within an organization or society. It refers to the structures and processes put in place to control, manage and steer a system and ensure that it operates in a transparent, accountable, and responsible manner. Over the past decade, the rise of blockchain technology has led to the emergence of a growing number of decentralized platforms that are governed less by platform owners and more through community efforts. The emergence of blockchain platforms offers a unique opportunity to examine alternative structures for platform governance and to develop a theory around the value of centralized, semi-decentralized, and decentralized governance. Drawing on mechanism design theory, we evaluate the trade-offs between centralization and decentralization and hypothesize semi-decentralization as a higher-performing governance structure. It has been identified by a systematic literature review, in which 189 papers on

M. Ruiz and P. Soffer (Eds.): CAiSE 2023 Workshops, LNBIP 482, pp. 132–144, 2023.
https://doi.org/10.1007/978-3-031-34985-0_14

governance mechanisms are discussed, that governance design in digital platforms is scarcely researched [3]. This is further supported by a systematic literature review [9] on conceptual modeling for digital business platforms that existing conceptual modeling languages are not satisfactory in designing blockchain governance. Therefore, we propose *DECENT* [7], a method that allows for designing decentralized governance. *DECENT* is developed in the philosophy that we as society have the responsibility in creating transparency in how rules of engagement are decided. We refer and coin the field in understanding and creation in rules of engagement between actors as Decentralized Governance. *DECENT* has been developed through a conceptual modeling approach and with real industry strength cases such as P2P energy trading, cryptocurrency and fiat money creation. Our long-term research goal is computational governance and to create a foundational structure to solidify *DECENT* towards a domain specific language (DSL). In order to achieve our long-term goal, we want to create a deeper semantic understanding of the *DECENT* meta model. We do so by formalizing the *DECENT* meta model in order to get a better understanding of the *DECENT* concepts and their relations. The paper is organized as follows. In Sect. 2 we explain related work. In Sect. 3, we explain our research approach, in Sect. 4 we motivate why decentralized governance requires a knowledge engineering approach and present the *DECENT* model and the definitions. In Sect. 5 we present the mathematical formalization, in Sect. 6 we evaluate and answer the research question. We conclude the paper in Sect. 7.

2 Related Work

The first step towards decentralized governance conceptualization occurred in the Bitcoin and Ethereum ecosystem, followed by various Decentralized Autonomous Organizations (DAOs). However while these decentralized ecosystems promise a decentralized governance structure, this is in fact not entirely true, as the decision making structure is often still rather centralized [4], and moreover restricts itself to decision making only, ignoring the process that happens before actual governance decisions are taken. In [3] the authors present a systematic literature overview in which 189 papers are discussed on governance design mechanisms, and stated that governance design in digital ecosystems is rarely investigated. Inter alia, the authors concluded: (1) There is no governance design and modeling approach (2) Decentralized Governance is a design decision (3) Governance design is crucial for ecosystem design and (4) Governance design is the right mechanism to create value and evolve ecosystem design [3]. Moreover, the authors present [3], amongst others the following future research directions: Which artifacts affect governance design decisions? Which mechanisms are used to implement and conceptualize governance design decisions? Which role does a party have in governance design? What are the power relation structures in governance design? We address the aforementioned research directions in our *DECENT* method. *DECENT* allows to represent and conceptualize decentralized governance design decisions. Our vision is that a decentralized ecosystem can only succeed if the governance design structure is also decentralized. In mathematics, the notion of patterns is also studied. A mathematical pattern is created by defining concepts as a set of numbers arranged in a sequence that are related to each other in a specific rule. These patterns demonstrate the relations between concepts and their structural behaviour. These rules define a pathway to calculate or solve problems [1]. Patterns could also be applicable in the field of governance, though there still does not exist much work on the topic. A pattern is a general, reusable solution to a commonly occurring problem within a given context. A pattern can be used as a basis for designing concrete solutions that are customized to address particular problems. Patterns have been used for many different purposes, e.g. architectural patterns, software patterns, and behavioural patterns. Overall, patterns can be applied in a wide range of fields and contexts to improve design, solve problems, and make informed decisions. An example of a pattern could be a board that is composed of representatives from the actors that it governs and has control of only one mechanism, which is a penalty for a symbolic monetary amount. An instance of this pattern is the Swedish Press Council[1]. Another example could be an organization that governs solely by awarding a certificate and letting actors decide for themselves whether or how to value this certificate. An instance of this pattern is the Marine Stewardship Council[2]. DECENT is well positioned to provide a structure for representing governance patterns, as it includes all the fundamental governance constructs. Meta governance refers to the practice of governing the governance itself. It is about designing, implementing, and monitoring systems and processes in complex and dynamic environments, where traditional forms of governance may be inadequate or insufficient. Today, meta governance has become increasingly important for states that find their own bureaucracies inappropriate for producing and providing certain kinds of services. Instead, they leave this production and provision to complex networks of companies, authorities and other organizations. The organizations in the networks undertake much of the work of governing by implementing policies and regulating themselves. The role of the state is solely to govern these organizations, to a large extent in a light-weight approach, which may include the development of frameworks, standards, and best practices.

3 Research Approach

In this paper we follow the research approach of mathematics [1]. Mathematics is about exploring patterns, structures, concepts, relationships and rules. We express DECENT as a mathematical notation because this allows us to make the relations and behavior between concepts more explicit. The long term research goal of DECENT is to evolve it further into a DSL. In order to achieve our long term goal we first focus on the DECENT meta model concepts as presented in Fig. 1, We express DECENT mathematically by following a descriptive static approach as inspired by [8]. Therefore we formulated the following research question: **RQ**: Can we mathematically formalize the DECENT meta model?

[1] https://www.wikiwand.com/en/Swedish_Press_Council

[2] https://www.msc.org/

4   DECENT Knowledge Engineering

The physical world is merging with the digital world rapidly and boundaries between these worlds are becoming more ambiguous and duality is occurring. It is not clear which actor is taking the decision and which actor is controlling the ecosystem at hand. More importantly, it is not transparent in how digital assets are created, consumed, stored and traded. This entails that mutual dependencies are occurring to orchestrate an ecosystem and that company or a customer is dependent at the ecosystem as a whole. The discussion in the value of digital asset creation and consumption is sparked with the introduction of Bitcoin philosophy that proposes that the value of the asset at hand is not limited only at asset creation, but there is also value in how the asset is consumed, traded and stored. Furthermore, with the rise of crypto-currency we have entered the age of computational trust. However, by giving algorithms the definition and task of executing trust is a risk factor in itself. From our consultancy experience in the blockchain world, we see that even though an ecosystem can be designed decentralized, power concentration still occurs at the technology provider and automatically at the design of decentralized ecosystems. This inherently causes the ecosystem to be probably never decentralized even though the philosophy mandates that. How to orchestrate and design the decision making of an asset and consequently the digital ecosystem that the asset is part of, we define it as a governance design decision. Blockchain technology and its most known use-case Bitcoin provides an use case that enables trust between peers thus eliminating the trusted third party(TTP). By eliminating the ttp the control and decision making structure of the ecosystem changes significantly because its not led centrally anymore. Governance is an imposed control system that decides the rules to steer behavior of actors which were previously formally decide by one actor first. Once the TTP is eliminated, Governance moves gradually towards decentralization thus requires a design method to decide on the system collectively. We want to develop and proposing a standard in how to design decentralized governance for ecosystems that are decentralized in its nature. In order to facilitate digital asset and ecosystem design in where decision making is decentralized over multiple actors we propose DECENT [7]. The abbreviation DECENT stands for Decentralization.

DECENT Meta Model. In [6] it is stated that a model is always part of a meta model and a model cannot exist on itself as it has to be connected to the overall meta model design goal approach. As we see it, decentralized governance is a future required state that needs to be developed. Decentralized governance is a new emerging research field which requires formalization and its corresponding semantics. As there is currently no language and uniform standard yet that allows to design decentralized governance [3, 9]. The development and positioning of DECENT relies heavily on knowledge engineering. As in [2] it is proposed that knowledge engineering contributes in linking data, software and stakeholders, this is exactly our design approach and vision for DECENT.

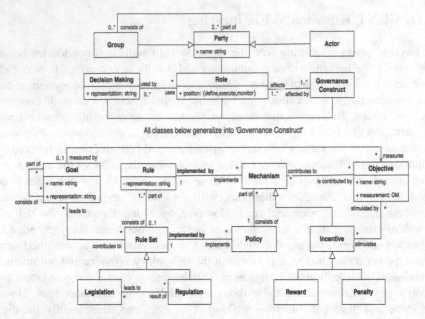

Fig. 1. *DECENT* Meta Model for Decentralized Governance Design

Our long term goal is to develop computational governance, but in order to achieve that goal we first have to develop the knowledge in how to design decentralized governance. With *DECENT* we focus on creating transparency in how rules of engagement are decided. Furthermore *DECENT* promotes design values such as open standards, transparency and democracy. In order to create transparency in how rules of engagement are designed we take a conceptual modeling approach. This will also eliminate the dependency on technology providers and create an equal field in terms of knowledge in how the decision making will be designed and executed for the decentralized ecosystem at hand. We state that a conceptual model can be understood by every actor and is superior to the written language. A conceptual model surpasses the written language and software coding. It is important that every actor has an equal basis and we want to achieve that by introducing *DECENT* a domain specific language that is not centralized, does not rely on coding, and is an uniform language that is lightweight and tractable. We take the *DECENT* design approach as rules can be interpreted subjective and a design approach eliminates ambiguity to a large extent. It reduces dependency as every actor speaks the same *DECENT* language. Uniformity is achieved between all actors. A graphical language by any means is always superior to the written language and can be understood by every actor in the design process of creating rules. *DECENT* allows to design collective ownership, promotion of open standards, strengthen our democracy, and transparency of rules. We present *DECENT* meta model in Fig. 1 and discuss the definitions in Table 1.

Table 1. *DECENT* Meta Model Definition

DECENT Concept	Definition
Group	Consists of multiple entities and can be identified based on shared characteristics, such as a common goal. A group consists-of one or more parties and can play multiple roles
Actor	An actor is an entity perceived by itself and the environment as economically independent
Party	Abstraction of an actor and a group. It can play several roles as one unit of control regarding decision making in relation to governance construct
Role	A party has one or more roles, which can be 'determining' 'executing' and 'monitoring' and relates to a governance construct. A role is played-by a party
Decision Making	Refers to a collection of different methods used by a party to take a decision. Decision making is used-by a role
Governance Construct	Abstraction and generalization of other concepts in the *DECENT* meta model namely decision making, rule, rule set, mechanism, policy, goal, objective, and incentive
Rule	Defines what is permitted or prohibited. A rule can be part-of (multiple) rule-set(s)
Mechanism	Implements a rule, is part-of a policy, contributes-to reaching an objective, generalization of incentive, contributes to satisfaction of a goal
Policy	A policy is a plan for action which implements a rule set
Goal	Formulated ambition to fulfill, for which a party has committed resources for. Goal is stated qualitatively to allow measurement of the goal by an objective
Objective	Measure and realizes achieving the qualitatively stated goal. To stimulate behavior that will lead towards achieving a goal via an objective, incentives are formulated
Legislation	Defined by the government, which is a group formulating the law. A citizen and companies have in their 'executing' role the duty to obey the law
Regulation	Is a defined action to monitor and regulate the implementations of laws
Rule Set	Coherent set of rules that consists of legislation and regulation
Incentive	Is a stimulation to achieve objectives and adhere to rules. It has an expression stating the reward or penalty. It is a mechanism, and as such can implement a rule. It is the generalization of penalty and reward and stimulates to reach an objective
Penalty	Is a sanction if objectives are not met and rules are not adhered
Reward	Is a motivation to achieve objectives

5 Formalization of *DECENT*

Our goal for this paper is to formalize and to demonstrate the decentralized nature of the *DECENT* meta model. This will also contribute in developing the correct notion for the *DECENT* graphical notation. We will explain each *DECENT* concept and its related governance structures through a mathematical notation. We have derived three

Decentralized Governance Processes (DGP) based on the mathematical expression of the *DECENT* meta model.

DGP1 Group, party, actor, their associated role [define, execute, monitor] and the decision making procedures change in a way that is not predictable.

DGP2 A party, that consists of group and actor, uses decision making to modify governance construct according to their role.

DGP3 Governance construct modify group, party, actor, their associated roles and the decision making procedure.

Processes **DGP2** and **DGP3** emerge naturally from the diagrams in Figs. 1. **DGP2** represents the action of the upper block (group, party, actor, role and decision making) on the lower (governance constructs), and **DGP3** represents the action of the lower block on the upper. Process **DGP1** takes into account the possible random evolution of the modeled environment.

The standard approach to model mutual, simultaneous influences between parts of a deterministic system is based on the theory of dynamical systems, where laws of evolution can be expressed by means of differential equations (see, for instance, [8]). The absence of a differential structure and the potential unpredictable nature of those processes leads us to use a hybrid discrete-continuous approach. In order to understand the rationale of the *DECENT* meta model we position it as *DECENT* Time.

Decentralization 1. [Time Structure]
Time is a 4-tuple $(T, \{r_i\}_{i=1}^{\infty}, \{s_i\}_{i=0}^{\infty}, \{t_i\}_{i=0}^{\infty})$ where:

(T1) T is the closed half-line $[0, +\infty) \subset \mathbb{R}$.
(T2) $\{r_i\}_i$, $\{s_i\}_i$, $\{t_i\}_i$ are sequences in $\mathbb{R}$.
(T3) $0 < s_0 < t_0 < r_1 < s_1 < t_1 < r_2 < s_2 < t_2 < \dots$.

A point $t \in T$ will be called instant. Instants r_i, s_i, t_i will be called crucial instants. Time is the totality of all instants related to each other via the concepts of past and future. An instant can be thought as a precise moment in time. The introduction of the sequences in (T2) and the partition of T in (T3) have a specific reason.

Process **DGP1** happens at instants r_i.
Process **DGP2** happens at instants s_i.
Process **DGP3** happens at instants t_i.

Property (T3) ensures that **DGP2**, **DGP3**, **DGP1** happen exactly in that decentralized order. **DGP2** comes first according to the underlying philosophy of *DECENT*. In order for governance to be fair, first goals are set, then policies and regulation are created in order to facilitate their achievement. **DGP3** comes after **DGP2** because parties are immediately influenced by the governance constructs they have created. Finally, **DGP1** acts as a reset after random changes. We will now formalize, by using mathematical notation, the *DECENT* concepts as presented in Sect. 4.

Decentralization 2. [Group-Party-Actor Structure]
The Group-Party-Actor structure is a 4-tuple $(E, \mathcal{Ac}, \mathcal{G}, \mathcal{P})$.
(GPA1) E is a nonempty set of finite cardinality. Its elements are called entities.

(GPA2) $\mathcal{A}c$, $\mathcal{G}$ are families of nonempty subsets of E, whose elements are called, respectively, **Actors** and **Groups**, that satisfy:

GPA2.1 $\mathcal{A}c \cup \mathcal{G}$ is a covering of E, that is $E = \bigcup_{p \in \mathcal{A}c \cup \mathcal{G}} p$.
GPA2.2 $\forall A \in \mathcal{A}c$. $\#A = 1$.
GPA2.3 $\forall G \in \mathcal{G}$. $\#G > 1$.

(GPA3) $\mathcal{P} = \mathcal{A}c \cup \mathcal{G}$ is a family of subsets of E. Its members are called Parties.

Property GPA2.1 states that every entity belongs to a group or an actor.

Properties GPA2.2 and GPA2.3 highlight the main difference between an actor and a group. The former models entities perceived as independent, the latter describes an aggregation of entities.

GPA2.2 and GPA2.3 imply $\mathcal{A}c \cap \mathcal{G} = \emptyset$. So an actor is not a group, and a group is not an actor.

Property (GPA3) states that a party is either an actor or a group, hence translating the relation "actors extend parties" and "groups extend parties".

We remark that it is possible that a group G is the union of $k \in \mathcal{N}$, $k \geq 2$ distinct groups ("a group can be more groups").

Decentralization 3. [Role Assignment Structure]

Let $(E, \mathcal{A}c, \mathcal{G}, \mathcal{P})$ be a group-party-actor structure. Let $\mathcal{G}cs$ be a governance constructs structure and $\mathcal{G}c$ be the set of governance constructs (see Decentralization 7).

Let $Ro = \{$**define**, **execute**, **monitor**$\}$ be a set of strings, that are called roles. A role assignment is a subset $\mathcal{R}oa$ of $\mathcal{P} \times Ro \times \mathcal{G}s$.

(RoA1) Every party, every role and every governance construct appears at least in one 3-tuple of $\mathcal{R}oa$.

(RoA2) Let $G \in \mathcal{G}$. Suppose G is the union of $k \geq 2$ pairwise distinct groups $G_1, \ldots,$ $G_k \in \mathcal{G}$. Let $i, j \in \{1, \ldots, k\}$, $i \neq j$. Then $\forall r_i, r_j \in Ro$, $\forall c_i, c_j \in \mathcal{G}s$. $(G_i, r_i, c_i), (G_j, r_j, c_j)$ $\in \mathcal{R}oa \Rightarrow (r_i, c_i) \neq (r_j, c_j)$.

Property (RoA2) has a precise meaning. If "a group is k distinct groups", they pairwise either have different roles, or have the same role but related to different governance constructs.

Decentralization 4. [Goal-Objective Structure]

A Goal-Objective structure is a 3-tuple $(Go, \mathcal{G}o\ Obj)$.

(GOb1) Go is a finite, nonempty set of strings

(GOb2) $\mathcal{G}o$ is a subfamily of $2^{Go} \setminus \emptyset$, whose elements are called **Goals**.

(GOb3) Obj is a function that associates to every $\Gamma \in \mathcal{G}o$ a set

$\Omega = \mathrm{Obj}(\Gamma) \subset \mathbb{R}^{n(\Gamma)}$, where $n(\Gamma)$ is a positive natural number.

For $\Gamma \subset Go$, $\mathrm{Obj}(\Gamma)$ will be called the **Objective** associated to the goal Γ.

(GOb2) States that every goal is associated to numeric parameters. This formalizes the fact that an objective measures and realises achieving a qualitatively stated goal. We remark that it is possible that a goal Γ in $\mathcal{G}o$ is the union of $k \in \mathbb{N}$, $k \geq 2$, distinct goals ("a goal can be multiple goals").

Decentralization 5. [Rule Set Structure]

A rule set structure is a 5-tuple $(Ru, \mathcal{R}u, \mathcal{R}s, \mathcal{L}eg, \mathcal{R}eg)$.

(R1) *Ru* is a finite, nonempty set of strings.
(R2) *Leg*, *Reg* are two disjoint subfamilies of $2^{Ru} \setminus \emptyset$, that are called, respectively, legislation and regulation.
(R3) *Rs*, *Ru* are two subfamilies of $2^{Ru} \setminus \emptyset$ satisfying:

R3.1 *Ru*, *Rs* are coverings of *Ru*.
R3.2 *Rs* = *Leg* $\cup$ *Reg*.
R3.3 For every $P \in Rs$ there exist a positive natural k and $\rho_1, ..., \rho_k \in Ru$, such that $P = \rho_1 \cup \cdots \cup \rho_k$.
R3.4 For every $\rho \in Ru$. if $\sigma \neq \rho$ and $\sigma \subset \rho$, then $\sigma \notin Ru$.

An element of *Ru* is called a rule. An element of *Rs* is called a rule set.
Property (R1) formalises the fact that legislation and regulation are two differentconcepts.

Property R3.2 formalizes "legislation and regulation extends rule sets".
Property R3.3 formalizes the relation "rule sets consist of rules".
Property R3.4 implies that a rule ρ cannot be partitioned into strictly smaller rules.
A rule is an elementary concept.

Decentralization 6. [Mechanism Structure]
A mechanism structure is a 6-tuple $(M, Rw, Pn, , I, M, Pol)$, where:

(M1) M is a finite, nonempty set of strings.
(M2) *Rw*, *Pn* are two disjoint subfamilies of $2^M \setminus \emptyset$, whose elements are called, respectively, reward and penalty.
(M3) $I = Rw \cup Pn$.
(M4) M, *Pol* are two subfamilies of $2^M \setminus \emptyset$, whose elements are called, respectively, mechanism and policy, satisfying:
   M4.1 $I \subset M$.
   M4.2 For each $\varpi \in Pol$ there exist a positive natural k and $M_1, ..., M_k \in M$ pairwise distinct such that $\varpi = M_1 \cup \cdots \cup M_k$.
   M4.3 M, *Pol* are coverings of M.

Property (M3) states that incentive is either a reward or penalty.
In particular, from (M2), the two families are disjoint. Thus an incentive is either a reward or a penalty.

Property M4.1 formalizes the relation "incentives extend mechanisms".
Property M4.3 formalises the relation "a policy consist of mechanism".

Decentralization 7. [Governance Construct Structure]
A governance construct structure is a 14-tuple

$Gs = (Go, Go, Obj, Ru, Ru, Rs, Leg, Reg, M, Rw, Pn, , I, M, Pol)$.
(Gc1) $(Go, Go\ Obj)$ is a goal-objective structure.
(Gc2) (Ru, Ru, Rs, Leg, Reg) is a rule set structure.
(Gc3) $(M, Rw, Pn, , I, M, Pol)$ is a mechanism structure.

The three structures above are related to each other the following way.

(Gc4)There is a function impl: $\mathcal{R}u \to \mathcal{M}$.
(Gc5)There is a function IMPL: $\mathcal{R}s \to \mathcal{P}ol$.
(Gc6)There is a function stim: $\mathcal{I} \to \{\text{Obj}(\varGamma) \mid \varGamma \in \mathcal{G}o\}\}$.
(Gc7)There is a function contr: $\mathcal{M} \to \{\text{Obj}(\varGamma) \mid \varGamma \in \mathcal{G}o\}$.

The set of governance constructs is the disjoint union
$$\mathcal{G}c = \mathcal{G}o \sqcup \text{Obj}(\mathcal{G}o) \sqcup \mathcal{R}u \sqcup \mathcal{R}s \sqcup \mathcal{L}eg \sqcup \mathcal{R}eg \sqcup \mathcal{R}w \sqcup \mathcal{P}n \sqcup \mathcal{I} \sqcup \mathcal{M} \sqcup \mathcal{P}ol.$$

Decentralization 8. [Decentralized Evolution Structure]
For $\tau = 0$ or τ crucial instant, we have:

1. A group-party-actor structure $\Sigma(\tau) = (E(\tau),\ \mathcal{A}c(\tau),\ \mathcal{G}(\tau),\ \mathcal{P}(\tau))$.
2. A governance construct structure $\mathcal{G}s(\tau)$ and its associated $\mathcal{G}c(\tau)$.
3. A role assignment $\mathcal{R}oa(\tau) \subset \mathcal{P}(\tau) \times Ro \times \mathcal{G}c$.

Let η be the crucial instant that is consecutive to τ.
For every $G \in \mathcal{G}(\tau)$, for every $e \in E(\tau)$ we have functions below.

$$\Pi(\tau, G) : [\tau, \eta] \to \mathbb{R}^{N(\tau, G)} \quad N(\tau, G) \in \mathbb{N}$$
$$\pi(\tau, e) \ : [\tau, \eta] \to \mathbb{R}^{n(\tau, G)} \quad n(\tau, G) \in \mathbb{N}$$

The rationale behind this formalization is that, in the interval of time $[\tau, \eta)$, we are assuming that structures 1, 2, 3. Remain fixed. The evolution of the system in that interval of time is described by numerical parameters given by the functions $\Pi(\tau, \cdot)$ and $\pi(\tau, \cdot)$. When passing from a crucial instant to the consecutive, the structures in 1, 2, 3. Change accordingly to processes **DGP1, DGP2, DGP3**. Fix $i \in \mathbb{N}$, consider $s_i,\ t_i,\ r_{i+1}$. Let $\xi = r_i$ if $i > 1$ and $\xi = 0$ if $i = 0$. We will now discuss these processes hereafter. $(\underline{\xi \to s_i})$ At instant s_i process **DGP2** happens. We assume that $\varGamma (\xi) = \varGamma (s_i)$, while $\mathcal{G}c$ (s_i), $\Pi(s_i, \cdot)$, $\pi(s_i, \cdot)$ may be different from $\mathcal{G}s(\xi)$, $\Pi(\xi, \cdot)$, $\pi(\xi, \cdot)$. The process looks like that.

Parameters $\Pi(\xi)(\xi, G)(t)$, $\pi(\xi)(\xi, e)(t)$, with $P \in \mathcal{G}(\xi)$, $e \in E(\xi)$, $t \in [\xi, \eta)$ are analysed.

If objectives are not reached, that is, parameters do not belong to certain regions of $\mathbb{R}^{N(\xi, G)}$ and $\mathbb{R}^{n(\xi, e)}$ which depend on objectives, the decision making procedure modifies structures 2, 3 and functions Π and π in order to facilitate their achievement.

If objectives are attained, that is, parameters belong to the regions introduced above, after the decision making procedure, new goals can be set as well as new objectives. The other governance structures are modified in order to facilitate their achievement.

$(\underline{s_i \to t_i})$ At instant t_i process **DGP3** happens. We assume that $\varGamma (s_i) = \varGamma (t_i)$ and $\mathcal{G}s$ $(s_i) = \mathcal{G}s(t_i)$, while functions Π and π can be modified. The process looks like that.

For every $G \in \mathcal{G}(s_i)$, for every $e \in E(s_i)$, there exist R$(G, s_i) \subset \mathbb{R}^{N(si,\ G)}$ and $S(e, s_i)$ $\subset \mathbb{R}^{n(si,\ e)}$. Those regions depend on $\mathcal{G}s(s_i)$. For example, they may represent a forbidden behaviour of the system according to certain laws.

If there exists $G \in \mathcal{G}(s_i)$ such that $\Pi(s_i, G)([s_i, t_i)) \cap R(G, s_i) \neq \emptyset$ or there exists $e \in E(s_i)$ such that $\pi(s_i, e)([s_i, t_i)) \cap S(e, s_i)0 \neq \emptyset$ (for example, at a certain instant the parameters associated to a group belong to a forbidden region) then the functions Π and π are changed according to $\mathcal{G}s(s_i)$.

$(\underline{t_i \to r_{i+1}})$ At instant r_{i+1} process **DGP1** happens. The idea is that the groupparty-actor structure can change, but $\mathcal{G}s(t_i) = \mathcal{G}s(r_{i+1})$. In order to make sense of this process, we assume that there is a bijection $\Psi\colon \mathcal{P}t_i) \to \mathcal{P}(r_{i+1})$ such that:

$(\Psi\ 1) \forall G \in \mathcal{P}(t_i).\ (G,\ r,\ c) \in \mathcal{R}oa(t_i)$ if and only if $(\psi(G),\ r,\ c) \in \mathcal{R}oa(r_{i+1})$ $(\Psi\ 2)$ $\forall G \in \mathcal{G}(t_i).\ N\ (t_i,\ G) = N\ (r_{i+1},\ \Psi\ (G))$

6   Evaluation

In this section we present our observations following the formalization of the *DECENT* meta model.

Observation 1. DECENT Evolution of Time
We learned that time is an important requirement of decentralization. We have represented and derived that as Decentralized Governance Processes (DGP):

DGP1 Group, party, actor, their associated role Define, Execute, Monitor and the decision making procedures is non deterministic.
DGP2 A Party, that consists of Group and Actor, uses decision making to modify governance construct according to their role.
DGP3 Governance construct modify group, party, actor, their associated roles and the decision making procedure.

Observation 2. Decentralized Governance Structures
By explicitly expressing each *DECENT* governance concept, we see that a concept cannot exist on itself, this is again another element of decentralization. In the *DECENT* meta model several governance structures exist and how important the relation to the time structure is. We derived the following decentralized governance structures (DGS) based on the mathemathical expression.

DGS1 Time Structure
DGS2 Group-Party-Actor Structure
DGS3 Role Assignment Structure
DGS4 Goal-Objective Structure
DGS5 Rule Set Structure
DGS6 Mechanism Structure
DGS7 Governance Construct Structure
DGS8 Decentralized Evolution Structure

Observation 3. Incentive
DECENT concept incentive, which consists of reward and penalty, is a result that follows if a rule is adhered to or not respected. Therefore we consider that incentive should have a direct relationship with the *DECENT* concept Rule, as currently this is not the case.

Observation 4. Goals, Rules and Mechanisms
In *DECENT* a mechanism is defined as follows: "A mechanism contributes to (partial) satisfaction of a goal (via its associated rule, part of a rule set) in terms of reaching an objective", [7]. It is stated that a mechanism usually is process- oriented and can be represented, for example, by a BPMN model. While many governance mechanisms are indeed process-oriented, there are also those that go beyond processes. In order to address the diversity of mechanisms, it could be helpful to distinguish between different kinds of mechanisms. We expect that the graphical notation of *DECENT* will make the mechanism part more explicit.

Observation 5. Meta Governance
A question is if *DECENT* could model cases of meta governance and self governance, where systems can govern both themselves and other systems. This question relates to the definition of decentralized governance: "the set of rules a system has to obey, and which are set by another system", [7]. The definition distinguishes between a governing system and a governed system. However, the *DECENT* meta model does not yet explicitly include classes for these systems.

7 Conclusion

In this paper we presented the *DECENT* meta model and formalized it by taking a mathematical approach. The formalization will lead to an improved *DECENT* meta model, a better understanding of the governance structures and the ability to present these governance structures coherently. This formalization will serve as an input for the *DECENT* graphical notation, which we will create by employing the meta^2 modeling tool ADOxx. We will do so in collaboration with OMiLAB [5]. To emphasize the decentralized nature of the *DECENT* meta model we are considering in creating a BPMN model, as decentralization is also a process modeling question.

Acknowledgement. We thank Yulu Wang from Vrije Universiteit Amsterdam and Alexander V"olz from the University of Vienna for the feedback.

References

1. Brown, R., Porter, T.: The methodology of mathematics. The Mathematical Gazette
2. Buchmann, R.A., Karagiannis, D.: Enriching linked data with semantics from domain-specific diagrammatic models. Bus. Inf. Syst. Eng. **58**, 341–353 (2016)
3. Chen, L., Tong, T.W., Tang, S., Han, N.: Governance and design of digital platforms: A review and future research directions. J. Manage. (2022)
4. Goldsby, C., Hanisch, M.: The boon and bane of blockchain: getting the governance right. Calif. Manage. Rev. **3**, 141–168 (2022)
5. Karagiannis, D., Buchmann, R.A., Burzynski, P., Reimer, U., Walch, M.: Fundamental conceptual modeling languages in omilab. Domain-Specific Conceptual Modeling: Concepts, Methods and Tools, pp. 3–30 (2016)

6. Karagiannis, D., Burzynski, P., Utz, W., Buchmann, R.A.: A metamodeling approach to support the engineering of modeling method requirements. In: 2019 IEEE 27th International Requirements Engineering Conference (RE), pp. 199–210. IEEE (2019)
7. Kaya, F., Gordijn, J.: Decent: An ontology for decentralized governance in the renewable energy sector. In: 2021 IEEE 23rd Conference on Business Informatics (2021)
8. Moretti, V.: Meccanica Analitica. Springer (2020)
9. Tsai, C.H., Zdravkovic, J., Stirna, J.: Modeling digital business ecosystems: a systematic literature review. Complex Syst. Inform. Model. Quart. **30**, 1–30 (2022)

Using Knowledge Graphs for Record Linkage: Challenges and Opportunities

Andreas S. Andreou[1], Donatella Firmani[2], Jerin George Mathew[2(✉)],
Massimo Mecella[2], and Michalis Pingos[1]

[1] Cyprus University of Technology Limassol, Limassol, Cyprus
{andreas.andreou,michalis.pingos}@cut.ac.cy
[2] Sapienza Università di Roma, Rome, Italy
{donatella.firmani,jeringeorge.mathew,massimo.mecella}@uniroma1.it

Abstract. In this paper, we explore how Knowledge Graphs (KGs) can
potentially benefit Record Linkage (RL). RL is the process of identifying
and resolving duplicate records across different data sources, including
structured, semi-structured, and unstructured data (e.g., in data lakes).
RL is a critical task for information systems that rely on data to make
decisions and is used in a wide variety of fields such as healthcare, finance,
government and marketing. Due to recent advances in machine learning,
there has been a significant progress in building automated RL methods.
However, when dealing with vertical applications, featuring specialized
domains such as a particular hospital or industry, human experts are still
required to enter domain-specific knowledge, making RL prohibitively
expensive. Despite KGs can be powerful tools to represent and derive
domain-specific knowledge, their application to RL has been overlooked.
Inspired by a healthcare case study in the Republic of Cyprus, we aim at
filling this gap by identifying challenges and opportunities of using KGs
to reduce the effort of solving RL in vertical applications.

1 Introduction

The increasing value of data to individuals, organizations, and businesses is rev-
olutionizing decision-making, problem-solving, and innovation. However, information systems face challenges in storing and analyzing vast amounts of heterogeneous data coming from multiple sources, such as humans, processes and
devices (e.g., IoT devices), and different formats such as text, tables and images.
Novel approaches such as data lakes, on the one hand, can mitigate this problem
by allowing flexible storage of data from disparate sources such as databases and
file systems, but on the other, they can lead to duplicate or conflicting information about real-world entities, such as persons or machines, making it difficult to
obtain a complete and accurate understanding of the application domain. Record
linkage (RL) is the process of identifying and linking records that correspond
to the same real-world entity across multiple data sources to extract valuable
insights, in a wide variety of application scenarios, from traditional databases to
afore-mentioned data lakes [7]. RL is used in a broad range of domains, including healthcare, finance and government. For example, in healthcare, RL can

M. Ruiz and P. Soffer (Eds.): CAiSE 2023 Workshops, LNBIP 482, pp. 145–151, 2023.
https://doi.org/10.1007/978-3-031-34985-0_15

Fig. 1. Illustrative example of a RL task on Electronic Health Records.

help to identify patients who have been treated at multiple hospitals or clinics, and to ensure that their medical records are accurate and up-to-date. Over the years, researchers in the data management and the information systems community have developed different RL methods, including probabilistic methods [13], rule-based methods, and machine learning (ML) based methods [6]. Advances in natural language processing and increasing investments in data-driven information systems have fueled interest in RL in the last few years, leading to significant progress when dealing with highly descriptive data such as e-commerce and bibliographic datasets. Unfortunately, when dealing with vertical applications that are specific to a particular domain (e.g., healthcare or a particular industry) RL techniques must be tailored to take into account the unique characteristics of the data. This requires domain-specific knowledge which nowadays is provided by human experts, making RL in those applications significantly more expensive.

Our Contribution. We envision how Knowledge Graphs (KGs) could reduce the effort in solving RL in vertical applications and describe specific opportunities and challenges for research in this direction. KGs are a powerful approach to manage domain-specific knowledge and their potential of capturing complex relationships and hierarchies that are often present in vertical applications has been demonstrated in a multitude of applications [3]. Yet, the integration of readily available KGs into RL algorithms to improve their accuracy remains largely unexplored. We utilize examples from a healthcare case study in the Republic of Cyprus to provide a tangible illustration of our vision. We believe that the benefits of KGs extends effortlessly to other RL domains.

2   Background and Related Work

We now provide the simplest definition of RL, without loss of generality. Given two data sources, U and V, the goal of RL is to find all pairs of records $u \in U$, $v \in V$ that refer to the same real-world entity. Many RL approaches employ at their base a binary classifier: given records u, v the classifier predicts a *match* if u and v refer to the same entity and *non match* otherwise.

Figure 1 shows an illustrative example of an RL task in the healthcare domain where we need to identify patients. Differences in the anagraphic data can be handled with available RL techniques while information such as Treatment and Drug require domain-specific knowledge for correct disambiguation. In real-world

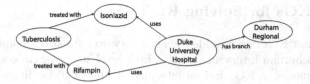

Fig. 2. A schematic representation of a KG as a directed labelled graph.

applications, healthcare dataset can include also patients' medical history and lab results in a variety of formats. In our case study, datasets include lab results in structured format and Bilateral carotid duplex scannings (images).

A Knowledge Graph (KGs) is a graph-based store of real-world information, where the set of nodes represent entities and edges are labelled with semantic relations; two entities h and t linked by an edge with relation r form a *fact*, i.e., a directed labelled edge $\langle h, t, r \rangle$, where h is the head and t is the tail. Figure 2 shows a schematic representation of a KG in the healthcare field. Consider again Fig. 1: by knowing from the KG that (i) Rifampin and Isoniazid are used in combination to treat the same condition and (ii) the hospital in record 1 is a branch of the hospital in record 2, we can automatically predict *match*.

Related Works. Several works have explored and proposed solutions in the intersection of RL and KG. We can distinguish between two directions, one focusing on the use of RL to augment an existing KG, and another one that instead leverages the semantics encoded in the KG to design new RL methods. Works related to the first direction include [11], which presents and evaluates methods for incrementally constructing a KG from multiple data sources using RL and [10], which discusses the different phases of KG construction that require the use of RL, such as when integrating new data into an existing KG or when merging information from two or more KGs, and proposes a RL model that can be applied in these settings. For the second research direction, we include [9] that investigates the usefulness of graph embeddings learned from a KG as input for ML classifiers for RL and [2] that proposes a comprehensive pipeline to extract textual features from images in order to build a KG and the learned KG embeddings for a downstream RL task. All these works focus on the usage of KG Embeddings or KGEs, that are low-dimensional vector representations of nodes and edges in the KG. KGEs can enable ML algorithms to operate on the KGs more efficiently but they have known drawbacks such as lack of interpretability, biased results (especially for rare entities) and limited support to KG updates. We also note that there are in literature RL methods that can use semantics relations, such as those in the KG, these techniques are often general-purpose and their effectiveness in vertical domains is still under investigation. In this paper, we discuss advantages that KGs may bring to RL in the most general setting, without solely restricting to the use of KGEs. In fact, some of the opportunities outlined in Sect. 3 might rule out the use of KDEs, requiring a transparent, unbiased and continuous access to the evolving KG.

3   Using KGs for Solving RL Tasks

We envision that KGs can provide the necessary domain-specific knowledge with minimal or no human intervention. At a high level such system comprises three blocks: a RL model, a KG, and an intermediate block to facilitate communication between the RL model and the KG. More specifically, if the KG is stored in a graph database, the intermediate block would translate the queries from the RL model into graph database queries (e.g. SPARQL). For instance, when processing the pair of records in Fig. 1, the RL model can submit to the intermediate block values of non-matching attributes, e.g., "Rifampin" and "Isoniazid" and "Duke University Hospital" and "Durham Regional Hospital". Then the block, by querying the KG can return paths connecting related entities such as $\{\langle$Durham University Hospital, Uses, Rifampin$\rangle, \quad \langle$Durham University Hospital, Uses, Isoniazid$\rangle\}$ and the singleton path $\{\langle$Durham University Hospital, has branch, Durham Regional$\rangle\}$. Finally, paths can be used in the RL model for learning similarities in vertical application. We now discuss opportunities (OPs) and challenges (CHs) in this setting.

OP1: Improving Accuracy. In our example, without domain-specific knowledge, patient records with different date, time, hospital name and treatment could be erroneously classified as non-match. Human experts are currently required to add specific rules to prevents such mismatches. However, a KG such as the one in Fig. 2 could provide additional information on hospital structure and therapies to identify that both records refer to the same patient. Many domain-specific KG are already available (e.g. the PyKEEN repository https://github.com/pykeen/pykeen) and more are coming thanks to recent progresses in the fields of automatic KG construction and completion [14].

CH1: The main challenges are (i) mapping values of records (e.g., an hospital name) to entities in the KG and (ii) learning which relations are relevant to the linkage process (e.g., analogies of treatments and branching of hospitals)

OP2: Data Augmentation. State-of-the-art techniques for RL are predominantly based on Deep Neural Networks. While these methods have demonstrated remarkable performance in practice, they can be as good as the labelled data fed to them. Unfortunately, manually acquiring enough non-trivial labelled data in vertical applications can be prohibitively expensive. Synthetic data generation and dataset augmentation techniques are often used in such scenarios [1] but they can yield non-realistic entries if not properly guided by domain knowledge. To address this issue, after identifying which relations are relevant to the linkage process, domain-specific KGs can be used to perturb available labelled data while preserving their semantics. For instance, one specific treatment could be replaced with an analogous one, and lab results could be generated by taking into account a coherent set of medical conditions.

CH2: The completeness and quality of the KG is critical, as incomplete information can lead to unrealistic synthetic data. Moreover the generated synthetic data may be too specific and as a result, the RL model may not be able to generalize well to new scenarios.

OP3: Temporal Variability. One important aspect of real-world data is its continuous evolution over time. For example, in the healthcare sector, patient data can change constantly due to various factors such as new treatments, hospitalisations, and the development of new medical conditions. Temporal Record Linkage (TRL) is a variant of the traditional RL problem aimed at linking records over time [5] such as the same patient across decades. Most methods for TRL are based on a time decay function that aims at capturing the effect of time elapsing on value evolution for the records. For instance, let us consider the records in Fig. 1 and let us assume the existence of a third, older record referring to the same patient but with a lower age value. In this case, a TRL approach would assign a lower importance to the age feature of the third record when attempting to match the entries in Fig. 1. Domain-specific temporal KGs [3] may provide a more robust solution for the TRL task as these KGs are explicitly designed to incorporate the temporal axis in the graph structure. By using these KGs, the accuracy of the RL algorithms might significantly improve.

CH3: Research challenges include discovering relevant time-sensitive relations without human intervention (e.g. the age feature in the previous example) and properly weighting such time-sensitive features during the RL task based on their update frequency and their history in the temporal KG.

OP4: Multiple Modalities: Most RL methods are focused on a single modality, such as textual data. However there is a significant lack of work on Multimodal RL (MRL), i.e. a variant of the RL problem where records comprise different modalities, which is often crucial in vertical applications, such as our healthcare case study, where tabular, text and image data coexist. The most recent MRL work we are aware of is [12], dealing with pairs of records containing text in one source and images on the other. On the other hand, there are several works on handling different modalities in the KG community, spanning from building a multimodal KG [4] to multimodal KG representation learning [8]. Incorporating these multimodal techniques from the KG community might foster the development of novel MRL approaches.

CH4: In this context a major barrier is designing methods at the intermediate block level that conveniently translates the multimodal values in the RL records for querying the (possibly) multimodal KG.

OP5: Explainability: The growing trend of devising and implementing large ML models for RL tasks has brought significant improvement in accuracy at the cost of transparency, which can prevent their application in healthcare and other critical decision-making domains, such as finance and government. Existing methods to explain RL results, such as [15], aims at mitigating RL opacity. Unfortunately their results are limited to either the record pair at hand or an additional subset of the dataset used to train the RL model. For instance, let us consider the toy example in Fig. 1 and assume we have an accurate model for RL that predicts these two records to be a matching pair. An explainability framework might unveil that those two records are matching due to the name, surname, treatment and hospital name features. However, it might be unclear why the hospital name is such a relevant feature for the matching outcome. In this context, using a KG from the same domain as the RL task (e.g. the KG in Fig. 2) can potentially give access to a broader set of contextual data that can be used to design more effective and intuitive explanations.

CH5: Challenges include identifying relevant information in the KG to help explaining the RL prediction as well as developing algorithms to automatically extract relevant information from the KG and integrate it with the RL model.

4   Concluding Remarks

In this paper we discussed how exploiting Knowledge Graphs for Record Linkage in vertical applications can bring several advantages for specific, vertical domains, such as healthcare, and explored the main benefits of such integration. We believe that KGs may empower RL task by improving their accuracy while reducing effort of human experts, providing high-quality training data for RL algorithms, improving the handling of temporally-changing features and multimodal data and finally potentially provide better explanation for the predictions made by ML based RL models. We also identified the main challenges when pursuing application of domain-specific KGs to RL. We leave the investigation of such challenges to a future work.

Acknowledgments. This work was partly supported by the SEED PNR 2021 grant FLOWER, Sapienza Research Project B83C22007180001, the European Union Next-Generation EU (PIANO NAZIONALE DI RIPRESA E RESILIENZA (PNRR) – MISSIONE 4 COMPONENTE 2 initiative "Future Artificial Intelligence Research" – FAIR and the Horizon 2020 project 857420 DESTINI. Jerin George Mathew is financed by the Italian National PhD Program in AI.

References

1. Ebraheem, M., Thirumuruganathan, S., Joty, S., Ouzzani, M., Tang, N.: Distributed representations of tuples for entity resolution. PVLDB **11**(11), 1454–1467 (2018)
2. Gautam, B., Terrades, O.R., Pujadas-Mora, J.M., Valls, M.: Knowledge graph based methods for record linkage. Pattern Recogn. Lett. **136**, 127–133 (2020)
3. Ji, S., et al.: A survey on knowledge graphs: representation, acquisition, and applications. IEEE Trans. Neural Networks Learn. Syst. (2021)
4. Kannan, A.V., et al.: Multimodal knowledge graph for deep learning papers and code. In: CIKM, pp. 3417–3420 (2020)
5. Li, P., et al.: Linking temporal records. PVLDB **4**(11), 956–967 (2011)
6. Li, Y., Li, J., Suhara, Y., Doan, A., Tan, W.C.: Deep entity matching with pre-trained language models. PVLDB **14**(1), 50–60 (2020)

7. Maccioni, A., Torlone, R.: KAYAK: a framework for just-in-time data preparation in a data lake. In: Krogstie, J., Reijers, H.A. (eds.) CAiSE 2018. LNCS, vol. 10816, pp. 474–489. Springer, Cham (2018). https://doi.org/10.1007/978-3-319-91563-0_29

8. Mousselly-Sergieh, H., Botschen, T., Gurevych, I., Roth, S.: A multimodal translation-based approach for knowledge graph representation learning. In: *SEM, pp. 225–234 (2018)

9. Obraczka, D., Schuchart, J., Rahm, E.: Embedding-assisted entity resolution for knowledge graphs. In: Second International Workshop on Knowledge Graph Construction (2021)

10. Pujara, J., Getoor, L.: Generic statistical relational entity resolution in knowledge graphs. arXiv preprint arXiv:1607.00992 (2016)

11. Saeedi, A., Peukert, E., Rahm, E.: Incremental multi-source entity resolution for knowledge graph completion. In: Harth, A., Kirrane, S., Ngonga Ngomo, A.-C., Paulheim, H., Rula, A., Gentile, A.L., Haase, P., Cochez, M. (eds.) ESWC 2020. LNCS, vol. 12123, pp. 393–408. Springer, Cham (2020). https://doi.org/10.1007/978-3-030-49461-2_23

12. Sarkhel, R., Nandi, A.: Cross-modal entity matching for visually rich documents. arXiv preprint arXiv:2303.00720 (2023)

13. Steorts, R.C.: Entity resolution with empirically motivated priors. Bayesian Anal. 10(4), 849–875 (2015)

14. Sun, Z., Vashishth, S., Sanyal, S., Talukdar, P., Yang, Y.: A re-evaluation of knowledge graph completion methods. In: ACL, pp. 5516–5522 (2020)

15. Teofili, T., Firmani, D., Koudas, N., Martello, V., Merialdo, P., Srivastava, D.: Effective explanations for entity resolution models. In: ICDE, pp. 2709–2721. IEEE (2022)

Employing Knowledge Graphs for Capturing Semantic Aspects of Robotic Process Automation

Ștefan Uifălean[(⊠)]

Babeș-Bolyai University, Cluj-Napoca, Romania
stefan.uifalean@stud.ubbcluj.ro

Abstract. The demand of automating mundane user tasks in business processes has been accelerated recently. There's a growing interest in making Robotic Process Automation more intelligent by embedding richer explicit knowledge in robotic reasoning and User Experience procedural knowledge can become a key enabler for this. The paper reports on a Design Science Research project introducing Knowledge Graphs to connect User Experience processes with contextual resources from enterprise repositories in order to feed procedural bots.

This paper addresses a need to manage procedural knowledge pertaining to the User Experience that must be mimicked in RPA projects. It does this by capturing and exploiting semantic links of front-end usage processes across a semantic repository of such processes. This is deployed as a demonstrator that introduces an intermediary navigation layer over an RDF graph persisted from an RPA-focused UX diagrammatic language that operates very close to the business domain. The demonstrator highlights the benefits of a semantic graph view on User Experience and the associated context. It simulates the robotic process of realizing a task where UI elements, external files and programs need to be called during process execution therefore they must be traceable from User Experience steps. Linking the visual appearance of GUI elements and file/data resources as knowledge for procedural execution turns this into a domain-specific process modeling and management approach.

Keywords: Resource Description Framework · Domain-Specific Modeling · Model-Driven Software Engineering · Process Queries · User Experience

1 Introduction

The paper reports on a Design Science project led by a Software Outsourcing enterprise seeking a process automation solution for repetitive tasks in internal systems. Semantic technology and its governing standards, such as RDF [1] and SPARQL [2], have been adopted to bridge the gap between internal process descriptions and their metainformation to improve the organization's efficiency with some administrative tasks. This is intended to reduce manual operations by means of automating processes in a context-aware manner facilitated by a Knowledge Graph strategy. A model-driven navigator API informs automation steps orchestration and, in the long run, aims to increase in-house interoperability of tools and data sources through an approach that mixes low-code process automation and User Experience semantics.

M. Ruiz and P. Soffer (Eds.): CAiSE 2023 Workshops, LNBIP 482, pp. 152–162, 2023.
https://doi.org/10.1007/978-3-031-34985-0_16

An early vision of this was originally presented as a poster at ISD 2022 [3], where a metamodel of User Experience linked to usage resources was introduced. It formulated a project-specific, non-standard treatment to representing Robotic Process Automation (RPA) / User Experience (UX) process models utilizing the RDF format. The DSR iteration at the core of this paper adds a demonstrator and an API capturing semantic aspects of those models to inform automation and analytical scenarios with a particular flavor of model-driven engineering. Procedural usage knowledge is stored in a GraphDB [4] triplestore using SPARQL for navigation and retrieval of front-end UI elements and resources. The demonstrator was deployed as a front-end fed by Spring Boot services to facilitate visual UX graph navigation in concordance with the custom metamodel, also leveraging linking to execution resources.

Consequently, the demonstrator offers a "process stepper" based on knowledge centered around competency questions of business relevance that accompanies a basic forward-backward process navigation. Considering a multi-process repository of such graphs, analytics can help assess the impact of a UX step or (file) resource in the whole organization across multiple UX process models intended to be automated by RPA. In addition to the traceability-enabled navigation, rule-based reasoning semantically enriches the modelled UX for purposes pertaining to the Knowledge Management needs of RPA projects. Centers of Excellence raise these needs as they monitor entire project lifecycle, requiring an integrative image of the automation portfolio in the enterprise context, since relying on commercial tools for RPA knowledge is not always feasible [5]. Live visual feedback from the linked sub-diagram of User Experience thus bridges a gap between RPA and Knowledge Management. This came as a requirement during the design cycle, as the other project teams that analyzed SotA automation software observed a deficiency: they deploy an RPA workflow of clicks and UI actions without contextualizing it and enabling design-time simulation or off-line analysis.

The remainder of the article is organized in accordance with the Design Science framework [6]: Sect. 2 discusses related research, Sect. 3 investigates the problem, defining objectives and outlining the treatment architecture. Section 4 includes design and implementation details for the suggested treatment and Sect. 5 shows some demonstration scenarios. Current assessment is confined to query-based competence, with a technical evaluation derived in Sect. 6. Conclusions end the paper.

2   Related Work

In previous work [7] a skeleton traversal app was introduced driven by Neo4J representation of BPMN. This time, we employ RDF graphs for navigating software GUI and retrieving knowledge assets attached to its operational workflows that add some UX domain specificity to BPMN. Hence, the present treatment solution follows the Model-Aware Engineering approach, which represents Software Engineering guided by querying models using RDF [8]. This is an engineering approach built around the Agile Modeling Method Engineering (AMME) framework discussed in [9], to which we also align the hereby presented visual modeling method. This is to induce flexibility about semantics of models as requirements evolve.

Early thoughts towards semantic business process management [10] revolved around the semantics of services utilized by processes. Since then, the need for tweaking standard procedural description modeling languages for knowledge representation has gained more support from the conceptual modeling community; see also [11] for on-the-fly ontology-based semantic augmentation of BPMN elements and [12] concerning the topic of semantic process modeling for ontology-aided BPMN and EPC modeling. Challenges of capturing domain-specific semantic aspects in [13] report queries on LPG to inform and provide semantical enrichment of systems medicine experimental data to benefit the patient. Analogous, we inform software and management by integrating business and UI descriptive data which is less volatile. More recently, [14] showed a process-aware application of BPMN models, transforming a surgery procedure into a checklist displayed in a dynamic HTML website. This also employs contextual knowledge from formal process descriptions.

The work of [15] summarizes the State of the Art in RPA tools – flows are stored and interpreted by an engine at execution time to eliminate human-computer interaction, replacing it with human-bot-computer interaction. Human-bot cooperation takes human reasoning and input into account as reported in [16] to trigger a multi-agent system which uses BPMN and Java to orchestrate robotic execution. This idea recently coined the term Hybrid Intelligence [17] - a key ingredient of the project's vision of producing both knowledge made available to human stakeholders and knowledge for knowledge-intensive bots/execution engines.

The problem of heterogeneity in the way RPA vendors define their system is addressed in [18] by presenting a common ontology that reunites all different names given to workflow components (based on previous [19] taxonomy) and procedures with the same objective but marketed differently. We overcome the interoperability issue by creating a software driving model base from the raw RPA flow enriched with UX and organizational semantics. The proposal of similarity search in [20] addresses the Knowledge Management scenario, inspiring future research on our behalf to discover common patterns in company RPA procedures and how User Experience influences over-all enterprise tasks efficiency. Authors of [21] state how AI techniques on existing RPA tools can induce improvement of operational and business processes of organizations, something that we currently achieve through rule-based reasoning over the Knowledge Graph. By integrating an RPA-based framework custom to knowledge flows in projects with a project management ontology the work in [22] highlights a bidirectional positive enhancement between automations and Knowledge Management in specific projects.

3 Problem Context, Statement and Treatment

Commercial solutions for RPA (either front or back-end) focus mostly on the recorded or emulated flow of user actions. Moreover, their interoperability is reduced since their workflow representation is not aligned to a standard like BPEL [23] for example, and force the user to stay in their ecosystem. Such execution flows can become part of an encompassing organizational knowledge graph to support novel Knowledge Management approaches, including assessing the criticality of usage procedures and digital resources used in the overall enterprise's automated capabilities.

Design Science Research addresses artifacts in context [6]. The company running this project contains a Service Desk business unit outsourced to serve customers having issues with various software. Along with other departments, they use internal tools that work with multiple data stores and host know-how or specific resources in textual form. An exemplary scenario is the administrative work of recording new job openings in their proprietary Project Management tool, a mundane task that needs to be done each time a new vacancy arises. From this scenario the demonstrator addressees the following requirements:

- To model contextual knowledge around an RPA flow in a domain-specific process modeling approach, considering the resources on which execution relies;
- To store this model in a serialized form that resembles the original graph form; the RDF version of diagram is obtained through a tool resulting from research in [24] and stored in a GraphDB repository;
- To enable the engineering of a semantic process execution engine driven by RPA/UX models; we developed an API to abstract such models at run-time;
- To use the enterprise's model base for informing Risk Management / Knowledge Management via semantic (SPARQL) queries;
- To induce flexibility such that the solution manifests agility to changing requirements; this is achieved by employing the AMME [9] framework.

The client company would spend too much time to craft such recorded scripts for each particular RPA scenario, and wants to leverage the User Experience knowledge that would be needed by an Intelligent software bot. Graph representations of RPA procedures should also take into consideration the user experience modifications on the screen while performing the UI-based task, as the company believes that common patterns in UX design can later become input for graph-based machine learning.

4   Treatment Design and Implementation

Figure 1 depicts the domain-specific metamodel to which the further abstracted Java class hierarchy for the demonstrator run-time adheres. The metamodel's classification of tasks carried on the UI of general software was derived from exemplary transcripts of recorded usage flows: the first was a video walkthrough of Add New Role task in enterprise's proprietary project management web app, and later a complex activity centered around creating a new channel in Microsoft Teams. This may have to be extended with the help of AMME in future iterations.

Nodes in a model can be instances of supertype Workflow, Resource or UI. *WorkflowElements* are chained into an RPA logically delimited flow/sub-diagram. Connecting them, edges from *ResourceElements* represent formal semantics of RPA step dependencies. Our Graph API layer instantiates objects from these two hierarchies. *UIElement* concepts forming UX chain provide semantic inference support through SPARQL queries, holding metainformation (*that current tools lack*) about graphical morphing of the GUI layout context) in which a robotic process execution is carried.

Of the RDF serialization file from exported model, only the properties/data exclusively relevant to the RPA/UX domain enter the instantiation of Java objects (filtered by the schema in Fig. 1). Every instance of a concept that is a Resource in database plane becomes a Node object in Java, but only a filtered amount of its properties out of

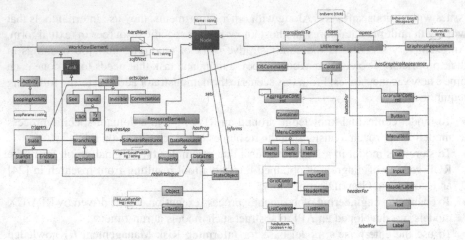

Fig. 1. Metamodel of Java mapping (Graph schema)

the triples that intersect those defined in the metamodel are attached as its fields. Every relation simple or complex (with embedded properties) gets its own Java object instance of the specific type from the metamodel and embeds two fields for source and target Nodes. To cover this separation an API method to get collections of relations based on a reference node at either side of them has been developed.

We designed a demonstrator module, NetworkPlotter, to generate a directed graph from a selection of triples in the RPA sub-flow, starting from a root node and going depth-first using a specified depth. Using the intermediary layer it makes recursive queries to model's RDF serialization in GraphDB constructing a network rendered via *VisJS* [25] front-end library.

The graph-driven traversal demonstrator's operation flow commences by calling an endpoint that fits a description of an RPA flow sub-diagram StartState (similar to a BPMN event). Using this reference node, the application launches a "node browsing session" phase. At each step during model navigation, the app renders characteristics of current UX step and its adjacent context - both inbound and outbound connections from/to RPA sub-diagram extracted concept instances. They are retrieved through SPARQL queries and mapped using the LPG-like abstraction layer to the following implemented types: workflow (Task, State, Branch) and resource (Software or external Data). The state of navigation is changed by accessing a hyperlink pointing to a proximal Node entity, then rendering template detailed previously is reloaded with information retrieved through the Middleware regarding the new node. This traversal, thus, happens in a loop and the user interacts explicitly with the app.

After implementation evaluation of several DSR cycles we found that simply focusing on next/previous connections is a generalist graph scenario blind to the semantic richness of knowledge captured in a network of UX models. Three new prompts have been included in the *Knowledge* panel of existing Graph Traversal Simulator. One exploits a SPARQL proximity query by retrieving the URI property locating a file required by an Action, and another analogous for retrieving the path of a program that needs to be called during flow execution. Lastly, a semantical deduction for rendering a picture of the UI appearance of the element targeted by an Action. If a particular procedure step is found to bear business-relevant knowledge, this semantic enhancing of the user experience is produced through addition of a panel to the DOM. It informs the user about the file or screenshot dependency and allows to click a button that will make an Operating System call to open the file for him/her or render the image in parallel with the process state description.

Our Java API's primary service methods fetch either a node with properties or all relationships of a reference node while interacting with the graph database and the front-end representation. The middleware is a Spring Boot Java implementation of an MVC architecture, with a Data Access Layer (DAL) for GraphDB communication and utility methods adapting underlying triple store retrieved results into a specific Object-Oriented pseudo-LPG view. Thymeleaf Views power front-end rendering.

5 Demonstration Scenario

Figure 2 shows the RPA/UX model before and after the RDF transformation. It depicts the scenario where a company worker registers a new opening in their internal Project Management tool. Following instructions in the left-side model implies interactions with UI/UX elements also visible in the diagram. Activity microflows named "Get to Projects" and "Get to project" help the user reach a listing of projects managed by the company, assisted by a cognitive See Action inside former Activity to discover the submenu containing it. Consequently, the user can select the specific project on which the new role will open. Lack of strictness in step succession is differentiated by using *softNext* relation (which means that the order was observed/preferred) instead of *hardNext* (which means that the order is imposed).

The atomic Action of the later Activity, "(Click) _p_projectName", provides an instruction for an execution engine to replace a parameter at run-time with the actual name of the project and access the specific entry from the "Project Name List". This last UIElement is depicted in the visual model, connected by the *actsUpon* relation.

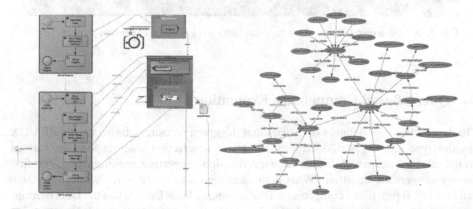

Fig. 2. UX process model and resources (left) and the RDF version for a fragment of it (right)

Preserved in RDF form are properties of concepts, a typical one used in ADOxx [26]-sourced metamodels being *ns0:name* for concept label. Depicted Activity instances are, in hierarchical order given by the flow direction: "Get to Projects" - > "Get to project" - > "Get to team". The containment relation is platform-induced without drawing it, depicted using RDF predicate *ns0:Is_inside*, as for "Visible project grid" and "(See) Projects grid". These are StartState and Action concepts connected through said property towards their parent microflow described by IRI:Activity-55278 and name "Get to project".

The front-end demonstrator is depicted in Fig. 3. Left side shows the process stepper demo gradually revealing each step of the process with its immediate context (nodes, required resources, etc.). Some additionally inferred information is isolated in the right panel – namely dependencies in the form of a rendered screenshot and locally opening text file or program. Screenshots of GraphTraversal component simulations have been taken in various steps of the model traversal. For node accessed in top-left side, the entire taxonomy is concatenated in the first heading. The process reached a Task of type LoopingActivity named "Loop _p_fields" mentioning "all fields" and requiring a local file containing a model serialization. Taking the bottom-left sided resource, there exist 4 child nodes that have an Is_inside connection. Using the links under Access column the user navigates to pointed node, thus changing the state of the traversal context.

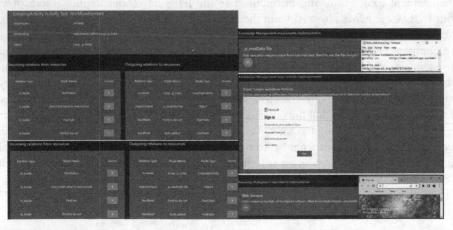

Fig. 3. Model-driven UI app graph traversal (left) and simulated execution prompts (right)

6   Query-Based Competence Evaluation

To demonstrate the richness of queries that the graph repository based on the RPA/UX model type can support, Table 1 illustrates a selection that respond to various retrieval, traversal and business-oriented decision-supporting requirements. The first query answers the question "What is the description of the resource with given name and type?". It provides a competent way of managing knowledge when the label descriptor is known, e.g. in the context of a Center of Excellence where a particular resource has to be put under lens to begin with the navigation analysis. We employ it in our demonstrator to answer the requirement of traversing the RPA flow by parameterizing it to seek the node marking the starting event of the robotic process (bearing fixed name across models). The second query feeds proximity graph navigation, since the demonstrator front-end links to Node instances in the model repository based on their IRI. Thus, it answers the question "What is the description of the resource uniquely described by given id?". In the third row a parameterized query retrieves only the statements that represent a property relation to another resource, based on source node. It feeds a query construction method in the Graph API filter that is applied at run-time that checks the provided direction of the reference resource (is it the source or the target of a simple relation). These first three queries address the requirement of adapting to the volatility in project requirements by building an abstraction layer framework that would minimize the need to rewrite SPARQL queries and replace them with pure high-level imperative language. They are used in the top-level interfacing methods.

The last query answers the question"What does the UI element on which an RPA Action operates look like?". The result is the value of an attribute set at modeling-time (a resource identified either locally to modeler's machine or remotely). This addresses the requirement of having traceable resources on which process execution relies for further project management within an RPA Center of Excellence. In current iteration of the treatment, it enhances the user's visual experience of the process traversal front-end demonstrator.

Table 1. Examples of model-enabled queries

Query explanation	Example SPARQL definition	Run-time benchmark
Find resource that has input **type and label**; retrieve the **triples** in which it is a subject (For Concepts)	PREFIX rdf: <http://www.w3.org/1999/02/22-rdf-syntax-ns#> PREFIX ns0: <http://www.taskmate.eu/mm#> select * where { ?iri rdf:type ns0:StartState . ?iri ns0:Name "Started flow" . ?iri ?p ?o . }	150ms
Find resource with input **IRI**; get the **triples** in which it is a subject (For Concepts and Relations)	PREFIX : <http://www.taskmate.eu/ewaanr#> SELECT * WHERE { ?iri ?p ?o . FILTER (?iri = :hardNext-30027-Keep-Type__p_field_value) . }	130ms
Find outwards-directed **simple Relation** where identifier of **source** resource **node** is known	PREFIX : <http://www.taskmate.eu/teamsv2#> PREFIX rdf: <http://www.w3.org/1999/02/22-rdf-syntax-ns#> PREFIX cv: <http://www.comvantage.eu/mm#> SELECT * WHERE { ?outgoingNodeIri ?propRelIri ?incomingNodeIri . FILTER (?outgoingNodeIri = :Action-43292-Access_Teams_app) . # Required Semantic filtering to keep only prop outgoing relations # Subject has IRI - guaranteed in an RDF statement, verify object # Double assert that object is an IRI and an instance of a concept FILTER (EXISTS {?incomingNodeIri rdf:type rc:Instance_class}) .	117ms
For **Action id**, find affected **UIElement**, retrieve **picture** location if defined UX appearance	PREFIX : <http://www.taskmate.eu/ewaanr#> PREFIX ns0: <http://www.taskmate.eu/mm#> SELECT ?PictureURI WHERE { ?actionIri ns0:actsUpon/ns0:hasGraphicalAppearance/ns0:PictureURI ?PictureURI . FILTER (?actionIri = :Action-26404-See_Login_window) . }	170ms

7   Conclusion

The paper reports on a Design Science project where an API and front-end navigator were built to empower knowledge navigation based on visual models capturing User Experience represented to the level of granularity needed by RPA projects. This solves limits of commercial RPA ecosystems by permitting processes to link with metainformation pertaining to execution environment and potentially expanding to enterprise ontologies. It addresses a project-specific requirement of using knowledge graphs to facilitate UX analytics and infer common microflows so that enterprises can minimize the time spent to create and adapt workflows for their administrative internal tools. The intermediary mapping over the Knowledge Graph permits lower-code customizing of model-driven software that integrate resources and know-how private to the company with agility to requirements change in mind.

In future DSR iterations there remains to develop an automation engine that navigates GUIs according to this visual description and uses semantically connected resources to parameterize and inform the execution and a chatbot governing it. As per [27] none of the RPA engines available on the market provide a form of Automated Reasoning, which is enabled by our tool through the management of diagrammatic models on an RDF graph repository.

Acknowledgements. The presented work has received financial support through the project: Integrated system for automating business processes using artificial intelligence, POC/163/1/3/121075 - a Project Cofinanced by the European Regional Development Fund (ERDF) through the Competitiveness Operational Programme 2014–2020.

References

1. RDF 1.1 Semantics. https://www.w3.org/TR/2014/REC-rdf11-mt-20140225/ last (Accessed 14 March 2023)
2. SPARQL 1.1 Query Language. https://www.w3.org/TR/2013/REC-sparql11-query-201 30321/ last (Accessed 13 June 2022)
3. Uifălean, Ş., Ghiran, A.-M., Buchmann, R.A.: User experience modeling method for a vision of knowledge graph-based process automation. In: Proceedings of the 30th International Conference on Information Systems Development (ISD2022). Association for Information Systems (AIS) eLibrary (2022). https://aisel.aisnet.org/isd2014/proceedings2022/kno wledge/12
4. GraphDB by Ontotext. https://graphdb.ontotext.com/ last (Accessed 10 June 2022)
5. Hartikainen, E., Hotti, V., Tukiainen, M.: Improving software robot maintenance in large-scale environments–is center of excellence a solution? IEEE Access **10**, 96760–96773 (2022). https://doi.org/10.1109/ACCESS.2022.3205420
6. Wieringa, R.J.: Design Science Methodology for Information Systems and Software Engineering. Springer Berlin Heidelberg (2014). https://doi.org/10.1007/978-3-662-43839-8
7. Uifălean, Ş., Ghiran, A.-M., Buchmann, R.A.: From BPMN models to labelled property graphs. In: Proceedings of the 30th International Conference on Information Systems Development (ISD2022). Association for Information Systems (AIS) eLibrary (2022). https://aisel. aisnet.org/isd2014/proceedings2022/knowledge/2

8. Buchmann, R.A., Cinpoeru, M., Harkai, A., Karagiannis, D.: Model-aware software engineering - a knowledge-based approach to model-driven software engineering: In: Proceedings of the 13th International Conference on Evaluation of Novel Approaches to Software Engineering, pp. 233–240. ScitePress (2018). https://doi.org/10.5220/0006694102330240
9. Buchmann, R.A., Karagiannis, D.: Agile modelling method engineering: lessons learned in the ComVantage research project. In: Ralyté, J., España, S., Pastor, Ó. (eds.) The Practice of Enterprise Modeling. Lecture Notes in Business Information Processing, vol. 235, pp. 356–373. Springer, Cham (2015). https://doi.org/10.1007/978-3-319-25897-3_23
10. Hepp, M., Leymann, F., Domingue, J., Wahler, A., Fensel, D.: Semantic business process management: a vision towards using semantic Web services for business process management. In: IEEE International Conference on e-Business Engineering (ICEBE 2005), pp. 535–540. IEEE (2005). https://doi.org/10.1109/ICEBE.2005.110
11. Laurenzi, E., Hinkelmann, K., van der Merwe, A.: An agile and ontology-aided modeling environment. In: Buchmann, R.A., Karagiannis, D., Kirikova, M. (eds.) PoEM 2018. LNBIP, vol. 335, pp. 221–237. Springer, Cham (2018). https://doi.org/10.1007/978-3-030-02302-7_14
12. Thomas, O., Fellmann M.A., M.: Semantic process modeling – design and implementation of an ontology-based representation of business processes. Bus. Inf. Syst. Eng. 1, 438–451 (2009). https://doi.org/10.1007/s12599-009-0078-8
13. Lysenko, A., Roznovăț, I.A., Saqi, M., Mazein, A., Rawlings, C.J., Auffray, C.: Representing and querying disease networks using graph databases. BioData Mining. 9, 23 (2016). https://doi.org/10.1186/s13040-016-0102-8
14. Ryniak, C., Burgert, O.: Automatic generation of checklists from business process model and notation (BPMN) models for surgical assist systems. Current Direct. Biomed. Eng. 6 (2020). https://doi.org/10.1515/cdbme-2020-0005
15. van der Aalst, W.M.P., Bichler, M., Heinzl, A.: Robotic process automation. Bus. Inf. Syst. Eng. 60(4), 269–272 (2018). https://doi.org/10.1007/s12599-018-0542-4
16. Sadik, A.R., Goerick, C., Muehlig, M.: Modeling and simulation of a multi-robot system architecture. In: 2019 International Conference on Mechatronics, Robotics and Systems Engineering (MoRSE). pp. 8–14. IEEE (2019). https://doi.org/10.1109/MoRSE48060.2019.8998662
17. Dellermann, D., Ebel, P., Söllner, M., Leimeister, J.M.: Hybrid intelligence. Bus. Inf. Syst. Eng. 61(5), 637–643 (2019). https://doi.org/10.1007/s12599-019-00595-2
18. Völker, M., Weske, M.: Conceptualizing bots in robotic process automation. In: Ghose, A., Horkoff, J., Silva Souza, V.E., Parsons, J., Evermann, J. (eds.) ER 2021. LNCS, vol. 13011, pp. 3–13. Springer, Cham (2021). https://doi.org/10.1007/978-3-030-89022-3_1
19. Martínez-Rojas, A., Barba, I., Enríquez, J.G.: Towards a taxonomy of cognitive RPA components. In: Asatiani, A., et al. (eds.) BPM 2020. LNBIP, vol. 393, pp. 161–175. Springer, Cham (2020). https://doi.org/10.1007/978-3-030-58779-6_11
20. Dijkman, R.M., Dumas, M., García-Bañuelos, L.: Business process graphs : similarity search and matching. In: Sakr, A. and Pardede, E. (eds.) Graph Data Management: Techniques and Applications. pp. 421–439. IGI Global (2011). https://www.igi-global.com/gateway/chapter/www.igi-global.com/gateway/chapter/58621
21. Ribeiro, J., Lima, R., Eckhardt, T., Paiva, S.: Robotic process automation and artificial intelligence in industry 4.0 – A literature review. Proc. Comput. Sci. 181, 51–58 (2021). https://doi.org/10.1016/j.procs.2021.01.104
22. Koch, O., Buchkremer, R., Kneisel, E.: Graph databases and robotic process automation: achieving improvement in project knowledge management. In: BLED 2020 Proceedings. (2020). https://aisel.aisnet.org/bled2020/31
23. Web Services Business Process Execution Language. http://docs.oasis-open.org/wsbpel/2.0/wsbpel-v2.0.html last (Accessed 19 April 2023)

24. Karagiannis, D., Buchmann, R.A.: A Proposal for Deploying Hybrid Knowledge Bases: the ADOxx-to-GraphDB Interoperability Case. In: Proceedings of the 51st Hawaii International Conference on System Sciences. pp. 4055–4064 (2018). https://doi.org/10.24251/HICSS.2018.510
25. vis.js - A dynamic, browser based visualization library. https://visjs.org/ last (Accessed 04 Oct 2022)
26. ADOxx Metamodelling Platform (2023). https://www.omilab.org/adoxx/ (2023) (Accessed 14 Mar 2023)
27. Viehhauser, J.: Is Robotic process automation becoming intelligent? early evidence of influences of artificial intelligence on robotic Process automation. In: Asatiani, A., et al. (eds.) BPM 2020. LNBIP, vol. 393, pp. 101–115. Springer, Cham (2020). https://doi.org/10.1007/978-3-030-58779-6_7

BC4IS and DGD

International Workshop on Blockchain and Decentralized Governance Design for Information Systems (BC4IS'23 and DGD'23)

CAiSE has a long history of research into advanced computer systems. As such, the CAiSE community recognizes the emergence of the Decentralized Web 3.0, and acknowledges that this development goes hand in hand with Blockchain and Decentralized Governance Design. Decentralized Web 3.0 is the next evolutionary step of the internet, and it is defined by focus on end-user sovereignty, which is expressed in decentralized design, which can be achieved through several advanced computer systems and technology such as blockchain. With the introduction of blockchain technology we entered the age of computational trust, in which network regulation is possible without a centralized party. Without a centralized actor, a self-organizing ecosystem requires a decentralized design approach; we refer to that as Decentralized Governance Design. Decentralized web 3.0 requires an innovative and computational approach in developing computer systems that will align with blockchain technology architectures. Blockchain technology offers a wide variety of opportunities to enable new kinds of collaborations and organizations, and to improve existing ones. Engineering blockchain-based systems is a task that is particularly complex, and that requires specific considerations, along with more traditional information systems engineering questions. In this context, research around the definition of requirements for, development, use and evolution of blockchain-based information systems is particularly relevant.

The workshop "Blockchain and Decentralized Governance Design for Information Systems" (BC4IS and DGD) featured a Keynote on the topic of blockchain by Felix Härer. This was followed by a session with two papers on the topic of Blockchain Governance Modeling: "Blockchain Governance Design - A Computer Science Perspective", "The MEV Saga: Can Regulation Illuminate the Dark Forest?", and the PhD Presentation by Fadime Kaya "A first view on DECENT a domain specific language to design Blockchain governance". In addition, there was a session on Blockchain for Information Systems, in which the paper "Regulation-Friendly Privacy-Preserving Blockchain Based on zk-SNARK" was presented.

June 2023

Victor Amaral de Sousa
Sarah Bouraga
Corentin Burnay
Geert Poels
Yves Wautelet
Jaap Gordijn
Fadime Kaya

Organization

BC4IS Workshop Co-chairs

Sarah Bouraga	University of Namur, Belgium
Victor Amaral de Sousa	University of Namur, Belgium
Corentin Burnay	University of Namur, Belgium

BC4IS Workshop Steering Committee

Monique Snoeck	KU Leuven, Belgium
Stéphane Faulkner	University of Namur, Belgium
Wim Laurier	University of Saint-Louis - Brussels, Belgium

BC4IS Workshop Program Committee

Michael Adams	Queensland University of Technology, Australia
Antoine Clarinval	University of Namur, Belgium
Jean-Noël Colin	University of Namur, Belgium
Ghareeb Falazi	University of Stuttgart, Germany
Felix Härer	University of Fribourg, Switzerland
Nicolas Herbaut	University Paris 1 Panthéon-Sorbonne, France
Giovanni Meroni	Technical University of Denmark, Denmark
Georgios Palaiokrassas	Yale University, USA
Pierluigi Plebani	Politecnico di Milano, Italy
Anthony Simonofski	University of Namur, Belgium
Christian Sturm	University of Bayreuth, Germany

DGD Workshop Co-chairs

Geert Poels	Ghent Universiteit, Belgium
Yves Wautelet	KU Leuven, Belgium
Jaap Gordijn	Vrije Universiteit Amsterdam, The Netherlands
Fadime Kaya	Vrije Universiteit Amsterdam, The Netherlands

DGD Workshop Program Committee

Bryant Gilot	University of Tübingen, Germany
Alexander Volz	University of Vienna, Austria
Francisco Javier Pérez	Universidad Rey Juan Carlos, Spain
Glenda Amaral	Free University of Bozen-Bolzano, Italy
Wim Laurier	UCLouvain Saint-Louis – Bruxelles, Belgium
Pedro Paulo Barcelos	Free University of Bozen-Bolzano, Italy
Mirko Zichichi	Universidad Politécnica de Madrid, Spain
Nadia Pocher	Universitat Autònoma de Barcelona, Spain

Regulation-Friendly Privacy-Preserving Blockchain Based on zk-SNARK

Lei Xu[✉], Yuewei Zhang[✉], and Liehuang Zhu

School of Cyberspace Science and Technology, Beijing Institute of Technology,
Beijing, China
{xu.lei,yueweizhang,liehuangz}@bit.edu.cn

Abstract. Recently, blockchain has attracted much attention from industries, due to its good characteristics such as decentralization and tamper proofing. To ensure that sensitive transaction data are not disclosed to the public, many privacy protection methods have been proposed for blockchain, which generally conflicts with regulatory requirements. To resolve such a conflict, in this paper we propose a privacy-preserving account-based blockchain system which supports auditing on transactions. The proposed system protects the privacy of a transaction via homomorphic encryption. The validity of the transaction is guaranteed via zero-knowledge proof. Especially, details of a transaction are presented in form of ciphertexts on the public ledger, which can be decrypted by regulatory authorities. We have implemented a demo of the proposed system using the Substrate framework. Simulation results show that the system has acceptable performance.

Keywords: Blockchain · Privacy Preserving · Regulation Compliance · Homomorphic Encryption · Zk-SNARK

1 Introduction

In recent years, blockchain technology has developed rapidly and is expected to provide key services in many fields [9]. A blockchain is a distributed ledger technology consisting of a growing list of records, called blocks, that are securely linked together using cryptography. Blockchain has the characteristics of decentralization, tamper proofing, and traceability. It can establish a trust relationship among different parties and has played an important role in the fields of finance, insurance, medical care, and supply chain security.

However, the openness of the public blockchain also brings privacy issues. For example, blockchain users in fields such as finance and medical care do not want their sensitive data stored on the blockchain ledger to be fully openly accessed. At the same time, data stored on the ledger may be required to accept legal and technical regulations [16]. For example, internal auditors in most companies should always have information about how the business is doing, and industries such as telecommunications and banking must provide courts with information when they receive a court request. There is a conflict between the need for protecting blockchain users' privacy and the need for supporting regulation.

M. Ruiz and P. Soffer (Eds.): CAiSE 2023 Workshops, LNBIP 482, pp. 167–177, 2023.
https://doi.org/10.1007/978-3-031-34985-0_17

Previous studies have tried to use technologies such as zero-knowledge proof [13] and homomorphic encryption [5] to solve the privacy issue, making it impossible for even blockchain operators to obtain the data. Zero-knowledge proof is a cryptographic method that allows a prover to prove to a verifier that a statement is true while avoiding communicating any additional information during the proof process. By using zero-knowledge proofs, the balance and the identity of an account and the amount associated with a transfer transaction can be hidden from the public. However, existing privacy-preserving approaches based on zero-knowledge proofs have the following problems. On one hand, since the transaction information is completely hidden, it is hard for regulatory authorities to conduct auditing. On the other hand, most zero-knowledge proof schemes need to consume a lot of computing resources and storage space, hence they are not preferred in practice.

In this paper, we propose a privacy-preserving blockchain system which enables regulatory authorities to supervise the transactions. There are already a few blockchain systems that can balance between privacy and regulation [7,8]. Most of them are based on the Unspent Transaction Output (UTXO) model. The system proposed in this paper is based on the account model. It utilizes the homomorphic encryption technique to hide the transaction amount and the balance of an account. To protect the identity of the sender and the receiver of a transaction, a set of addresses which contains the real address of the sender or receiver and some virtual addresses is constructed. And to ensure the correctness of transaction, the proposed system utilizes Zero-Knowledge Succinct Non-Interactive Argument of Knowledge (zk-SNARK) [1,10]. Specifically, details of a transaction, including the transaction amount, balance and the public keys of both parties of a transaction, are encrypted with the public key of the regulatory authority and stored on the blockchain, so that the regulatory authority can check if the transaction satisfies the regulation rules.

The rest of the paper is organized as follows. Section 2 reviews the related work. Section 3 introduces the system architecture. Section 4 describes the privacy protection mechanism. Section 5 presents the performance evaluation results. Section 6 concludes the paper.

2   Related Work

A number of privacy-enhanced blockchain systems have been proposed. Monero [14] is a decentralized cryptocurrency that uses ring signatures to hide transaction outputs and stealth addresses to hide the receiver's identity. The disadvantages of Monero are limited privacy protection and large transaction size. Zcash [12] uses a two-layer system with zero-knowledge proofs to ensure that transactions are not linked to senders, receivers, or amounts, but Zcash requires a trusted setup. Dash [3] uses a currency mixing mechanism called CoinJoin, but the process of currency mixing is relatively slow. Zether [2] uses an account model rather than a UTXO model, and realizes privacy protection using smart contracts without modifying the underlying blockchain system. ZETH [11] is

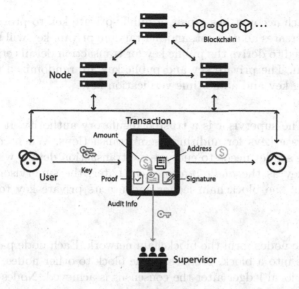

Fig. 1. A simple illustration of the proposed system.

another account-based blockchain system. ZETH implements the protocol of Zcash on top of Ethereum using smart contracts.

In order to solve the conflict between privacy and regulation, Garman *et al.* proposed DAP [6] which ensures compliance by introducing a privacy protection policy enforcement mechanism. However, such an approach is very inefficient. The PRCash system proposed in [15] has made some progress in efficiency, but it has sacrificed some privacy and auditability functions. PAChain [17] is an auditable consortium blockchain implemented using Hyperledger Fabric. It utilizes anonymous credentials, zero-knowledge range proofs, and additive homomorphic encryption. However, it is slightly lacking in sender privacy protection. Therefore, it is necessary to design an auditable blockchain system with high efficiency and comprehensive privacy protection.

3   Overview

3.1   System Model

As shown in Fig. 1, the proposed system includes the following components:

User. Users conduct transactions in the system and generate transaction information that can be audited in the future. Each user has only one account[1]. The account has a unique address which is a fixed-length string. The account may possess some tokens. We refer to the number of tokens as the *balance* of

---

[1] Unless otherwise specified, we use the two terms *user* and *account* interchangeably.

the account. Each account has a pair of public-private key to prove its identity. When the user creates an account, another random private key will be generated, which can be used to derive the public key for transaction details encryption and proof generation. The private key and public key are randomized to generate a one-time signing key and a one-time verification key.

Supervisor. The supervisor is a trusted regulatory authority. It has a pair of public and private keys for auditing users' transactions. When constructing a transaction, the sender needs to encrypt the transaction details with the supervisor's public key as the *audit information*. Later, the supervisor can get the transaction from the blockchain ledger and use its private key to decrypt the information.

Node. Multiple nodes form the blockchain network. Each node packages multiple transactions into a block, broadcasts the block to other nodes, and appends the block to its local ledger after the consensus is achieved. Nodes are deployed with smart contracts for verifying zero-knowledge proofs and updating balances of accounts.

3.2   Basic Workflow

Transfer Transaction. To conduct a transfer of tokens, the sender first uses its private key to generate a one-time signing key and a one-time verification key. Then, the sender encrypts the transfer amount with its public key. Meanwhile, in order to hide the identities of the sender and the receiver, some virtual addresses are created and mixed up with the address of the sender and the address of the receiver. Then sender also encrypts the transaction amount, balance, its public key and the designated receiver's public key with the supervisor's public key. After that, the sender runs the zk-SNARK protocol to generate a zero-knowledge proof, proving that the transaction is valid. Then the sender uses the one-time signing key to generate a signature for the combination of the ciphertexts, the proof, and the set of addresses. After preparing aforementioned data, the sender can construct a transaction to invoke the transfer function of the smart contract. The smart contract verifies the signature and the zero-knowledge proof. If both the signature and the proof are valid, the contract will utilize the homomorphic property to update the balance of the sender and the balance of the receiver. In the next section, we will describe in detail how the transfer is done in a privacy-preserving and auditable way.

Transaction Audit. If the transfer of tokens is successful, the corresponding transaction will be appended to the blockchain ledger. The sender, the receiver and the transfer amount are unknown to the public. If the supervisor wants to audit the details of the transaction, it can extract the encrypted audit information from the transaction and use its private key to decrypt it. After obtaining the plaintext transaction information, the supervisor can check if the transaction complies with the regulation rules.

4   Design Details of Transaction Flow

In the proposed system, the process of a transfer transaction mainly consists of two phases, namely transaction construction and transaction execution. Before constructing a transaction, the user must prepare necessary cryptographical materials. At a certain point, the supervisor will initiate an audit process.

4.1   Initialization

The main task of the initialization phase is key derivation. Each user in the system first generates its own private key sk. Then, the user can derive the public key pk and the address $addr$. The supervisor first generates its private key sv^*, and then derives its public key sv. The public key is published to all users.

4.2   Transaction Construction

We use the following example to illustrate the process of a transfer transaction. Suppose that a user Alice wants to transfer a certain amount of tokens to the user Bob via the smart contract. Let pk denote Alice's public key, sk denote her private key, and $addr$ denote her address. The current balance of Alice is denoted by b. The transfer amount is denoted by a. Bob's public key is denoted by $\overline{pk}$, his address is denoted by $\overline{addr}$, and his current balance is denoted by $\overline{b}$. As the sender, Alice wants to keep her identity, the receiver Bob's identity and the transfer amount private.

Encrypt Transaction Details. In order to hide the transfer amount and the account balance, Alice encrypts the transaction details with her public key pk and Bob's public key $\overline{pk}$. In order to improve the encryption efficiency as much as possible while maintaining the homomorphic property, the proposed system chooses the Lifted-ElGamal [4] asymmetric key encryption algorithm which has good compatibility with zero-knowledge proof. We define p to be a prime. Let $\mathbb{G}$ denote a group of order p. The generator of $\mathbb{G}$ is denoted as g. Let $\mathbb{Z}_p$ denote the integers modulo p. Let $\mathbb{Z}_p^\star$ denote the set of inverses in $\mathbb{Z}_p$. Let r denote a random uniform sample from the set $\mathbb{Z}_p^\star$. If b and b' are encrypted with the same public key pk to get ciphertexts $(C_L = g^b pk^r, C_R = g^r)$ and $(C_L' = g^{b'} pk^{r'}, C_R' = g^{r'})$ respectively, then $(C_L C_L' = g^{b+b'} pk^{r+r'}, C_R C_R' = g^{r+r'})$ is an encryption of $b+b'$ under pk.

Specifically, Alice uses her public key pk and Bob's public key $\overline{pk}$ to encrypt the transfer amount a respectively. The resulting ciphertexts are denoted as $C_{amount} \doteq \{(C, D), (\overline{C}, \overline{D})\}$. In order to make the transaction auditable, Alice uses the supervisor's public key sv to encrypt the audit information, including the transfer amount a, Alice's remaining balance $b' \doteq b - a$, the public keys pk and $\overline{\text{pk}}$. The resulting encrypted audit information are denoted as $C_{audit} \doteq \{C_a, C_{b'}, C_{\text{pk}}, C_{\overline{\text{pk}}}\}$.

Address Obfuscation. In order to hide her identity, Alice randomly generates several virtual addresses $\{addr_0, addr_1, \ldots\}$ each of which has the same format as her real address addr. The number of virtual addresses can be pre-configured. For nodes in the blockchain network and other potential privacy attackers that can access the ledger, the real addresses of Alice and Bob are indistinguishable from those virtual addresses. As a result, given a transaction, attackers cannot determine the identities of the sender or the receiver.

Generate Zero-knowledge Proofs. Since the transfer amount is encrypted, nodes in the blockchain network has no way to check the validity of the transfer. Therefore, Alice needs to construct a zero-knowledge proof. The proof is essentially a statement. With this proof, Alice can convince the blockchain nodes that the transfer is valid without disclosing additional information other than the statement.

Given the transfer amount a, Alice's remaining balance b', Alice's keys pk and sk, Bob's public key $\overline{\text{pk}}$, the supervisor's public key sv and the maximum allowed transaction amount Max, Alice needs to prove the following things.

1. The transfer amount is a non-negative value, namely $a \in [0, \text{Max}]$.
2. Alice's remaining balance b' is a non-negative value, namely $b' \in [0, \text{Max}]$.
3. All ciphertexts are well formed and encrypt the same value a. That is, the following equation must hold:

$$C = g^a \text{pk}^r \wedge \overline{C} = g^a \overline{\text{pk}}^r \wedge D = g^r \wedge C_L/C = g^{b'} (C_R/D)^{\text{sk}} \wedge \text{pk} = g^{\text{sk}}. \quad (1)$$

4. Each element of the audit information $(a, b', \text{pk}, \overline{\text{pk}})$ is encrypted by the supervisor's public key sv. That is, the following equation must hold:

$$C_a = g^a \text{sv}^r \wedge C_{b'} = g^{b'} \text{sv}^r \wedge C_{\text{pk}} = g^{\text{pk}} \text{sv}^r \wedge C_{\overline{\text{pk}}} = g^{\overline{\text{pk}}} \text{sv}^r. \quad (2)$$

The proof π constructed by Alice is given by

$$\begin{aligned}
\pi : \{(\text{pk}, \overline{\text{pk}}, \text{sv}, & C_L, C_R, C, D, \overline{C}, C_a, C_{b'}, g; \text{sk}, a, b', r) : \\
& a \in [0, \text{Max}] \wedge b' \in [0, \text{Max}] \wedge \\
& C = g^a \text{pk}^r \wedge \overline{C} = g^a \overline{\text{pk}}^r \wedge D = g^r \wedge \\
& C_L/C = g^{b'} (C_R/D)^{\text{sk}} \wedge \text{pk} = g^{\text{sk}} \wedge \\
& C_a = g^a \text{sv}^r \wedge C_{b'} = g^{b'} \text{sv}^r \wedge \\
& C_{\text{pk}} = g^{\text{pk}} \text{sv}^r \wedge C_{\overline{\text{pk}}} = g^{\overline{\text{pk}}} \text{sv}^r\}.
\end{aligned} \quad (3)$$

Table 1. Fields in the transaction.

Field	Symbol	Description
Sender	$\{\mathsf{addr}, addr_0, \ldots\}$	Set of Alice's address and virtual addresses
Receiver	$\{\overline{\mathsf{addr}}, \overline{addr_0}, \ldots\}$	Set of Bob's address and virtual addresses
Amount	C_{amount}	Encrypted transfer amount
Audit	C_{audit}	Encrypted audit information
Proof	π	Zero-knowledge proof
Signature	$\sigma_{transfer}$	Generated by Alice using a one-time signing key
Key	pk'	Alice's one-time verification key

Sign the Transaction. Before executing a transaction, Alice uses her private key sk and public key sk to generate a pair of one-time signing key sk' and one-time verification key pk' through a randomization process. The one-time keys are used to ensure the anonymity of the transaction signature. Define a message $m = (\{\mathsf{addr}, addr_0, addr_1, \ldots\}, \{\overline{\mathsf{addr}}, \overline{addr_0}, addr_1, \ldots\}, C_{amount}, C_{audit}, \pi)$, Alice uses her one-time signing key sk' to sign m, and the result is denoted by $\sigma_{transfer}$. Then, Alice constructs a transaction to invoke the transfer function defined in the smart contract. The contents of the transaction are shown in Table 1.

4.3 Transaction Execution

Validity Verification. To make sure the transaction is valid, the smart contract needs to use the one-time verification key pk' obtained in the transaction to perform the following verification on $\sigma_{transfer}$ and π:

1. The transaction is correctly signed by the one-time signing key sk' and can be correctly verified by pk', namely there is

$$\mathsf{Verify}_{\mathsf{pk}'}(\sigma_{transfer}) = \mathsf{True}. \tag{4}$$

2. The zero-knowledge proof π is valid, namely there is

$$\mathsf{Verify}_{\mathsf{pk}'}(\pi) = \mathsf{True}. \tag{5}$$

Update Balance. If the transaction passes the verification, the smart contract will perform homomorphic calculations to update Alice's and Bob's account balances. Given the transaction amount encrypted with Bob's public key $\overline{C} = g^a \overline{\mathsf{pk}}^r$, the encrypted new balance of Bob can be calculated through $g^b \overline{\mathsf{pk}}^r \overline{C}$. Similarly, given the transaction amount encrypted with Alice's public key $C = g^a \mathsf{pk}^r$, the encrypted new balance of Alice can be calculated through $g^b \mathsf{pk}^r / C$. The smart contract updates the balances of both parties simultaneously to avoid inconsistencies.

Table 2. Transaction overhead.

Item	Length (bytes)
Key	32
Address	32
Encrypted Amount	64
Signature	64
Zk-proof	192

4.4 Transaction Audit

When this particular transaction from Alice and Bob needs to be audited, the supervisor first extracts the audit information from the transaction, and then uses its private key sv^* to decrypt the encrypted audit information $\{C_a, C_{b'}, C_{\mathsf{pk}}, C_{\overline{\mathsf{pk}}}\}$. After obtaining plaintext audit information $\{a, b', \mathsf{pk}, \overline{\mathsf{pk}}\}$, the supervisor can carry out the auditing. Since only a decryption operation is required, obtaining the audit information can be very efficient. In order to further improve the efficiency, the supervisor can perform the decryption operation in parallel.

In this paper, we assume that the supervisor is able to protect its private key from unauthorized access, which is also an important prerequisite for ensuring the security of the audit information on the blockchain ledger. With the zero-knowledge proof generated by the sender of a transaction, we can ensure that the audit information required by the supervisor has been correctly encrypted using the supervisor's public key. If an attacker deliberately constructs an unauditable transaction without audit information, the transaction cannot pass the validity verification. That is to say, the proposed system ensures that all transactions are auditable.

5   Performance Analysis

In order to evaluate the performance of the proposed system, we have developed a demo system based on the Substrate framework[2] and simulated the transfer transactions. The experiments are conducted on a laptop with Intel Core i7-1165G7 4.7 GHz and 16 GB RAM.

5.1   Results and Discussion

As shown in the Table 2, in the proposed system, all keys have the same size (32 bytes). The size of the zero-knowledge proof is 192 bytes. The size of the signature is 64 bytes. The size of an account address is 32 bytes. The size of a ciphertext is 64 bytes.

---

[2] A blockchain framework for developing customized blockchains.

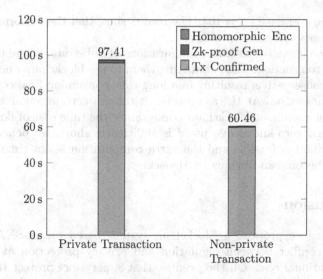

Fig. 2. Performance of private and non-private transactions.

For a transfer transaction which follows the transaction flow described in Sect. 4, the operations that occupy computing resources can be divided into three parts, namely key distribution, homomorphic encryption, and zero-knowledge proof generation. Since the key distribution can be performed offline, the main time-consuming operations are concentrated in the latter two parts. We use the `std::time::Instant` provided by the Rust standard library to measure the time spent by each part of the system and see if the time consumed by the extra computation in our transfer transaction is low enough in the whole transaction.

As shown in Fig. 2, the encryption operation takes 171 ms in total, and generating a zero-knowledge proof takes 1,536 ms. However, the total time taken for the transaction to be confirmed and appended to the ledger is as high as 97 s. As a comparison, for a non-private coin minting transaction, the homomorphic encryption operation takes 48 ms, the generation of zero-knowledge proof takes 587 ms, and the total time for the transaction to be confirmed and appended to the ledger is 60 s.

For the transaction audit part, decrypting data from the chain is only an ordinary asymmetric decryption operation, and it can be completed offline, so it is not included in the performance analysis.

5.2   Substrate Framework

In order to find out why it takes a long time for a transaction to be confirmed and appended to the ledger, we built a Substrate single-node development chain, and used the API to send 50,000 transfer transactions to test its transaction processing capability. The test results show that the average Transactions Per Second (TPS) is 168. Then, we conducted the same test on a multi-node development chain, and the average TPS is 164. The results show that the performance of the Substrate framework is acceptable.

Currently, we use the default configurations of Substrate, where the strategy of packaging transactions and submitting them to the blockchain under low load is relatively conservative, resulting in a long time-consuming final completion of the entire transaction. At the same time, it takes a certain amount of time to reach a consensus among blockchain nodes. Since the time cost of homomorphic encryption and zero-knowledge proof is sufficiently short, we believe that the proposed method is feasible and the extra computation is not time consuming and will not become an obvious bottleneck.

6   Conclusion

In this paper, we propose a blockchain system based on zk-SNARK which resolves the conflict between regulation and privacy protection at an acceptable computational cost. On the premise that supervisors protect their private keys from unauthorized access, transaction amount and user's identity on the blockchain ledger can be kept private, and can only be obtained by the supervisor when it conducts the auditing. We combined homomorphic encryption, zero-knowledge proof, and asymmetric encryption techniques to implement an early experimental version of the system, and analyzed its performance. The results show that the performance is acceptable.

Acknowledgements. This work was supported in part by the National Defense Basic Scientific Research Program of China under Grant No. JCKY2019602B013 and No. JCKY2018602B015, and in part by the Beijing Natural Science Foundation under Grant No. M21035.

References

1. Bitansky, N., Canetti, R., Chiesa, A., Tromer, E.: From extractable collision resistance to succinct non-interactive arguments of knowledge, and back again. In: Proceedings of the 3rd Innovations in Theoretical Computer Science Conference, pp. 326–349 (2012)
2. Bünz, B., Agrawal, S., Zamani, M., Boneh, D.: Zether: towards privacy in a smart contract world. In: Bonneau, J., Heninger, N. (eds.) FC 2020. LNCS, vol. 12059, pp. 423–443. Springer, Cham (2020). https://doi.org/10.1007/978-3-030-51280-4_23
3. Duffield, E., Diaz, D.: Dash: a privacycentric cryptocurrency (2015)
4. ElGamal, T.: A public key cryptosystem and a signature scheme based on discrete logarithms. IEEE Trans. Inf. Theory **31**(4), 469–472 (1985)
5. Feng, Q., He, D., Zeadally, S., Khan, M.K., Kumar, N.: A survey on privacy protection in blockchain system. J. Netw. Comput. Appl. **126**, 45–58 (2019)
6. Garman, C., Green, M., Miers, I.: Accountable privacy for decentralized anonymous payments. In: Grossklags, J., Preneel, B. (eds.) FC 2016. LNCS, vol. 9603, pp. 81–98. Springer, Heidelberg (2017). https://doi.org/10.1007/978-3-662-54970-4_5
7. Li, Y., et al.: Toward privacy and regulation in blockchain-based cryptocurrencies. IEEE Network **33**(5), 111–117 (2019)

8. Lin, C., He, D., Huang, X., Xie, X., Choo, K.K.R.: PPChain: a privacy-preserving permissioned blockchain architecture for cryptocurrency and other regulated applications. IEEE Syst. J. **15**(3), 4367–4378 (2020)
9. Maesa, D.D.F., Mori, P.: Blockchain 3.0 applications survey. J. Parall. Distrib. Comput. **138**, 99–114 (2020)
10. Parno, B., Howell, J., Gentry, C., Raykova, M.: Pinocchio: nearly practical verifiable computation. Commun. ACM **59**(2), 103–112 (2016)
11. Rondelet, A., Zajac, M.: Zeth: On integrating zerocash on ethereum. arXiv preprint arXiv:1904.00905 (2019)
12. Sasson, E.B., et al.: Zerocash: decentralized anonymous payments from bitcoin. In: 2014 IEEE Symposium on Security and Privacy, pp. 459–474. IEEE (2014)
13. Sun, X., Yu, F.R., Zhang, P., Sun, Z., Xie, W., Peng, X.: A survey on zero-knowledge proof in blockchain. IEEE Netw. **35**(4), 198–205 (2021)
14. Van Saberhagen, N.: Cryptonote v 2.0 (2013)
15. Wüst, K., Kostiainen, K., Capkun, V., Capkun, S.: PRCash: centrally-issued digital currency with privacy and regulation. IACR Cryptol. ePrint Arch. **2018**, 412 (2018)
16. Yeoh, P.: Regulatory issues in blockchain technology. J. Finan. Regul. Compliance **25**, 196–208 (2017)
17. Yuen, T.H.: PAChain: private, authenticated & auditable consortium blockchain and its implementation. Futur. Gener. Comput. Syst. **112**, 913–929 (2020)

Blockchain Governance Design a Computer Science Perspective

Yulu Wang[✉], Fadime Kaya, and Jaap Gordijn

Vrije Universiteit Amsterdam, Amsterdam, The Netherlands
y50.wang@student.vu.nl, {f.kaya,j.gordijn}@vu.nl

Abstract. Blockchain-based DAOs and governance frameworks have emerged, however limited research has been done on the governance foundations of blockchain networks. In blockchain networks decisions are made through a collaborative and consensus building design mechanism. Such a governance process is complex, dynamic, and challenging. This paper presents blockchain governance design from a computer science perspective. We do so by exploring concepts such as decentralization, blockchain governance, Decentralized Autonomous Organization (DAO) and a novel modeling approach on blockchain governance namely DECENT. In this paper, we presented why conceptual modeling is a design requirement for blockchain governance. Researchers can use the DECENT modeling approach as a reference framework for blockchain governance design, such as empirical and comparative case studies.

Keywords: Blockchain Governance · DAO · Digital Platform Governance · Decentralized Governance Design

1 Introduction

Decentralization has been a growing trend in recent years, with an increas ing number of entities moving from centralized towards decentralized systems [2, 4, 19, 26]. Kaya et al. define [18] decentralized governance (DG) as a collection of parties who work cooperatively and competitively to satisfy customer needs, and in which decision power is fairly distributed over a (sub)set of parties in the ecosystem [1, 10]. This approach has several potential benefits [8, 13] and we can consider decentralization and the emergence of DG as a response to the limitations of centralization and the need for a more flexible and adaptable ecosystems. Blockchain technology can be seen as an important driver in the conceptualization and adaption in the field of decentralized governance [25, 26]. Along with the development of blockchain technology, the idea of web 3.0 as a new iteration of the World Wide Web is proposed[1]. Web 3.0 aims to build a more open, decentralized and user-centric internet [6]. Blockchain network governance, which also can be seen as decentralized governance, involves decision-making and resource allocation through a decentralized network of participants, this is a key feature of Web 3.0. Although many

---

[1] https://www.wired.com/story/web3-gavin-wood-interview/.

M. Ruiz and P. Soffer (Eds.): CAiSE 2023 Workshops, LNBIP 482, pp. 178–185, 2023.
https://doi.org/10.1007/978-3-031-34985-0_18

blockchain-based DAOs and blockchain networks have emerged, very limited research has been done on the theoretical foundations and model validation of the decentralized ecosystem design [7]. Also, current blockchain networks still face issues in the actual implementation process [12, 29]. Our long term research goal is to develop a domain specific language (DSL) for DECENT, that allows a systematic approach in designing decentralized governance for blockchain networks. The research goal of this paper is to present blockchain governance design from a computer science perspective.

This paper is structured as follows. In Sect. 2, we explain our research approach. Section 3 presents conceptual modeling to design blockchain governance, Sect. 4 presents our conclusions, limitations, and suggestions for further research.

Table 1. Research Selection Criteria

Pub Year	Keyword Selection Criteria	Reference
2011–2018	DACs, DAOs, Blockchain, Design principle	[1, 4, 9, 10]
2019–2021	Model construction, DGD frameworks	[8, 11, 13, 16–18, 25, 26, 29]
2022–2023	BGD, Conceptual modeling	[2, 3, 5–7, 12, 15, 21, 23, 24, 28]

2 Research Approach

The research goal of this paper is to present blockchain governance design from a computer science perspective. We do so by exploring the concepts and developments of blockchain networks, DAO and conceptual modeling. We selected the PRISMA methodology [20] as our research approach. Research question and detailed steps are presented as follows:

RQ: Why is Conceptual Modeling Relevant for Blockchain Governance Design (BGD)?

Step 1 - Identification. Our preliminary study starts with publications presented by DISE lab[2]. We searched literature by keywords like DG, DAO framework, blockchain governance, conceptual modeling and the 'snowball' method [27] is applied. As BGD is an emerging research domain we cannot only limit ourselves to google scholar, but also focus on relevant websites, conference, white papers and reports. The total number of retrieved literature records is 1645.

Step 2 - Screening. Our research domain is focus on the computer science perspective. Records discussed from a economic, business or political perspective are excluded. We screen these literature records mainly by abstract and keywords. The number of records excluded in this part is 649.

---

[2] https://dise-lab.nl/.

Step 3 - Eligibility. The number of remaining literature records after being assessed for eligibility is 97. We keep 29 records closely related to the area of DG, DAOs framework, meta governance design and co-area of conceptual modeling and blockchain governance design.

Step 4 - Included. We analyzed 29 literature records ultimately. After indepth reading and critical understanding of the selected records, we can answer our research question. Research selection criteria are summarized in Table 1.

3   Conceptual Modeling for Blockchain Governance Design

3.1   Blockchain Networks in DAO Design Philosophy

In this section, we first discuss blockchain networks that employs a DAO design philosophy which contains the concept of decentralization. Also, some design flaws has been identified and summarized. Secondly we present DECENT which is a novel and innovative conceptual modeling approach for blockchain gover- nance design (BGD).

Blockchain Governance Networks.
In this subsection, we discuss many blockchain-based DAOs and blockchain networks in DAO design philosophy and identified some design flaws from them. *Compound*[3] is a decentralized financial (DeFi) platform which key feature is loan rates are automatically adjusted. Decisions in Compound are made via smart contracts, and token holders have governance rights. [12].

Uniswap[4] is the largest decentralized exchange (DEX) platform allowing users to trade crypto currency tokens without intermediaries [12], but its decision making structure is still centralized.

Ethereum Name Service (ENS)[5] is a decentralized domain name service system, which is more decentralized compared to Compound and Uniswap [12].

Aragon[6] is a DApp that facilitates the creation and management of DAOs. It provides a modular governance framework while this framework does not provide a governance coordination mechanism [11].

MakerDAO[7] is a DeFi project combines functions from voting to execution and issuing governance passes [5]. Due to off-chain coordination mechanism, it suffers from the inevitable drawbacks like progressive centralization of governance, increased governance costs and reduced governance initiative of participants[8]. *Moloch DAO*[9] is a governance framework emerged to crowdfund and allocate funds for Ethereum infrastructure projects. Moloch DAO V2 adds a multi-pass system and many mechanisms

---

[3] https://compound.finance/.
[4] https://app.uniswap.org/.
[5] https://ens.domains/.
[6] https://aragon.org/.
[7] https://makerdao.com/.
[8] https://makerdao.com/zh-CN/whitepaper/.
[9] https://dao.molochdao.com/.

which has improved the degree of distribution and governance stability while problems like malicious proposal attacks and the long governance decision cycle still existed.

DAO stack[10] aims to solve the scalability problem in governance and focuses on effective distributed decision-making through its proposed Holographic Consensus decision system[11].

Design Flaws. There are many design flaws existed in blockchain governance networks: (1) Difficulty in balance between decentralization and efficiency. Competing points of interest for different stakeholders can lead to decision-making bottlenecks and inefficiencies [3, 7]. (2) Incomplete decentralization. Many ecosystems claiming decentralization do not achieve it in practice, and decentralization should extend to processes preceding governance decisions [12, 15]. (3) The issue of scalability. The underlying blockchain technology limitations [22] can lead to scalability issues as usage grows, resulting in slow and expensive transactions [21]. (4) Application scenarios and function of blockchain network governance are limited. Limited exploration of real-life scenarios with disintermediation and distributed requirements [7], and a lack of new modules on governance framework platforms restrict the overall governance efficiency and quality [24].

(5) The potential legal risks [9, 28].

3.2 Conceptual Modeling Method

Blockchain governance design (BGD) is clearly an emerging research domain and it has been identified that there is a need and requirement for a conceptual modeling method which allows to design blockchain governance [8, 23]. A conceptual modeling approach is a method used to design and represent complex systems in a simplified approach. In the context of BGD, conceptual modeling is useful as it can be used to design and represent complex, decentralized systems for DAOs that is easy to understand and analyze. This contributes to identify potential problems or issues with the design and to determine how it can be improved [16] already at an early stage. Conceptual modeling can represents the governance structure and the design decisions of a DAO as a set of artifacts and their inter-relationships. These artifacts can include elements such as decision-making mechanisms, regulations and incentives. In this way, it is possible to understand how the different artifacts interact and how it contribute to the overall functioning of the organization. A novel and innovative approach to design blockchain governance has been recently introduced by taking a conceptual modeling approach. This method to design blockchain governance is coined as DECENT [16].

DECENT Introduction. Kaya et al. states that finding an appropriate sound governance solution for a decentralized ecosystem is a design problem [17]. Due to the different application fields and environments of ecosystems, from the perspective of model development, they face different contexts, and the required system components will also be different. In order to avoid serious problems such as centralization of the system, low efficiency or loss of fairness the governance structure can be conceptualized in a clear

---

[10] https://daostack.io/.

[11] https://medium.com/daostack/holographic-consensus-part.

approach that is understood by every actor in the decentralized ecosystem. In order to explore the topic of DGD, authors have founded "DECENT" [15, 16] and presented in Fig. 1. DECENT[12] is developed with the vision that it is a societal and economical responsibility to create ecosystems that promote equity in how we set the rules of participation. DECENT is a conceptual modeling method that will allow an actor or a group who is not proficient in programming languages or technology to conveniently and easily design an ecosystem collaboratively. DECENT employs a conceptual modeling approach, and this type of an approach (machine-processable formalization) will enable the idea of a decentralized ecosystem to be more widely disseminated and applied. For different decentralized projects, the resulting proprietary decentralized governance model will be considered the product of a rigorous design process [17]. DECENT is positioned within the generic modeling method framework as proposed by [14]. DECENT can be used to describe specific governance models, i.e. conceptual models. All governance models are based on real-life research subjects, which can be seen here as abstracted and aggregated from requirements analysis in specific domains such as DeFi, P2P Energy, and Decentralized Social Media.

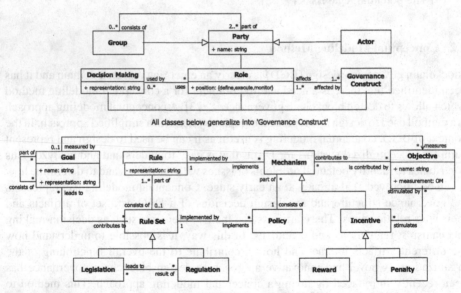

Fig. 1. DECENT meta model [16]

DECENT Meta Model. Kaya et al. positions and presents the relevant design artifacts for decentralized governance as the DECENT meta model [15, 16]. DECENT is lightweight and easy-to-handle with a well-defined set of decentralized governance concepts. It responds to the design needs of developing governance structures and aims to provide an easy-to-understand modeling environment and tools for users having the desire to design and built a decentralized ecosystem. Figure 1 shows its meta model as

---

[12] https://dise-lab.nl/.

a UML class diagram, consisting of attributes, associations, generalizations (is-a) and constraints. The DECENT meta model provides a clear and structured approach to defining governance structures and relationships. An important aspect of the DECENT meta model is the multiparticipant approach, which differs from a single participant involved in coordinating system decisions and operations. Each participant has a specific role to define, implement and monitor, and these roles constrain each other, influence each other and complete the whole process of governance design decisions under the influence of other institutional rules.

DECENT Governance Models. The DECENT governance model belongs to the domain of conceptual models and can be seen as a bridge between the real world and the DECENT meta model in the overall meta modeling approach [14]. Governance consultants are expected to use the DECENT modeling language as a descriptive tool to conceptually decompose and abstract real-world study subjects (banking, social software, etc.) according to the context and characteristics of the desired decentralized ecosystem in order to present a concrete, specific DECENT governance model. Decentralized governance as a new field of research has not yet emerged as an unified, authoritative definition. Process of multiple participants working together to understand rules and create rules is called decentralized governance, and it is positioned as a design product. The study of BGD by adopting a conceptual modeling approach contributes to the understanding and design of structured governance and unification across industry and as a research domain.

4 Conclusion

This paper on blockchain governance design contribute to a perspective for thinking about the development direction and quantitative criteria of future blockchain network governance design in a noval conceptual modeling approach. The development of internet technologieshas driven the field of decentralized governance from theory to practice, with the emergence of many blockchain-based DAOs and blockchain networks in DAO design philosophy. Some design flaws could be identified from them. Finding the most adapted governance solution for decentralized ecosystems in different application domains and environments is a design problem, and DECENT employs a conceptual modeling approach to provide a useful solution for analyzing, discussing and developing a reference framework and structured foundation for blockchain network governance. DECENT has already been applied in the domains of peer-to-peer energy trading and digital currency development [15, 16]. A conceptual modeling method helps to identify potential problems in decentralized ecosystem design and determine how to improve them already at an early stage. Also it can be understood and applied by every actor with no reliance on the technology provider to prevent powerful concentrations in developing the governance decision structure. Since our long-term research goal is to develop the DECENT modeling language, we provide a detailed description of the DECENT establishment concept and the metamodel built according to the conceptual modeling approach (Sect. 3.2).

Limitations. The sources we have selected are mostly related to computer science. We excluded sources from a business and political perspective and this can potentially affect the generalizability of our results.

Future research. Blockchain network governance requires further exploration from a theoretical foundation and technical development perspective. We will contribute to the design philosophy of DECENT by extending it towards a domain specific language (DSL).

References

1. Arrun̄ada, B., Garicano, L.: Blockchain: The birth of decentralized governance. Pompeu Fabra University, Economics and business working paper series **1608** (2018)
2. Axelsen, H., Jensen, J.R., Ross, O.: When is a dao decentralized? Complex Syst. Inf. Model. Q. **31**, 51–75 (2022)
3. Bellavitis, C., Fisch, C., Momtaz, P.P.: The rise of decentralized autonomous organizations (daos): a first empirical glimpse. Venture Capital, pp. 1–17 (2022)
4. Bossert, T.J.: Decentralization of health systems: Challenges and global issues of the twenty-first century. Decentralizing health services: a global perspective, pp. 199–207 (2014)
5. Brennecke, M., Guggenberger, T., Schellinger, B., Urbach, N.: The de-central bank in decentralized finance: a case study of makerdao. In: Proceedings of the 55th Hawaii International Conference on System Sciences (2022)
6. Chen, C., et al.: When digital economy meets web 3.0: applications and challenges. IEEE Open J. Comput. Soc. (2022)
7. Chen, L., Tong, T.W., Tang, S., Han, N.: Governance and design of digital platforms: a review and future research directions on a meta-organization. J. Manag. **48**(1), 147–184 (2022)
8. Chen, Y., Richter, J.I., Patel, P.C.: Decentralized governance of digital platforms. J. Manag. **5**, 1305–1337 (2021)
9. Chohan, U.W.: The decentralized autonomous organization and governance issues. Available at SSRN 3082055 (2017)
10. Faguet, J.P.: Decentralization and governance. World Development **53**, 2–13 (2014). https://doi.org/10.1016/j.worlddev.2013.01.002, https://www.sciencedirect.com/science/article/pii/S0305750X13000089, decentralization and Governance
11. Faqir-Rhazoui, Y., Arroyo, J., Hassan, S.: A comparative analysis of the platforms for decentralized autonomous organizations in the ethereum blockchain. J. Internet Serv. Appl. **12**(1), 1–20 (2021)
12. Fritsch, R., Mu̇ller, M., Wattenhofer, R.: Analyzing voting power in decentralized governance: who controls daos? (2022). https://doi.org/10.48550/ARXIV.2204.01176, https://arxiv.org/abs/2204.01176
13. Gordijn, J., Kaya, F., Wieringa, R.: A call for decentralized governance of fair ecosystems. J. Serv. Manage. Res. (06 2021)
14. Karagiannis, D., Kühn, H.: Metamodelling Platforms. In: Bauknecht, K., Tjoa, A.M., Quirch-mayr, G. (eds.) EC-Web 2002. LNCS, vol. 2455, pp. 182–182. Springer, Heidelberg (2002). https://doi.org/10.1007/3-540-45705-4_19
15. Kaya, F., Amaral, G., Blanco, F.J.P., Gordijn, J., Makkes, M.X., der Linden, T.V.: An ontological exploration of central bank digital currency governance design. In: Proceedings of the BLED conference (2022)

16. Kaya, F., Gordijn, J.: Decent: An ontology for decentralized governance in the renewable energy sector. In: Almeida, J.P.A., Guizzardi, G., Montali, M., Proper, H.A. (eds.) Proceedings 2021 IEEE 23rd Conference on Business Informatics, CBI 2021. pp. 11–20. IEEE (2021)

17. Kaya, F., Gordijn, J., Wieringa, R., Makkes, M.: Governance in peer-to-peer networks is a design problem. In: Laurier, W., Poels, G., Roelens, B., Weigand, H. (eds.) Proceedings of the 14th International Workshop on Value Modelling and Business Ontologies (VMBO 2020). CEUR (2020)

18. Kaya, F., Gordijn, J., Wieringa, R.J., Makkes, M.X.: Exploring governance in a decentralized energy trading eco-system. In: Bled eConference, p. 19 (2020)

19. Litvack, J., Wallack, J., Ahmad, J., Institute, W.B.: Decentralization Briefing Notes. WBI working papers, World Bank Institute (1999). https://books.google.nl/books?id=1 slAQAA-MAAJ

20. Moher, D., Liberati, A., Tetzlaff, J., Altman, D.G., PRISMA Group*, T.: Preferred reporting items for systematic reviews and meta-analyses: the prisma statement. Annals of internal medicine 151(4), 264–269 (2009)

21. Nelaturu, K., Du, H., Le, D.P.: A review of blockchain in fintech: taxonomy, challenges, and future directions. Cryptography 6(2), 18 (2022)

22. Sampedro, M.C., Alcalde, A.H., Lago-Pen̄as, S., Mart́ınez-V́azquez, J.: Extreme events and the resilience of decentralized governance. Tech. Rep., Universidade de Vigo, GEN-Governance and Economics research Network (2022)

23. Tsai, C.H., Zdravkovic, J., Stirna, J.: Modeling digital business ecosystems: a systematic literature review. Complex Syst. Inf. Model Q. 30, 1–30 (2022)

24. Tullney, V., et al.: Decentralized platform ecosystems-development barriers and their implications on design approaches (2022)

25. Wang, S., Ding, W., Li, J., Yuan, Y., Ouyang, L., Wang, F.Y.: Decentralized autonomous organizations: Concept, model, and applications. IEEE Trans. Comput. Soc. Syst. 6(5), 870–878 (2019)

26. Wang, S., Ouyang, L., Yuan, Y., Ni, X., Han, X., Wang, F.Y.: Blockchain-enabled smart contracts: architecture, applications, and future trends. IEEE Trans. Syst. Man, Cybernet.: Syst. 49(11), 2266–2277 (2019)

27. Wohlin, C.: Guidelines for snowballing in systematic literature studies and a replication in software engineering. In: Proceedings of the 18th international conference on evaluation and assessment in software engineering, pp. 1–10 (2014)

28. Wronka, C.: Financial crime in the decentralized finance ecosystem: new challenges for compliance. J. Financ. Crime 30(1), 97–113 (2023)

29. Ziolkowski, R., Miscione, G., Schwabe, G.: Decision problems in blockchain governance: old wine in new bottles or walking in someone else's shoes? J. Manag. Inf. Syst. 37, 316–348 (2020)

The MEV Saga: Can Regulation Illuminate the Dark Forest?

Simona Ramos[1]([⊠]) [iD] and Joshua Ellul[2] [iD]

[1] Universitat Pompeu Fabra, Barcelona, Spain
`simona.ramos@upf.edu`
[2] University of Malta, Msida, Malta

Abstract. In this article, we develop an interdisciplinary analysis of MEV which desires to merge the gap that exists between technical and legal research supporting policymakers in their regulatory decisions concerning blockchains, DeFi and associated risks. Consequently, this article is intended for both technical and legal audiences, and while we abstain from a detailed legal analysis, we aim to open a policy discussion regarding decentralized governance design at the block building layer - as the place where MEV occurs. Maximal Extractable Value or MEV has been one of the major concerns in blockchain designs as it creates a centralizing force which ultimately affects user's transactions. In this article, we dive into the technicality behind MEV, where we explain the concept behind the novel Proposal Builder Separation design (PBS) as an effort by Flashbots to increase decentralization through modularity. We underline potential vulnerability factors under the PBS design, which open space for MEV extracting adversarial strategies by inside participants. We discuss the shift of trust from validators to builders in PoS blockchains such as Ethereum, acknowledging the impact that the later ones may have on users' transactions (in terms of front-running) and censorship resistance (in terms of transaction inclusion). We recognize that under PBS, centralized (dominant) entities such as builders could potentially harm users by extracting MEV via front-running strategies. Finally, we suggest adequate design and policy measures which could potentially mitigate these negative effects while protecting blockchain users.

Keywords: MEV · Decentralized Design · Blockchain

1 Introduction

A basic rule of blockchains is that the most up-to-date state of the system is represented by the longest chain, and rational miners (under PoW) or validators (under PoS) are incentivized to attempt to generate new blocks that extend the chain further in order to gain the next block reward (and any fees associated with transactions included in the block). The higher the computational power of a miner (under PoW) or staking power of a validator (under PoS) the higher the probability of acquiring the ability to execute the next block is. Miners (or validators) receive transactions from various users and also may broadcast submitted transactions to other miners (or validators). Given the

M. Ruiz and P. Soffer (Eds.): CAiSE 2023 Workshops, LNBIP 482, pp. 186–196, 2023.
https://doi.org/10.1007/978-3-031-34985-0_19

distributed and decentralized nature of the network, there is no way to know the order within which users' transactions were submitted—and therefore, it is up to the miners (or validators) to determine the order within which transactions are executed for the specific blocks a specific miner (or validator) is attempting to generate. Before transactions are included in a block, and after they are submitted into the network, they end up residing in a memory pool (mempool). Each miner (or validator) maintains its own mempool of pending transactions, and as discussed above, it is up to each individual miner (or validator) to decide on how to sort the transactions within the mempool. A node may decide to use a naive sorting strategy, where it simply appends transactions in the order the particular node received the transactions or it might perform a profit-maximizing strategies as discussed below.

The ability for miners (or validators) to order transactions turns them into a centralising force that creates an important challenge in the network which consequently impacts users. Miner (or maximum) extractable value (MEV) is a measure of the profit a miner (or validator, sequencer, etc.) can make through the ability to arbitrarily include, exclude, or re-order transactions within the blocks they produce—and, of course, miners (and validators) do their best to ensure they make maximum fees. As a result, this may lead to front-running, 'sandwiching' and other forms of market manipulation strategies, which can affect market prices, users' funds and the overall trust in the system. While MEV extraction can be considered an inherited part of the block building design, the evolution and adoption of Automated Market Makers (AMM) opened new arbitrage opportunities between crypto-asset markets bringing MEV to another level. Currently, statistics show that MEV is so pervasive that one out of 30 transactions is added by miners for this purpose [1], while sandwich attacks cost users more around 90 million dollars in 2022.

In traditional financial markets, user transactions are sequenced by a trusted and regulated intermediary in the order in which they are received. In a blockchain, by contrast, the updating of a block can be competitive and random. According to some critics, since these intermediaries can choose which transactions they add to the ledger and in which order, they can engage in activities that would be illegal in traditional markets such as front-running and sandwich trades, opening the discussion for the need of certain regulatory measures. There have been several open questions on whether current regulation on insider trading is directly transferable to MEV. Recently, the Bank of International settlements has emphasized this concern and asked for further regulatory research and adequate measures. From a general standpoint, MEV related challenges could be analyzed and potentially mitigated from two angles (one does not exclude the other):

1. by introducing technical solutions in the blockchain system and associated smart contracts, which includes developing incentive mechanisms under which the negative effects of MEV would be mitigated.
2. by introducing regulatory measures that could mitigate the negative impact of MEV and protect users and other affected parties.

Overall, in order to make effective policy, a solid understanding of the technicality behind MEV is needed as regulatory solutions can find it useful to follow the current development on the technical side - in order to understand where things could go wrong (e.g., where centralization may occur).

2 MEV Basics: The Dark Forest and Flash Boys 2.0

The ability of miners to access the mempool and rearrange transactions in accordance to perceived fee value has been at the core of MEV. In general, there are harmful and unharmful activities that involve MEV. For example, arbitrage and liquidations are noted as potentially bening activities (unharmful) which tend to promote market efficiency [2]. On the other hand, the harmful ones have predominated in market discussions as they have dramatically increased in the past few years costing users millions of dollars.

While some articles regarding MEV focus on miners as profit maximizing entities that utilize mempool information to generate extra profits [1], the current system design enables other adversarial entities to target user transactions by creating diverse types of attacks. For example, currently many users have suffered from adversarial actions (such as front-running, back running, sandwich attacks, etc.) done by very specialized 'Arbitrage Bots' that detect arbitrage opportunities across the network and replicate users transactions with a higher gas price hence managing to extract additional value, and overburden the system by creating bot-to-bot competition attacks. Arbitrage bots constantly monitor pending transactions in the mempool and are able to rapidly detect and exploit profitable opportunities.

As emphasized in one of the earliest articles on MEV- *"Ethereum is a Dark Forest"*, the authors explain a situation where front-running arises because the transaction broadcasted by the legitimate claimant to a smart contractual payment, can be seen and slightly altered by others—specifically, arbitrage bots—to direct token payment to an alternative adversarial owned wallet [3]. By offering higher transaction fees and leveraging on the lag involved in this process, these bots can have the same transaction recorded with an earlier time-stamp, on the same or on an earlier executed block than the legitimate claimant, hence making the bot's transaction valid and overruling the transaction of the legitimate claimer. This front-running example is very similar to the one described in [4]. There, front-running involves racing to take advantage of arbitrage opportunities that are created in the nanoseconds after someone engages in an asset purchase on financial markets but before the transaction has reached the market. Likewise, this type of front-running often occurs when bots try to take over arbitrage opportunities between cryptocurrency exchanges.

Alongside front-running, the most common MEV attacks also include back running, and sandwich attacks. Sandwich attacks are common adversarial technique. For a sandwich attack to occur, imagine that Josh wants to buy a Token X on a Decentralised Exchange (DEX) that uses an automated market maker (AMM) model. An adversary which sees Josh's transaction can create two of its own transactions which it inserts before and after Josh's transaction. The adversary's first transaction buys Token X, which pushes up the price for Josh's transaction, and then the third transaction is the adversary's transaction to sell Token X (now at a higher price) at a profit. Since 2020, total MEV has amounted to an estimated USD 550–650 million just on the Ethereum network [1]. MEV can also essentially increase the slippage in the trading price for users.

Slippage is a de facto a 'hidden price impact' that users experience when trading against an automated market maker (AMM). When trading via an AMM, the expected execution price can differ from the real execution price because the expected price depends on a past blockchain state, which may change between the transaction creation and its execution because of certain actions (e.g., front-running transactions).

3   PBS: How Does It Work and Why is it Important

Proposer/Builder Separation (PBS) is a blockchain design feature that divides block building into the roles of block proposers and block builders. Block proposal is the action of submitting a block of transactions for the approval of network validators, while block building is the action of transaction ordering. When a blockchain protocol separates these two actions, it simplifies the process of completing each task and allows actors to specialize in one or the other. On most blockchains, a singular actor completes both tasks. For example, before Ethereum completed 'The Merge' there was no proproposer/builder separation and miners had a sole control. Arguably, proposer/builder separation (PBS) mitigates these problems by splitting the block construction role from the block proposal role. In simplest terms, at first, users/searchers send transactions to block builders through public or private peer-to-peer transaction pools. A separate class of actors called **builders** are responsible for building the block bodies—essentially an ordered list of transactions that becomes the main "payload" of the block, and submit bids. **Block proposers** receive a block from their local block builder, and sign and propose it to the network. For their work, the chosen builder receives a fee from the validator after the execution of the block [5].

An important party in the block building ecosystem, Flashbots, play a crucial role in this system [5]. Considered a type of entity providing a public good, Flashbots focus on mitigating the existential risks MEV could cause to stateful blockchains like Ethereum. In essence, Flashbots provides a private communication channel between Ethereum users and validators for efficiently communicating preferred transaction order within a block. Flashbots connect users/searchers to validators while allowing them to avoid the public mempool.

As noted in Fig. 1 below, searchers (users) may send transactions via so called bundles through a block builder such as Flashbots itself. Bundles are one or more transactions that are grouped together and executed in the order they are provided. The builder simulates the bundles to ensure validity of transactions, and then builds a full block. In this way users can 'hide' their transactions (avoid public mempool) before they are publicly executed in a block. Hence, users/searchers can avoid potential front-running and other types of adversarial attacks by using Flashbots.

Whilst PBS is optional for validators, as they can decide to arrange transactions in their own way and extract MEV, PBS is beneficial for them as it minimizes validator computational overhead. Hence it is likely that rational validators would eventually resort to using PBS. However, PBS ultimately incentivizes builder centralization, shifting the need for validator trust to builder trust. In essence, PBS does not fully avoid front-running attacks, as these can still be done by builders. Builders can still act as searchers and include their own MEV extracting transaction, ultimately front-running the user's delegated transaction.

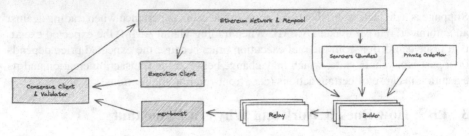

Fig. 1. PBS Design Scheme. Source: flashbots.net

In the effort to increase modularity and increase democratization amongst builders, Flashbots also introduced MEV-boost as part of the PBS structure. MEV-boost is open source middleware which helps create a competitive block-building market. MEV-boost act as a trusted party and aggregate blocks from multiple builders and identify the most profitable block to submit to the block proposer (validators). At the moment this part is far from truly decentralized. Data from mevboost.org shows that there are six major active relays currently delivering blocks in Ethereum, namely Flashbots, BloXroute Max Profit, BloXroute Ethical, BloXroute Regulated, Blocknative and Eden.

There are still certain risks that can occur from PBS. Identified risks include: *Builder Centralization; Builder/Relay Collusion and Malicious Relays.* Understanding the risks associated with centralization and collusion are important as they open a regulatory discussion as we explain in the next section. Arguably, a centralized builder/relay ecosystem, gains the ability for censorship and access to exclusive transaction order flow from which front-running types of attacks can be executed. Ultimately this creates market inefficiencies and impacts users negatively. For example, consider a wallet trying to send exclusive order flow to a single builder. For this order flow to be executed, it has to be included in a block on the blockchain which may take time. In order to avoid execution delays, a rational user will minimize this delay by sending the order to the builder with the highest inclusion rate, further increasing their dominance and centralization of the market. In that case, exclusive order flow would allow a builder, or small group of colluding builders, to capture the builder market, making it effectively uncompetitive. Also, a dominant builder would have a significant amount of private transaction information, allowing him to be in a more privileged position to extract MEV through front-running.

4   Can Regulation Illuminate the Dark Forest?

As demonstrated in the paragraphs above, MEV can negatively affect market participants—and to a large extent. Arguably MEV is still an under researched topic and has been shown to be an evolving force (as demonstrated through proposed changes for block building). Besides certain theoretically derived scenarios noted by [6], there are no other studies (to the best of the authors' knowledge) that investigate the impact of MEV on consumers/users/investors—an important factor that could merit regulatory intervention. Hence, we have resorted to looking at MEV from a security perspective - trying to understand when and how things could go wrong for users, in terms of attacks and vulnerabilities exploits (such as sandwiched user transactions) or in terms of transaction censorship (such as purposely excluding user transactions from the building block). We agree with [2] argument on the need for a more well-defined and detailed differentiation of the notion of what a "victim" is in an MEV scenario. In other words, someone that has been deprived of something that was rightfully theirs may not be the same as someone whose 'transaction or trade-based profit' decreased due to certain market movement. Arguably, regulation is not meant to protect users by enabling conditions for them to achieve profit maximizing. Also, this definition may be interpreted differently as non-adversarial forms of MEV extractions (e.g., liquidation) may still indirectly render a negative impact on users via its effect on the market as a whole. In this paper, we follow [7] and [2] differentiation of MEV under three broad categories: Monarch, Mafia and Moloch.

- "Monarch" extractable value refers to the more broadly accepted understanding of MEV, as value extractable due to the power to order and allocate (block) space.
- "Mafia" extractable value "arises when one agent (coalition of agents) gains an asymmetric knowledge of another agent's private information (asymmetric sophistication)."
- "Moloch" extractable value arises from inefficient coordination methods.

In the following sections, unlike [2] we focus mostly on Monarchs (which can extract value based on their ability to dominate transaction ordering) and Mafia—referring to value that arises when an entity has asymmetric information of users' transaction information. We look at these two occurrences as potentially being performed by 'insiders' such as builders due to their ability to create adversarial and market manipulative strategies in order to achieve profit maximizing.

4.1 Front-Running in Traditional Finance vs. DeFi

In traditional finance, front-running is considered unethical and often illegal. The premise of illegality is based on the notion that a trader possesses and acts on inside information to achieve personal gains. The non-public information concerning certain transactions ought to be of a 'material size' - meaning that it is significant enough to cause a price change in the futures or options contract and thereby allow the front-runner to profit [8]. An example of front-running in traditional finance is when a broker exploits significant market knowledge that has not yet been made public. This is similar to insider trading, with the minor difference that the broker works for the client's brokerage rather than inside the client's business [9]. In reality, front-runners profit by exploiting the discrepancy between the security's true value and its market value [8]. Consequently, the market price of the security being bought and sold does not reflect the true value of the security which distorts market efficiency. Enforcement of insider-trading regulations is currently a high priority for the Securities and Exchange Commission (SEC) [10].

The possibility that insider information has impacted cryptocurrency returns has been noted in [11], where the authors show the impact of cyber-attacks related news on price changes of the attacked cryptocurrency (in terms of abnormal losses). This example however mostly involves the centralized user-facing layer in the blockchain ecosystem (e.g., users trading via centralized exchange) where insider information can mostly be used by outsiders (e.g., hackers). Nevertheless, front-running at the block-building layer can be exploited by insiders - due to the ability of miners to arbitrarily include, exclude, or reorder transactions in blocks, allowing them to even place their own transactions when they identify a profitable opportunity. This can be seen to be a much more serious case of front-running as it is not due to abnormal temporal shocks to the system (such as an unexpected cyber-attack) but as a byproduct of the block-building design.

In essence, miners can be noted as possessing insider information, however this is due to the technical constraints that create a lag in the recording of transactions across all nodes in different geographical locations. For example, different nodes (e.g., a node in Australia and a node in Alaska) would not have a same view of the mempool's list of transactions, although there would be some overlap and similarities. This happens because every node receives transactions from different neighbouring nodes at different times.

When it comes to transaction ordering under the PBS designs, users send transactions to builders via a private channel. This gives builders the ability to have insider information over potential front-running opportunities. As noted in [5], a centralized builder ecosystem of a builder that dominates the market because of its outsized profitability gains the ability for censorship and access to exclusive transaction order flow. According to [2] under the PBS design, a user may send a transaction only to one builder, placing this entity in a privileged position and enabling them to treat user transactions as a kind of private order flow. The way the builder may arrange transactions could result in front-running or other types of adversarial attack which may impact the user's transaction gains negatively. Nevertheless, in this case there would be a loss of trust to the selected builder party which could disincentivize the user to send private flow transactions via this entity again.

4.2 Regulating Central Points in a Decentralized World

Nissembaum approaches trust and security in ICT as a conglomeration of two main factors, namely composed of insiders (e.g. miners, validators, builders, etc.) and outsiders (e.g. hackers), maintaining that very often issues can appear from an 'adversarial insider' behavior [12]. This perspective has been essential when analyzing blockchains, as the system operations are primarily maintained by 'insiders', whose dishonest or adversarial behavior may put the security and reliability of the system at stake [13].

The incentive design behind a blockchain system is crucial for its proper operation, however under certain premises of some blockchains networks, participants can engage in strategic behavior by exploiting profitable opportunities (e.g., MEV). On one hand, some non-malicious forms of 'collusive behavior', such as miners joining mining pools, may be essential for miners to beneficially participate in the system (e.g. due to the increased difficulty level of generating a block), although under certain premises mining pools can collude and act as a cartel and threaten the trustworthiness of the system. [14] argues that on-chain conduct may render issues of tortious liability for miners. However, treating miners as fiduciaries could discourage them from participating in what may be considered a socially beneficial project, due to a fear of potential liability, and without them contributing processing power the system risks disappearing.

Blockchain based ecosystem there might be little effectiveness of regulation of a system that is composed of a decentralized and distributed (also no-easily-identifiable) group of entities [15, 16]. Indeed, under the PoW design, regulating miners would be difficult due to their anonymity/pseudonymity trait. While a front-running activity can be noted on the chain, the pseudo-anonymous trait of miners makes it very difficult to regulate. As such, deterrence based on sanctioning in a decentralized setting may not be highly effective. According to [13], sanctioning measures are less likely to be effective in the cyber sphere where the identity of the attacker is uncertain and there are many unknown adversaries.

However, we note that whilst regulating decentralized networks of many different miners can be difficult, regulating small networks can be more easily achieved—since with enough investigative effort it may be possible to identify the few miners involved (e.g. pseudonymous illicit actors are often identified via some off-chain interaction). Indeed, such a small network would be decentralized only to those participants and outsiders would likely deem the network as 'centralized'—yet it is important to highlight that de/centralization is not a binary value, but is a spectrum (from a system being highly decentralized to less and completely centralized when involving a single actor).

Arguably, blockchain is a more complex ecosystem where different liability rules may apply depending on a careful distinction of the modularity of the layer and the given use-case. For example, under a PBS design the anonymity trait of builders is reduced. This is because, while anyone can be a miner, builder entities tend to be more organized due to the overhead needed in their operation.

Moreover, the lack of any single point of failure, dominance and control contributes to increasing the resilience of blockchain-based systems, while also making it more difficult for national laws to be enforced on them. Nevertheless, in practice, this might not be the case, as centralization has occurred in various segments across the blockchain ecosystem, including the block building layer. However, a propensity for centralization does not necessarily mean that the dominant entity would exert its power to over-run the system. In other words, while centralization is an undesired occurrence in decentralized systems, it doesn't necessarily mean that would negatively affect users. However, this situation may ultimately reduce the trust in the underlying ecosystem and disincentivize participation - which puts the system at a risk for survival.

Centralization of builders through collusion can happen under the PBS design which can allow builders to extract large amounts of MEV. As we note the previous section, an exclusive overflow leads to builder centralization, creating dead-weight loss on the user side as a consequence of the market inefficiencies. Furthermore, under the PBS design, there is possibility for builder collusion which could lead to increased interblock front-running due to profitable opportunities related to transaction ordering [5].

Overall, there are different types of front-running. In our case, there are two relevant categories: intrablock (frontrunning happens in the same block) and interblock (multi-block front-running). The former can be done (in general) with or without builder collusion. The second, on the other hand, is difficult to execute without collusion. Overall, if the builders' collusion seeks to maximize profits then the second type of front-runnings would occur, which would imply that the first would also occur. This creates a need to avoid collusion among builders, for which regulation can prove to be useful under certain conditions. Consequently if, a) adversarial builder collusion can be detected and b) regulation has means to detect and punish builders – than applying certain type of monetary sanctions may render useful in deterring malicious behavior (e.g., front-running). For example, in a simplistic game of two builders colluding (where payoff is higher for both than not colluding), and if there is a regulatory penalty for collusion when detected, then depending on the size of the front-running profit and size of penalty, builders may be disincentivized to collude and front-running will be reduced. In other words, a suitable size of penalty ought to be established depending on front-running profits for which builders would not be willing to risk and collude.

Another measure to reduce collusion is for governments or other trusted institutions to have their own builders, however this would imply a partial switch of trust in such trusted institutions and a potential for increase in censorship. Government interference at block building level has shown in practice to have negative impact on censorship resistance in blockchains. As noted, after OFAC (Office of Foreign Assets Control in the USA) sanctioned Tornado Cash and several Ethereum addresses associated with it, there was a noted difference in block building (transaction inclusion) – as blocks stopped including transactions coming from the mixer (non-OFAC compliant) [17]. This basically means that base layer participants would either exclude any sanctioned addresses in blocks they propose or refuse to attest to any blocks that include such sanctioned addresses. Another important insight is the presence of MEV-Boost in the blocks. Interestingly, most of the blocks involve a MEV-boost relay which is an essential part of the overall selection (and execution) of blocks that involves transaction ordering [18]. Arguably, sanctioning mixers does have an impact on overall transaction inclusion and block creation, ultimately affecting the decisions by the still heavily centralized block builders and relays (MEV-boosts) under the PBS proposed design. Also, imposing fiduciary duties may also render negative effects as a regulatory arbitrage may appear when operators may decide to register in a place of favorable jurisdiction while being able to operate in another [2].

Alternatively, a type of monitoring measure that can be used by governments to make sure that transaction ordering is random (hence no strategy for front-running) is to oblige builders to use TEE (Trusted Execution Environment). Such TEE code could be programmed and then audited by governments to assure transaction ordering takes place in the desirable manner (e.g., random). While this would in theory avoid front-running by builders, it would increase the overall cost of using the system, as it adds another step in the process (increasing fees) and would decrease overall welfare creation. Moreover, this could potentially incentivize spamming the builder, as a malicious player could send many transactions which would increase the likelihood of one of the transactions being placed in front of the targeted transaction. Overall, it is important to mention that regulatory measures placed at the block building layer in blockchains amounts to an 'inability' to report a transaction due to a fear of liability; not an ability to "fully block" it as it is usually done in traditional finance.

Arguably, trying to allocate 'potentially central points' in order to apply centralized (traditional) regulatory measures may show to be partially effective as it may undermine some of the most important traits of the system (such as censorship resistance). As maintained by [19] and cited by [20]: *"Trying to apply centralized solutions to decentralized problems fails. It fails to scale, and it fails to achieve any of the stated goals. Although, it does push the decentralized platforms to try to innovate elsewhere... The answer is really simple. If you want to solve decentralized problems, solve them with decentralized solutions...."*

An alternative with merits further discussion is the ability of the system for self-regulation. In line with Lessing's "code is law", an argument can be made for the ability for on-chain governance to incorporate certain constitutional (regulation-like) principles into its block-building design which would imply a certain level of regulation and protection from colluding and centralized powers. For example, as a desired outcome of the PBS design - if in the future a certain optimal is achieved as to create a competitive market for builders - a reputation system can be established as a form of self-regulation and user protection. In other words, a reputation system can be created where users could record if they suspect that any of their transactions were front-runned or sandwiched. This could serve as a security assurance for users, when selecting which builder to send their transaction to. Consequently, this type of system would reinforce trust in a potentially centralized setting. Likewise, on-chain incentive design suggestions imply a creation of a 'fee escalator system.' Under this system market inefficiencies seem to be corrected (in theory) as the user is put in a seemingly powerful position to run an auction "facing the other way" in the MEV supply chain. In other words, the situation can be flipped so that MEV extractors offer bids to users to execute their order. In line with [2], on-chain based self-regulation would avoid the high cost of regulatory intervention, such as monitoring, detection and enforcement of penalties.

5 Conclusion

In this article we dived into the technology underpinning MEV, shining light on the evolution of the block building design at the consensus layer. We explained the novel Proposal Builder Separation (PBS) design and underlined potential vulnerability factors associated with it - such as the potential for builder centralization and collusion in order to front run user's transactions and maximize profits. While we recognize that under PBS, centralized (dominant) entities such as builders could damage users (and the system) by extracting MEV via front-running types of attacks, it is a matter of a) technological detection techniques advancements and b) regulatory ability to identify and punish - that regulatory mechanisms could be established to protect users. Nevertheless, we warm over the potential negative effects of regulatory intervention due to their impact on censorship resistance. Likewise, taking into consideration the cost of regulatory supervision and enforcement, technical (detection-based techniques) measures may suffice. In other words, detection of malicious activities by builder would ultimately reduce the trust and confidence in this entity, reducing the number of users transacting through that network. Overall, this might have a short run negative impact on the network (and the amount of transactions being executed) until confidence is restored and certain safeguarding principles are established. Moreover, alluding to one of the main EU's objectives regarding new technology law: "to protect users, without withholding innovation", we argue that regulating at the base layer in public blockchains may disincentivize main participants to contribute effort (e.g., staking, computing power, code, equipment etc.) and thus pose a risk for the system to further centralize or disappear. Overall, on-chain measures such as reputation design and fee escalator system are suggested as viable and cost-effective.

References

1. Raphael, A., Frost, J., Vidal Pasto, J.M.: Miners as intermediaries: extractable value and market manipulation in crypto and DeFi. Bank of International Settlements (2022)
2. Barczentewicz, M.: MEV on Ethereum: A Policy Analysis. International Center for Law and Economics (2023)
3. Robinson, M., Konstantopoulos, G.: Ethereum is a Dark Forest (2020)
4. Philip,D., Steven,G., Tyler, K., Yunqi,L.: Flash Boys 2.0: Frontrunning, Transaction Reordering, and Consensus Instability in Decentralized Exchanges (2019)
5. Flashbots. Flashbots (2023). https://boost.flashbots.net/
6. Mazzora, B., Penna, N.: Constant Function Market Making. Social Welfare and Maximal Extractable Value (2022)
7. Sun, X.: This Is MEV. in DEVCON BOGOTA, Bogota (2022)
8. Markham, J.: Front-Running – Insider Trading Under the Commodity Exchange Act. Catholic University Law review (1989)
9. Jaffe, J.: Special information and insider trading. J. Bus. **47**(3), 410–428 (1974)
10. Securities and Exchange Commission. Final Rule: Selective Disclosure and Insider Trading.17 CFR Parts 240, 243, and 249.
11. Ramos, S., Pianese, F., Oliveras, E., Leach, T.: A great disturbance in the crypto: Understanding cryptocurrency returns under attacks. Blockchain Res. Appl. **2**(3), 100021 (2021)
12. Nissenbaum, H.: Securing trust online: Wisdom or oxymoron. (2001)
13. Ramos, S., Melon, L. Ellul, J.: Exploring blockchains cyber security techno-regulatory gap. an application to crypto-asset regulation in the EU. In: 10th Graduate Conference in Law and Technology, Sciences Po, Paris (2022)
14. Walch, A.: Call blockchain developers what they are: Fiduciaries. American Banker (2016)
15. Lessig, L.: Code and other laws of cyberspace (1999)
16. De Filipi, P., Wright, A.: Blockchain and the Law: The Rule of Code (2021)
17. Cointelegraph (2022). https://cointelegraph.com/news/ofac-compliant-blocks-on-ethereum-hits-three-month-low-of-47
18. Mevwatch (2023). https://www.mevwatch.info/
19. Antonopoulos, A.: In Harvard Law School Blockchain and FinTech Initiative Conference (2021)
20. Altschuler, S.: Should Centralized Exchange Regulations Apply to Cryptocurrency Protocols?. Stanford J. Blockchain Law Policy **1**, 92 (2022)

Correction to: Position Paper - Hybrid Artificial Intelligence for Realizing a Leadership Assistant for Platform-Based Leadership Consulting

Stella Gatziu Grivas, Denis Imhof, and Phillip Gachnang

Correction to:
Chapter "Position Paper - Hybrid Artificial Intelligence for Realizing a Leadership Assistant for Platform-Based Leadership Consulting" in: M. Ruiz and P. Soffer (Eds.): *Advanced Information Systems Engineering Workshops,* **LNBIP 482, https://doi.org/10.1007/978-3-031-34985-0_4**

In the originally published version of chapter 4 the author Phillip Gachnang and his affiliations are missing. This has been corrected.

The updated original version of this chapter can be found at
https://doi.org/10.1007/978-3-031-34985-0_4

Author Index

M. Ruiz and P. Soffer (Eds.): CAiSE 2023 Workshops, LNBIP 482, pp. 197–198, 2023.
https://doi.org/10.1007/978-3-031-34985-0

Printed in the United States
by Baker & Taylor Publisher Services

Printed in the United States
by Baker & Taylor Publisher Services